The Dutch Atlantic

Decolonial Studies, Postcolonial Horizons
Series editors: Ramon Grosfoguel (University of California at Berkeley), Barnor Hesse (Northwestern University) and S. Sayyid (University of Leeds)

Since the end of the Cold War, unresolved conjunctures and crises of race, ethnicity, religion, diversity, diaspora, globalization, the West and the non-West, have radically projected the meaning of the political and the cultural beyond the traditional verities of Left and Right. Throughout this period, Western developments in 'international relations' have become increasingly defined as corollaries to national 'race relations' across both the European Union and the United States, where the reformation of Western imperial discourses and practices have been given particular impetus by the 'war against terror'. At the same time hegemonic Western continuities of racial profiling and colonial innovations have attested to the incomplete and interrupted institutions of the postcolonial era. Today we are witnessing renewed critiques of these postcolonial horizons at the threshold of attempts to inaugurate the political and cultural forms that decolonization now needs to take within and between the West and the 'non-West'. This series explores and discusses radical ideas that open up and advance understandings of these politically multicultural issues and theoretically interdisciplinary questions.

Also available

Rewriting Exodus
American Futures from Du Bois to Obama
Anna Hartnell

Islam and the Political
Theory, Governance and International Relations
Amr G.E. Sabet

THE DUTCH ATLANTIC

Slavery, Abolition and Emancipation

Kwame Nimako and Glenn Willemsen

First published 2011 by Pluto Press
345 Archway Road, London N6 5AA

www.plutobooks.com

Copyright © Kwame Nimako and Glenn Willemsen 2011

The right of Kwame Nimako and Glenn Willemsen to be identified as the authors of this work has been asserted by them in accordance with the Copyright, Designs and Patents Act 1988.

British Library Cataloguing in Publication Data
A catalogue record for this book is available from the British Library

ISBN 978 0 7453 3108 9   Hardback
ISBN 978 0 7453 3107 2   Paperback
ISBN 978 1 8496 4615 4   PDF eBook
ISBN 978 1 7837 1484 1   Kindle eBook
ISBN 978 1 7837 1483 4   EPUB eBook

Library of Congress Cataloging in Publication Data applied for

This book is printed on paper suitable for recycling and made from fully managed and sustained forest sources. Logging, pulping and manufacturing processes are expected to conform to the environmental standards of the country of origin.

10 9 8 7 6 5 4 3 2 1

Published with the assistance of NiNsee

Designed and produced for Pluto Press by Chase Publishing Services Ltd
Typeset from disk by Stanford DTP Services, Northampton, England

In loving memory of
Glenn Frank Walther Willemsen (1948–2008)

Contents

Acknowledgements ix
Foreword xii
Stephen Small, UC Berkeley
Preface xix
Artwell Cain, NiNsee

1 **Introduction, Goals and Issues** 1
   Introduction and Goals 3
   Context and Concepts 4
   Importance and Relevance 6
   Overview of Chapters 8

2 **Transatlantic Slavery and the Rise of the European World Order** 13
   The Age of Banditry (1492–1648) 14
   Sovereignty and Chattel Slavery (1648–1789) 20
   Citizenship, Slavery and the 'Free Soil Ideology' 29
   Science and Chattel Slavery 41

3 **Chattel Slavery, Sugar and Salt** 52
   Slavery and the Making of Global Economy 52
   Slavery and Sugar 60
   Sugar and Suriname 64
   Pacification and Resistance 77

4 **Abolition without Emancipation** 87
   European and Systemic Context 87
   From Regulation to Intervention 90
   Modalities of Abolition: Progressive Control versus
      Transformative Change 97
   Abolition and Citizenship 112

5 **Trajectories of Emancipation: Religion, Class, Gender and Race** 123
   Religion and Emancipation 125
   Class and Emancipation 128

Gender and Emancipation	131
Race and Emancipation	134
The Immediate Aftermath of Abolition	147

6 **The Legacy of Slavery: The Unfinished Business of Emancipation** — 149
- Memory and Dignitarianism — 150
- Commemorators and Commemoration — 158
- Integration and Multiculturalism — 164
- NiNsee as a Contested Project — 170
- Museums and Galleries — 175
- Reparations — 178
- Anniversaries and Apologies — 181

7 **Conclusion: Parallel Histories and Intertwined Belonging** — 184
- Some Conclusions — 184
- A Final Note — 189

Bibliography — 191
Index — 201

Acknowledgements

The word 'debt' has different meaning in different settings. In the world of economics, finance and money, being in debt to a person or institution is an indication that you are in deep trouble; it means the person or institution you are indebted to has some power or control over you. However in other social relations and settings, being indebted reflects an appreciation of the humanity and generosity of others to you. It is in the latter context that I wish to express my indebtedness to the following people.

Let me begin by thanking Carla Willemsen-de Vries and Tamira Willemsen, the wife and daughter respectively of the late Glenn Willemsen, for allowing me to continue a project Glenn and I initiated before he passed away. They know that, after more than 25 years of close friendship and collaboration with Glenn, I was well placed to continue this project on his behalf. Carla and Tamira entrusted me with this work in Glenn's name in the belief that I would do justice to him. I hope I have not disappointed them.

I discussed this project with Eddy Campbell, then interim director of NiNsee, in August 2008. To facilitate its realization, he agreed to support it, giving me access to NiNsee's facilities and covering part of the cost. His successor, and the current director of NiNsee, Artwell Cain, gave his full backing when he assumed office in 2009. As friend and colleague, Artwell has consistently offered invaluable support. Ronny Rens, the office manager at NiNsee, and Denice Soekra, the executive secretary, gave me the necessary administrative support to facilitate my work. I discussed the project with Frank Dragtenstein and Humphrey Lamur in NiNsee corridors whenever the opportunity arose. My conversations with Cees Luckhardt enriched my understanding of salt production on Bonaire in the Dutch Antilles.

I would like thank a number of institutions and organizations which Glenn and I visited, either together or separately, for the opportunities they gave us to make presentations about material related to this book and for the feedback and comments received from panel respondents and audiences. These institutions include: the Center for Global Studies and the Humanities, Duke University; the Institute for Postcolonial and Transcultural Studies, University of Bremen; the Gilder Lehrman Center for the Study of Slavery, Resistance and Abolition, Yale University; the Wilberforce Institute for the Study of Slavery and Emancipation, University of Hull; the Department of African American Studies, University of California, Berkeley; Northwestern University; Maison des Sciences de l'Homme (MSH), Paris; and finally the NiNsee Symposia on Trajectories of Emancipation, which I have helped to organize.

Interactions with old and new friends and colleagues were invaluable in helping me develop my thoughts about a number of issues. Among them are: Robert Allen, Harald Axwijk, Dew Baboeram, Bill Banks, Hilary Beckles, Dalida Maria Benfield, Allison Blakely, Sabine Broeck, Jean Casimir, Michaeline Crichlow, Carlos Erselina, Philomena Essed, David Theo Goldberg, Lewis Gordon, Jane Gordon, Ramon Grosfoguel, Marina Grzinic, Enrique Dussel, Hardy Frye, Darlene Clark Hine, Charles Henry, the late Andre Gunder Frank, Dienke Hondius, Gerd Junne, Susan Legêne, Trica Keaton, Kamala Kempadoo, Abdul JanMohamed, Eric Mielants, Walter Mignolo, Claudia Milian, Chris Mullard, Tiffany Ruby Patterson, Mark Sawyer, Madina Tlostanova, Nelson Maldonado-Torres, Catherine Walsh, Gloria Wekker, T. Sharpley-Whiting, and Donna Driver-Zwartkruis.

My visits to the Liverpool International Slavery Museum, the London Docklands Museum, and the Museum of the African Diaspora in San Francisco gave me additional motivation to complete this project.

Eric Mielants prepared an English translation of Glenn Willemsen's book *Dagen van gejuich en gejubel* (*Days of Exultation and Jubilation*) (2006a), making it easier for me to integrate some material from the earlier book into the present one. Artwell Cain, Trica Keaton and Walter Mignolo read an early draft of the book and gave me useful tips and valuable feedback.

I am grateful to Ramon Grosfoguel, Salman Sayyid and Barnor Hesse for inviting me to submit the manuscript for the Decolonial Studies and Postcolonial Horizons Series published by Pluto Press. David Castle, the commissioning editor at Pluto Press, has been very flexible, patient and supportive. I also thank the three Pluto anonymous reviewers; they asked tough questions, which forced me to confront important issues.

As usual, my friend and colleague, Amy Abdou, my 'boss' as I affectionately call her, has stood by me all along. Her efficiency is outstanding. She is my first call for edits and feedback; during the past three years I have hardly finished any major work without seeking her opinion.

I cannot thank my friend and colleague Stephen Small enough. He knows this book from A to Z; he read all the draft chapters and the whole manuscript along the way and consistently gave me valuable feedback. This is reflected in his foreword.

I take this opportunity of thanking all these people and institutions; but that is not to suggest that any shortcomings in this book can be attributed to them.

Kwame Nimako
April 2011

Foreword

Stephen Small

At the start of the twenty-first century, those of us trying to tackle the enormity and legacy of what transpired during the European slave trade, slavery and colonialism must figure out how to unravel the tangled knots of fallacy, fiction and farce, which have so often masqueraded as facts in institutional representations and scholarly analysis. This is true for film and television; it is true for museums, exhibitions and galleries; it is true in education; and it has been true, also, for scholarship and publishing. Untangling these knots has not been easy. The weight of dead generations rests on our shoulders, and we are fighting against several centuries of biased and distorted representations and analysis. The nature and quality of the records in the archives, the criteria deployed to validate scholarship, the institutions and processes in place to fund research and regulate publication, and a context of continuing inequality, resource imbalance and political opposition – all remain in place to distract or constrain us. But we persevere. And even in my lifetime we have seen significant advances, as we seek to achieve a more comprehensive and multifaceted appreciation of the unfolding of human events that emerged from the European slave trade.

This is the context in which Kwame Nimako and Glenn Willemsen have produced their compelling book, *The Dutch Atlantic: Slavery, Abolition and Emancipation*. They begin with a conundrum: 'It is a paradox of modern times that the further we get from slavery, the more efforts are made to remember it, to commemorate it and to force it into the public realm.' This is true not only in the public realm, but also in the realm of scholarly production. And it is this paradox that shapes the contours of this book. In preparing their book they worked with both the pain and the joy from many decades of professional and personal experience, in full recognition of the legacy of the past, with insight and wisdom, and a profound realization of the desperate need to confront these issues with rigorous research. Readers will not be disappointed. And anyone familiar with the social and political context of the Netherlands today will be well aware of the opportunities and constraints.

It is common in the Netherlands (as it was in Britain until recently) for slavery to be thought of as something that happened over there, far away, not for very long, and with little consequence for Dutch society today. In this book, Nimako and Willemsen make a compelling argument to the contrary. They demonstrate that slavery and the slave trade are inextricably and irrepressibly part of Dutch society, its political traditions, its cultural fabric and its social formation; that slavery and the slave trade are absolutely integral to a full understanding of Dutch history and society; that they are like veins of blood running through the body politic of the nation; and that without closely examining these veins you can understand little of the life and functioning of the body politic, or of the nation itself. No doubt this contention will be a bitter pill for many Dutch people to swallow. It's a different kind of medicine from the one they've been taking for a long time. But it was a bitter pill for many Americans to swallow in the 1950s, after more than a century of representing US slavery as plantation melodies, moonlight and magnolias, and 'faithful slaves'. And it was a bitter pill for the British to swallow in the 1980s, after more than a century celebrating their kind and magnanimous abolition of the slave trade. And it will no doubt be a bitter pill for the French, Spanish and Portuguese to swallow, for they are yet to develop a critical literature on the role that they played in slavery, the slave trade and their legacies. But the Dutch, like the Americans and British before them, will find a way to swallow this pill. My experiences giving lectures and presentations and attending exhibitions on slavery and its legacies across the Netherlands since 2006 convince me that there are a great number of Dutch people who are ready to discuss slavery, and who want to know far more about what happened, and what the legacy is for today, than they have been told. The far more extensive activities being undertaken by NiNsee (the National Institute for the Study of Dutch Slavery and its Legacy) convey the same message. This is the nature of social change, as any informed consideration of social history and historiography clearly demonstrates.

One of the key lessons from this book is that in coming to terms with the role of the Dutch in the slave trade, slavery and its legacies it is necessary to ask questions of history and questions of historiography. Questions of history require us to establish the facts of what transpired under the slave trade and slavery, and in the shadow of its legacies, in the metropolis and in the colonies, even after independence. To do this we need evidence and data. We also need to think about how these facts are defined, identified, conceptualized, framed and interpreted. This in turn requires attention to theory. But questions of historiography extend across a much broader terrain. They compel us to confront questions about the nature of the research that tends to be done; that has been done; and is being done. And to ask why, among the innumerable questions that might be asked about history, certain questions have consistently been asked, and so many others have not been asked. Why is it, as Nimako and Willemsen ask, that Dutch historiography is dominated by questions of profits from the slave trade, on whether slavery economically benefited the Netherlands or not, and on whether the enslaved were mentally or morally suitable for legal freedom, and yet so little research has been carried out on violence and sexual abuse by the Dutch during slavery, on the culture, aspirations and dreams of the enslaved, their human agency, or on the pronounced limitations of legal abolition and freedom? Why is it that so few questions have been asked, and so little research has been done, on the legacy of slavery in the Dutch orbit, including in the metropolis itself? Why is it that the question of emancipation, so central to 'mainstream Dutch historiography', invariably avoids addressing the legal emancipation of the enslaved, or its implications? Only by focusing on questions of historiography can we begin to address these questions. Addressing history and historiography inevitably, indeed immediately, raises questions of epistemology. We may also ask about questions of authority and power in relation to knowledge production. And these too are questions, as you will read, that the authors do not shy away from.

There are scholars in the academy who believe that the best and most rigorous research and conceptual and theoretical innovation arise primarily from institutional dynamics intrinsic to the academy; from a community of scholars interacting with one another, researching, presenting, discussing, debating, challenging, refining and rewriting. Those of us inside the academy know and have benefited from this tradition. But anyone who is not blindfolded sees that this is only half the story; that much of what transpires inside the academy is directly shaped by personal and social forces outside it. The research and biographies of so many scholars reveal, in indubitable ways, how personal experiences, social relationships and political developments profoundly influenced their work. In their choice of topics and questions, in the assumptions they make, in their commitment, perseverance and dedication to the project at hand. Nowhere is this more evident than in the field of history. In the United States, it was not until the Civil Rights Movement and

Black Power, and the Women's Movement, that the assumptions, questions and research strategies in the history and historiography of slavery and its legacies carried out at top US universities forever changed. And in my home country, the United Kingdom, it was not until the migration and permanent settlement of hundreds of thousands of Black people from the Caribbean and Africa that fundamental transformations in scholarship and publishing on slavery and its legacies occurred. Diasporic connections, resources and linkages have been central in all these developments. It is no surprise, therefore, that some of the fundamental challenges to Dutch history and historiography on slavery and its legacies, that one sees today in the Netherlands, have been directly shaped by the arrival and settlements of hundreds of thousands of Black people from the Dutch Caribbean orbit and from Africa. This is true also in the realm of public history, as can be seen from the activities that led up to the unveiling in 2002 of the Nationaal Monument Slavernijverleden (National Slavery Monument) in the Oosterpark in Amsterdam, as well as from the establishment in 2003 of NiNsee. This book is a product of both sets of institutional dynamics.

This book brings evidence, analysis and insights that will be fascinating for those who know the literature on Dutch slavery closely, as well as for those who know little or nothing about it. It offers the most comprehensive analysis to date of the nature of Dutch slavery and the slave trade, legal abolition and formal emancipation, their relationship to slavery in other European nations, and their legacies in Suriname, the Dutch Antilles and the metropolis itself. It tackles questions of history; and it tackles questions of historiography. Nimako and Willemsen traverse an extensive terrain. They link slavery, the slave trade and its legacies in the Dutch Caribbean orbit to their counterparts elsewhere in the Caribbean, to sovereignty, state formation, citizenship and social identity in the Netherlands and across Europe, and to patterns of trade and emerging systems of international relations across Europe, Africa and Asia. The book describes the rise of modern world order, the place of the Dutch within it, and how slavery and the slave trade functioned in the system as a whole.

It addresses some of the distinctive features of the Dutch system in and of itself – including the pre-eminent role of the Dutch in operating the slave trade rather than in enslaving large numbers in their colonies – as well as the distinctive issues raised by consideration of salt as a product of consumption and circulation. It describes the nature of the slave trade and slavery in the various Dutch colonies from Suriname to the Antilles, including variations across these territories; and it analyses relations between the Dutch West Indies and the Dutch East Indies, economically, financially, and in terms of the interconnected system of production and consumption. It also identifies the aspects of Dutch slavery that were shared with other nations, including economic exploitation and racial domination, as well as the violence and brutality endemic to the system.

The authors question the accuracy, validity and usefulness of many key assumptions and concepts in current Dutch historiography on slavery and its legacies, including concepts like 'abolition' (which was legal in name and limited in scope) and 'emancipation' (which was never really tried, and is still unfinished). They argue that what happened was, in fact, '(legal) abolition without emancipation' which was tantamount simply to the 'removal of mastery' rather than to genuine freedom. As we know from the limited descriptions that exist on the post-abolition period, 'the end of slavery did not entail the end of injustice'. After all, it was Dutch master enslavers and their associates who received financial reparations. Instead the authors introduce the idea of 'unfinished trajectories of emancipation', a concept that resonates with many of the activities currently being organized across the Netherlands today. It is only by engaging with such conceptual issues, they suggest, that one can begin to understand the incessant historical and contemporary demands for reparations from the descendants of the enslaved, and the increasing scholarship being carried out on reparations – in the Dutch orbit, as well as in the United Kingdom and the United States.

They also pay attention to language and terminology, reminding us, as Walter Rodney once did, that it was Africans (not 'slaves') that were kidnapped; that Africans and their descendants were not 'slaves', but were 'enslaved' (*tot slaaf gemaakt*); and that it is more instructive to talk of 'master enslavers' than 'slave masters' (to convey the unceasing negotiation between social actors with different levels of power). Semantic matters, some would argue, but not me. Instead, as I have argued in my own work, I relish the ways in which such concepts challenge the assumptions and the framework of analysis that centuries of putative scholarly objectivity have bequeathed us. And these concepts humanize us. The phrasing 'Black' and 'non-Black' is not common in the mainstream media or in scholarly publications because it implies a fundamentally different conceptualization of race and hierarchy than does 'white' and 'non-white'.

In articulating their central argument Nimako and Willemsen introduce the idea of 'parallel histories and intertwined belonging', encountered by people who 'share the same space but have different experiences and memories'. Historically, in the castles that stored captives on the west coast of Africa, in the depths of the ships in the middle passage, on the auction blocks, in the geography of farms and plantations, Europeans and Africans have shared the same social spaces. And today, in the schools, streets and socially segregated neighbourhoods of Dutch urban areas – especially in Amsterdam, Rotterdam and the Hague – the descendants of Europeans and Africans also share similar social spaces. But their knowledge of slavery and its legacies and their receptivity to information, discussion and debate about this legacy, while intertwined and overlapping, reveal clear discrepancies. As this book demonstrates, the public history and collective memory of slavery and its legacies in the Netherlands today reveal marked differences that reflect differential access to political power and knowledge production. And despite Dutch official reluctance to discuss race, these institutional activities also reveal marked racial differences.

And the authors tackle the very concept of legacy – this amorphous, evasive, slippery idea – forcing us to confront its nature, provenance and purview. Depending on whom you ask – scholar, professor, schoolteacher, journalist or the proverbial woman on the street – the legacy of slavery is everywhere and nowhere. For many it ended shortly after slavery was legally abolished, in the conditions of emancipation. In part, this is why the Dutch prefer not to talk about race, but about ethnicity, about *autochtonen,* or natives (people who belong, with its implied notion of historical rights), as opposed to *allochtonen* (non-natives, aliens, those who don't belong). For others, such as Nimako and Willemsen, the legacy continues to this day, in the nature of state and social formation, in racial identities, stereotypes and discrimination. This is a far-reaching debate, with many implications.

These are controversial and emotive topics, and they don't make for light reading. Whether the questions are about history and historiography, or about public history and collective memory today, Nimako and Willemsen do not shy away from the controversies that such questions are likely to raise. Instead, they plunge deep into the murky and fathomless waters, confident that their rigorous research and conceptual innovations will provide the necessary breathing apparatus to sustain them. They are most direct, concrete and forthright in identifying, documenting and assessing the specifics of the Dutch orbit, telling us that today, in the Netherlands, '[t]he main legacy of slavery is emancipation as unfinished business'. I have no doubt that this book will make an indispensable contribution in the Netherlands to the research and teaching on slavery and its legacies; and to a broader understanding of Black European experiences. It will challenge assumptions, raise questions, stimulate debates, open eyes, and make people scratch their heads.

Finally some words about great colleagues – one of remembrance and one about the future. I knew Glenn Willemsen, his work at NiNsee, and his scholarship; and I had the good fortune and pleasure of meeting him several times. It was a tragedy to his family, friends, community and nation that Glenn died such an untimely death. My friendship and professional relationship with him had only just begun, and I'm sorry that it was cut short so tragically. We must be thankful for his work with NiNsee, and that he started such an important project; and we must find ways to honour and commemorate his memory. NiNsee began the Glenn Willemsen annual memorial lecture series on slavery and its legacies several years ago.

My friendship and professional relationship with Kwame Nimako continues. It will be clear to any reader who had made it to the end of this foreword that I consider Dr Nimako an outstanding intellect and scholar. I have learnt a great deal from him and a great deal from this book, and I admire his work. He is also my friend. This book demonstrates that he is a thinker with immense skills: a rigorous scholar, innovative theorist, and forthright writer. Nor does he shy away from tough questions. And he hasn't finished yet. This book promises to be just the first in a series of projects that insistently engage with enduring issues of history and historiography in evaluating slavery and its legacies.

Stephen Small is associate professor in African American Studies at University of California, Berkeley. He is the author of *Racialised Barriers: The Black Experience in the United States and England in the 1980s* (1994), and co-author of *Representations of Slavery* (2002) and *Race and Power: Global Racism in the Twentieth Century* (2001).

Preface

Artwell Cain

NiNsee is the only public history institute in the Netherlands solely devoted to the Dutch involvement in the Atlantic slavery and its legacy. Of course there are several institutions and individuals who work on, or pay attention to, similar subject matter; but that is not their core business.

NiNsee as a knowledge centre is structured around five main pillars. These are: (1) the planning and execution of research pertaining to the Dutch slavery past and its legacies; (2) the preparation and development of curricula and general educational information regarding the same; (3) the application of research findings to display and share knowledge through exhibitions in its gallery; (4) the creation of a space for gathering all relevant documents and other sources of information, whether print or audiovisual, that pertain to this history and its heritage; (5) and last but not least, the organization of annual commemoration ceremonies: the national commemoration and remembrance day for the abolition of Dutch slavery in the Caribbean in 1863 and the 'Breaking of the Chains' festival (Keti Koti) on 1 July; the commemoration of the Tula uprising in 1795 on 17 August; and also the UNESCO International Day for the Remembrance of the Slave Trade and its Abolition on 23 August.

In addition to these main activities, NiNsee also organizes bi-monthly public lectures. These lectures are given by regional, national and international scholars. Every June, NiNsee also organizes the Summer School on Black Europe, an intensive three week programme for graduate students from around the world, which examines the role and position, as well as the experiences and aspirations, of Black Europeans. This Summer School is followed by an annual two-day international symposium entitled 'Trajectories of Emancipation', which invites scholars from all over the world to discuss topics relevant to the legacy of slavery in the Netherlands and elsewhere. NiNsee also plays an important role in facilitating grassroots organizations to undertake their own activities. It works in cooperation with other institutions and organizations to realize joint objectives and shared results on a national and international level. These are just a few of the endeavours that are administered and/or facilitated by NiNsee (see www.ninsee.nl).

From the very start NiNsee has been using its unique position as a centre of knowledge in the Netherlands to make a difference. Our work is driven by knowledge, through research and education, learning and making information available locally, nationally and globally. We recognize knowledge production and dissemination as our core business. Our main goal is to reach as many people as possible and educate them on the Dutch slavery past and its legacies. Herein lies the key to furthering the emancipation of the diverse ethnic groups and individuals in the Netherlands. Enslavement was and remains a solemn history. It is a history that must be approached with full attention to the facts, and with appreciation to the sensitivity of the issues at hand. Now more than ever, in an age in which the internet and a host of new technological advances offer endless possibilities for accessing information, everyone has a responsibility to pay closer attention to the transatlantic slave trade and its contribution to Dutch history, historiography and cultural identity.

Kwame Nimako and Glenn Willemsen locate the issue of knowledge production in an interesting, profound and concise manner when they ask: 'Why were people who were not slaves classified as slaves in historical literature before they were enslaved? What is the difference between, capture, captivity, kidnapping, slaves and enslaved?' They set out to challenge our knowledge and mindset with regard to how we think, speak and write about those who were enslaved and, among other topics, about colonialism, emancipation, racism and citizenship. These to my mind are classical epistemological and soul-searching issues, which have continued to torment our minds. The question is whether after reading this volume we will be able to quench our intellectual and investigative quest for more knowledge. At the same time we are aware that the road is long and uneven. Knowledge on its own is never enough.

When I took over as the director of NiNsee after the tragic and untimely death of my predecessor, Glenn Willemsen, and first heard of this project I supported it wholeheartedly. Before taking up the helm at NiNsee, I had known Glenn as an academic and civil servant since the 1980s. I am also aware of the collaboration of Kwame Nimako and Glenn Willemsen since their days as colleagues at the Centre for Race and Ethnic Studies (CRES) at the Universiteit van Amsterdam. Thus when I was introduced to this project I had no doubt that Kwame could carry it on to its logical conclusion. I have not only supported this project as director of NiNsee, but I have also closely followed its evolution.

I think that for those who question why Atlantic slavery should be remembered and commemorated, the answer can be found in this book. This is a biting narrative.

Artwell Cain is director of NiNsee.

1
Introduction, Goals and Issues

At the turn of the twenty-first century, the unwavering efforts of predominantly black Dutch groups in the Netherlands have put the legacy of Dutch slavery on the national political agenda. These efforts have brought the discourse on the legacy of slavery in the Netherlands into the public domain and have simultaneously given it an emotional charge, culminating in the unveiling of the National Slavery Monument on 1 July 2002 in Amsterdam. The physical monument was followed by the establishment in 2003 of a slavery institute, namely, the National Institute for the Study of Dutch Slavery and its Legacy (NiNsee).

When Glenn Willemsen became the first director of NiNsee (in August 2003), he found himself in a situation in which he had to explain to the Dutch public what NiNsee was and why the abolition of Dutch Atlantic slavery on 1 July 1863 should be remembered and commemorated in the Netherlands. In order to answer some of these questions he decided to write a book, *Dagen van gejuich en gejubel (Days of Exultation and Jubilation)* (2006a). The main purpose of the book was to answer two questions: what happened on the day of legal abolition in the Netherlands, Suriname and the Dutch Antilles; and how did the demand for a slavery monument and institute come about? Willemsen was also interested in the notion of freedom, namely, how various parties, including the state, the enslavers and the enslaved, interpreted the notion of freedom. I (K.N.) supported him in researching the book and gave him feedback as he wrote the book.

What was also not anticipated when Willemsen became the director of NiNsee was the number of invitations he would receive from various civil society groups, including student groups, to give lectures on the Dutch involvement in the transatlantic 'slave' trade and slavery. It was clear that there was widespread interest amongst the Dutch public, especially young people, for information about the role of the Dutch in the 'slave' trade. After such lectures he was frequently asked to recommend a book for further reading. Obviously there are several books on the Dutch involvement in the transatlantic 'slave' trade and slavery. But he realized that what was needed was a comprehensive book, one that would give an overview of the complexity of the subject. It was against this background that he invited me to collaborate with him in writing such a book. However, in February 2008, during the process of researching and working on the book, Glenn Willemsen passed away. This was a tragic loss to his family, to me personally, and to the Black community in the Netherlands. Since the basic contours of the book had already been delineated and part of the research had been done, I decided to complete it. I felt that there was still a desperate need for a book of this kind, and that its publication would make a significant contribution to the debate on slavery and its legacy in the Netherlands.

This leads us to several questions. The first question that arises is: what exactly happened on that famous day of emancipation, 1 July 1863, in Suriname, the Dutch Antilles and the Netherlands? This question was dealt with extensively by Willemsen (2006a), so we only reflect on it briefly in this book. More relevant here is another question, namely, what is the genesis of this passion that strives to keep alive the events of emancipation day – especially among the descendants of those who were enslaved? And what sustains such a passion? Then there is the question of why the white part of the population in the Netherlands experiences this day so differently from the way that black Dutch men and women experience it. Next, we expand on why the first of July has never really become 'this happy day in Dutch history' which the editors of the *Utrechtsch Provinciaals en Stedelijk Dagblad* (2 July 1863) had anticipated. And finally, we expand on why slavery in the Dutch Antilles is not commemorated on 1 July in the same way as it is in Suriname. In the Dutch Antilles, 17 August, a date of uprising among the enslaved, is remembered; why are there several dates for the remembrance of Dutch slavery?

To the best of our knowledge this is the first book that discusses and analyses Dutch slavery, legal abolition and issues related to emancipation in an integrated fashion. Existing works tend to analyse these issues separately, chronologically (Emmer 2005, Postma 1990). But these massive and far reaching phenomena were fundamentally and inextricably integral to one another. An integrated analysis of the functioning of Dutch slavery and the 'slave' trade, and of its legal abolition and the circumstances of emancipation, promises far greater insights into how the system functioned as a whole and into the distinctive features of the Dutch experience, when compared with the roles of Britain, the United States, Spain and Portugal. And an integrated analysis of the kind provided in this book is able to offer far more penetrating insights into the roles of these phenomena in the formation of modern systems of international relations.

Much of the existing research on Dutch slavery focuses on the Dutch involvement in the transatlantic 'slave' trade, with emphasis on the transportation of African captives on Dutch ships to the Caribbean and the Americas (van Danzig 1968, Postma 1990, de Heijer 1997. The literature on legal abolition and emancipation in the context of the legacies of slavery is limited (Siwpersad 1979, Oostindie 1996, van Stipriaan 1996, Willemsen 2006a). We focus on slavery itself because the transportation (slave trade) was a means to an end (slavery). In turn slavery was a means (production) to an end (consumption). We are also interested in the decision-making processes, namely, the planning and designing of the 'slave' trade and slavery. It will become clear below that some of the decisions culminated in the signing of treaties between European nations. Atlantic slavery also contributed to new social formations and social thought. This implies that more people were involved in the 'slave' trade and slavery than just those who actually implemented the system. And we examine the legacy of slavery, including its reach into the institutions and collective activities of organizations and groups in the Netherlands and beyond at the present time.

INTRODUCTION AND GOALS

Most countries in Africa, Europe and the Americas acknowledge the place of the transatlantic 'slave' trade and slavery in their histories during the past 400 years. Each region has acknowledged the part that it played in this unequal division of labour. Europe was the location of ideas, design, planning and innovations in slavery and the slave trade; Africa was the source of banditry, abduction and the captivity of vulnerable peoples (Rodney 1974); the Caribbean and the Americas were the sites of production by enslaved labour (James 1980); and Europe again was the destination of the consumption of the goods produced by the enslaved (Williams 1994). All elements of this network of nations and international relationships were irrepressibly racialized (Banton 1977; Miles 1982).

This book carries out a systemic and coherent interrogation of the involvement of the Dutch in the transatlantic 'slave' trade and slavery system and it assesses the consequences of this involvement for contemporary society and social thought. By 'systemic' we imply a process that became intertwined with nation state formation, not only in the Netherlands but also across Europe and beyond. By 'coherent' we imply consideration of the 'slave' trade and slavery as a totality; in other words, that the 'slave' trade and slavery were much more than an economic system – that they became part of a social and cultural system that was taken for granted by those who dominated it. A fundamental social component of this system was racism (Williams 1994). In turn most of the documents on the 'slave' trade and slavery had taken it for granted that Africans had to be enslaved.

Modern European expansion and colonization was also a consequence of rivalry among Europeans, so it is necessary to study and analyse both processes (rivalry and colonization) simultaneously (Palmer and Colton 1978; Huntington 1993; Tilly 1986 and 1990). The European countries that were involved in the Atlantic 'slave' trade and slavery did so under national flags. Also the lands that were acquired to put the enslaved to work without consent and contract were acquired in the name of nations. Thus we begin our interrogation by looking at the formation of nation states in Europe, including the Netherlands, in relation to the transatlantic 'slave' trade and slavery system.

European populations had to be mobilized to implement policies that facilitated the 'slave' trade and slavery. Also the European countries developed laws that facilitated the 'slave' trade, slavery and colonization; an international legal framework was called into being that made the 'slave' trade and slavery a legitimate business enterprise in the eyes of European leaders and many of its citizens. One of the major goals of this book is to analyse the place of the Dutch nation state in these processes and the consequences of these developments for contemporary society and social thought, including the ways in which discussion of race is addressed or marginalized.

CONTEXT AND CONCEPTS

The context of this book is the formation of the Dutch nation state and the social formation that emerged as a consequence of the transatlantic 'slave' trade and slavery system. One of our conclusions is that this has given rise to *parallel histories* and *intertwined belonging*. People who have parallel histories and intertwined belonging share the same space but have different experiences and memories. With regard to the transatlantic 'slave' trade we see that the captives shared the same ship as their captors (intertwined belonging) but the histories of how they boarded the ship and the conditions they experienced on board were fundamentally different (parallel histories); in a similar vein the enslaved might have inhabited the same space on a plantation as the enslaver (intertwined belonging), but the histories of how the enslaved and the enslaver ended up in the same space and the division of labour (imposed by the enslaver on the enslaved) also differed fundamentally (parallel histories). These parallel histories and intertwined belonging in turn gave rise to a different understanding and different notions of freedom and emancipation. For the enslaver and the nations that enslaved others, freedom may have implied the freedom to enslave others; for the enslaved, freedom may have meant finding a place that they could call home without being hunted and dehumanized and humiliated. Thus, in the context of Dutch history, we have different emancipation trajectories. The key concepts that will serve as a guide in articulating the trajectories of emancipation are: sovereignty, citizenship, science, racism, chattel slavery, freedom and legal abolition. The formal abolition of slavery made citizenship (as opposed to common space) an intertwined belonging and parallel memories (as opposed to different experiences) parallel histories.

The book is based on a wide range of primary and secondary sources. In the literature on slavery, career historians legitimately place emphasis on salvaging archive material (Eltis et al. 1999, Richardson 1985, Walvin 1973, Lovejoy 2000, den Heijer 1997, Klooster 1997, Postma 1990, Dantzig 1968). Analyses of slavery based on archival sources have provided important insights. There is no doubt that these efforts are laudable. But they also have limitations, sometimes severe limitations. We recognize that while archives give us a window to the past they do not necessarily have the last word on human history and agency. A view from a window – one window – does not provide the necessary panorama for understanding the phenomena of slavery, legal abolition and emancipation as a whole. It is now acknowledged that in writing about powerless people, drawing on archival and conventional published sources alone is not enough (Hochschild 2006, Wolf 1982; Wallerstein 1974; Frank 1998: 178; Trouillot 1995). As more people gain access to institutions of education, especially communities with histories of oppression and enslavement, they question the history that has been passed down to them and in some cases forced down their throats (Rodney 1974, Davidson 1980, Mignolo 2007).

Besides, data in the archives were collected for a variety of different purposes. In addition, career historians use data selectively; they use data that suit their needs and leave out those data that they consider irrelevant (Willemsen 2006a). Decisions about what to include and exclude are typically presented as being based on 'objective' or 'valid' criteria. But we have a great deal of evidence to demonstrate that such decisions have frequently been based on subjective criteria, and often for reasons of bias and distortion (Collins 1991). Anyone conducting research on slavery should be aware that the vast majority of data in the archives were not recorded by the enslaved, nor for the enslaved. Neither was the opinion of the enslaved sought. In fact the concept of 'slave trade' was imposed on captives. There is no evidence, even from the sources of the enslavers, that the Africans who were chained and transported across the Atlantic Ocean to the Americas were slaves in Africa before they arrived in the Americas. Thus throughout this book, all mention of 'slave trade' and 'slavery' refers to the abduction and enslavement of Africans in the so-called 'New World' of the Americas from 1500 until the 1880s. We find that in contemporary discourses, academic and public, the notions of 'slave trade' and 'slavery' have become conceptually inflated and universalized in ways that often act as an impediment to their analysis. So in our efforts to write a more comprehensive history of these phenomena, and to do so in an integrated way, we find it imperative to embrace a far greater range of primary and secondary data than can be found in the typical archives. For instance data that was used by the state to compensate enslavers before the legal abolition of slavery can also be used by the descendants of the enslaved to claim reparations. Archives on their own cannot do this.

IMPORTANCE AND RELEVANCE

The issues surrounding the transatlantic 'slave' trade and slavery have become far more enduring than many people thought. This is true in the academy and scholarship, and it is also true in a wide range of public institutions, and in a wide range of communities. This book is an attempt to contribute to, and address, some of the questions related to why the issues surrounding the transatlantic 'slave' trade and slavery have not yet gone away, and why they are not likely to go away anytime soon. It thus appears that it is more relevant to address the question of how to deal with this history than that of how to bury it. This is true for the case of career historians. But we believe that it is also true with regard to those social movements that commonly demand that this history be told. It is a paradox of modern times that the further we get from slavery, the more efforts are made to remember it, to commemorate it and to force it into the public realm (Small 1994b; Nimako and Small 2010).

A review of current global trends in *post-* and *anti-slavery* issues reflects diverse positions on the topic and trends. *Post-slavery* refers to the fact that slavery, especially European-initiated and -led chattel slavery, was at a given point in history a legal institution before it was rendered an illegal institution (Tibbles 1994). In this book, we speak of anti-slavery, because there are those who consider slavery as unfinished business; forms of slavery still exist. There are also those who view emancipation as unfinished business.

On the basis of these two opposing interrogations of slavery, we can distinguish five movements or trends: the remembrance and commemoration movement; the reparations movement; the anniversaries and apologies trend; the museum heritage and artefacts trend; and the new anti-slavery movement.

The *remembrance and commemoration* movement, located in Black communities across the diaspora, has consistently recognized slavery and its legacies, with many activities beginning the very moment that slavery was legally abolished (Fryer 1984; Campbell 1985; Brundage 2005; Clark 2005).

The second movement, *reparations*, is primarily Black-led. It has branches located in Great Britain and emerging branches in the Netherlands. Reparations have had a significant presence in Black communities, with only intermittent attention in the wider public domain.

The third trend is that of *anniversaries and apologies*. This trend is a recent development, having begun mainly in the last 15 years, with examples in Great Britain and the United States and, much more recently, indications that it is taking root in the Netherlands. There have been formal apologies in Britain and the United States, but at the time of writing no formal apologies in the Netherlands.

The fourth trend is the *museum heritage and artefacts* trend, which is predominantly elite and white-led, and focuses on the legacy of slavery in terms of its objects, artefacts, art and physical infrastructure (AWAD 2009). But in the United States since the 1950s, in the Caribbean since the 1960s, in Britain since the 1990s and in the Netherlands in the last ten years, there has been more willingness to acknowledge the role of slavery and the 'slave' trade in the acquisition of such artefacts (Nimako and Small 2010). Social mobilization of Black communities proved to be the critical catalyst in bringing about this change of face.

The fifth and final movement is the *new anti-slavery movement*, whose trajectory lies in the 'old' slave trade abolition movement of eighteenth- and nineteenth-century Britain. The new anti-slavery movement, which has branches located in Britain and North America (with emerging branches in the Netherlands), is primarily white-led and focuses on vulnerable groups across the world today, especially women and children. This movement is the most visible publicly. But in comparison with the first four movements it is both distinctive and unique, because it remembers slavery primarily as a metaphor and a foil, to highlight the trafficking and exploitation of what it defines as the 'new slaves' of the modern world. In other words its main focus is on contemporary slavery, rather than the European 'slave' trade in Africans and the slave systems that developed across the Americas.

While each of these movements or trends explicitly engages with issues of slavery, the 'slave' trade and their legacies, they differ in several major respects, including their assumptions, their conceptualization of slavery and its continuing relevance to achieving full emancipation and justice for people of African descent, and in their organizational forms. They are also different in the nature of their access to political power and knowledge production processes. We take all five trends into account, but place most emphasis on the first, as it is most relevant to the discussion of the Netherlands.

These trends highlight the need to draw systematically on secondary and other sources of information. Not only do we get part of the secondary sources from primary sources, but also it is incontestable that living people also make history. This is not a question of perspectives, because irrespective of a view point, there is no indication, from archives or secondary sources, that those who were enslaved gave themselves up voluntarily to be enslaved.

OVERVIEW OF CHAPTERS

In the present chapter, after describing the origins of the research and work for this book, we introduced the idea of 'parallel histories and intertwined belonging' as a central organizing feature of the book. We questioned the nature, scope and value of archival material in analyses of slavery to date, and suggested that a full understanding of what really transpired must search beyond the parameters which have been set by Dutch historiography, and must look at evidence

INTRODUCTION, GOALS AND ISSUES   9

outside the archives. Finally we identified five movements or trends in post-slavery analysis, and briefly described their main contours.

Chapter 2 deals with the global context of the transatlantic 'slave' trade and slavery and the position of the Netherlands therein. We see that the initiative, planning and designing of the system were located in Europe. The European world order that emerged between the sixteenth and twentieth centuries laid the foundations for the interstate system and international law as we know them now, which came to be dominated by European states.

Some of the issues that are addressed in this chapter include: the role chattel slavery played in shaping and fostering national sovereignty and citizenship in Europe; how the transatlantic 'slave' trade and slavery were rationalized and justified; and how slavery, the formation of nation states in Europe and citizenship reinforce each other.

As European citizens became freer, non-Europeans became less free. We show how European dominance led to the concept of the superiority of the European man and in turn to modern racism, sanctioned by state power and violence.

Chapter 3 is devoted to consideration of the goods produced by the enslaved, and the conditions under which such goods were produced, which in fact was the primary purpose of the 'slave' trade and slavery by those who practised it. Specifically we describe how the colonization of the Americas led to the production of goods (e.g. silver) that became global commodities, exchanged as far as Asia, reinforcing trade and strengthening European states. These developments in turn facilitated the eventual colonization of both Asia and Africa. We also explore the relationship between consumption and production – the production of goods by the enslaved and their consumption by Europeans and by the enslaved themselves. We describe the horrors of slavery in the production processes, including repression, pacification and resistance.

We examine the uneven cycles through which slavery went – from the height of productivity of slavery-based plantations in the Dutch Caribbean in the seventeenth and eighteenth centuries to their decline in the early nineteenth century, the latter being the period when the Dutch East Indies colony (Indonesia) was at the height of its productivity. We explain how plantation owners in the Dutch West Indies delayed the abolition of slavery while demanding compensation for the loss of their human property, and we detail some of the ways in which the Dutch state acquired resources from their East Indies colony to compensate the enslavers. We challenge the view that legal abolition of slavery happened because slavery was not profitable to the Dutch people in general, and the Dutch state in particular.

In Chapter 4 we describe the conditions of legal abolition in the Netherlands by comparing the process and outcome with similar patterns in Great Britain. Unlike Great Britain, the Netherlands never experienced a mass movement against slavery and only very small numbers of people were active in the public debate or politically engaged in this issue. We explain that this was because the 'slave' trade and slavery took place far from the daily life and scope of most Dutch people, and consequently did not penetrate the collective consciousness.

We draw a clear distinction between abolition and emancipation. We speak of (legal) abolition without emancipation because, despite the fact that some Dutch scholars have regarded them as equivalent, the two terms did not (and do not) mean precisely the same thing. The first covers a historical event: the enslaved obtained their legal freedom; the second indicates a process rather than a distinctive moment in history. In fact, the end of slavery did not entail the end of injustice – it was the plantation owners who obtained compensation for the loss of their 'human machines', while most of the enslaved finished the period of slavery with little more than the clothes on their backs, without economic means and with no real political rights.

Chapter 5 is devoted to the issues of racialized emancipation, and various ways in which emancipation has been conceptualized – in particular, the notion of emancipation as understood by mainstream Dutch historiography. We show that for historical, cultural and emotional reasons, the term 'emancipation' has different connotations for different groups. In the history of the Netherlands, three events are primarily associated with this term: the political emancipation of the Catholics, the emancipation of the working class and the political emancipation of women. The first two of these, Catholic and working-class emancipation, gave rise to what became known in Dutch political history as pillarization. In Suriname and the Dutch Antilles, however, 'emancipation' is primarily linked to the abolition of slavery on 1 July 1863. We link the various notions to one another, as well as exploring the processes of assimilation, integration and segregation that followed from them.

In Chapter 6 we argue that the main legacy of slavery is emancipation as unfinished business. We demonstrate that the historical day associated with emancipation has been and continues to be dealt with very differently in the Netherlands and its former colonies, Suriname and the Antilles. In the Netherlands, until the final decades of the twentieth century, the problem of Dutch slavery and its legacy remained a non-issue in the public domain as well as in the collective memory of Dutch society. Among the majority Dutch population almost no one discussed it and, apart from the work of a handful of Dutch historians, a pervading silence enveloped the subject. By contrast, in the Surinamese and Antillean communities living in the Netherlands, it remained an important and recurring topic of conversation. These different approaches reflected different histories and different access to power and knowledge production in the Netherlands as compared with Suriname and the Dutch Antilles.

With mass migration from the former plantation colony of Suriname in the mid 1970s (the time of its independence), the Netherlands had its past, particularly slavery, quite literally delivered to its door. Collective memory expressed in the Afro-Dutch community, which predominantly settled in the big cities of Amsterdam, Rotterdam and The Hague, led to the creation of a number of organizations whose primary function was to commemorate 1 July and the legacy of slavery and to celebrate abolition with a range of activities. Mobilization and interactions with the Dutch government led ultimately to the 'Nationaal Monument Slavernijverleden' and the establishment of NiNsee and to Slavery Emancipation Day.

In the final chapter we draw four conclusions from the book as a whole. The first is of conceptual and methodological relevance and can be formulated as follows. The Atlantic world has had an enormous influence on state formations in Europe, Africa and the Americas. Atlantic slavery was an important, if not the major, constituent part of these formations. Thus Atlantic slavery is relevant to a full understanding of state formation, social formations and social thought in Europe, including the Netherlands.

The second conclusion is that Atlantic slavery has had an enormous influence on the functioning of the world economy, and the role of Europe and the Netherlands therein. The Atlantic economy, which was built around chattel slavery, became complementary to the Asian and European economies.

Our third conclusion is that the Atlantic slavery has given rise to parallel histories and intertwined belonging, which in turn lead to a different understanding and different notions of freedom and emancipation. The key concepts relevant to understanding these issues are: sovereignty, citizenship, science, racism, chattel slavery, freedom and legal abolition.

Our final conclusion involves the relationship between the Atlantic 'slave' trade and slavery on the one hand, and knowledge production on the other. The unequal access to power that followed the legal abolition of slavery ensured that it was the former master enslavers – and the white elites in the metropolis of each empire – who were able to portray their version of how slavery and the 'slave' trade ended, and of the meaning and significance of the legacy of slavery. And in doing so they have assigned most value and validity to knowledge produced from archives, while marginalizing knowledge produced from other sources. Access to power and knowledge production still remains unequal in the twenty-first century, but the dominant view that reigned for so long, frequently one-sided and even hegemonic, is now facing fundamental challenge, as the descendants of the former enslaved write their own histories, and do so in ways that alter our understanding of Dutch history. And in this process, they challenge the unquestioned validity of knowledge produced in archives. This book which I have completed, inspired by the work of Glenn Willemsen, is part of that parallel history and intertwined belonging. This makes emancipation an unfinished business.

2
Transatlantic Slavery and the Rise of the European World Order

This chapter examines the relationship between Atlantic slavery and the rise of the European world order. Europe, and those countries outside Europe that are considered to be part of the Western world, came to be distinguished from other regions and peoples of the world as a 'modern world' after Christopher Columbus crossed the Atlantic Ocean and landed in the Caribbean in 1492.

Text book accounts of this event tell us that Columbus ended up in the Americas by accident; he and his crew were actually looking for a shorter route to India or Asia (Palmer and Colton 1978). The events that unfolded after this historical accident were to transform a region considered geographically as part of the Asian peninsula and to give rise to a European world order. In this context, 'European world order' refers to an international political–economic system that emerged between the sixteenth and twentieth centuries and laid the foundations for an international legal framework and system, including maritime and company law as we now know them, that came to be dominated by European states and people of European descent around the world (Wallerstein 1974).

Chomsky reflected on the world order at the end of the twentieth century in the following terms: 'Writing on the world order in 1991, one can hardly ignore the approaching end of the first 500 years of a world order in which the major theme has been Europe's conquest of most of the world' (Chomsky 1993: 141).

It can be argued that chattel slavery went hand in hand with the process of European conquest of most of the world and the making of the European world order. As will be clear below, some of the important treaties in the making of the European interstate systems also took Atlantic slavery into account. Equally important to note is that the development of the interstate system went hand in hand with the international division of labour in the transatlantic 'slave' trade and slavery which we described in Chapter 1: Europe was the location of ideas, design, planning and innovations; Africa was the source of captive Africans for enslavement; the Caribbean and the Americas were the sites of production, and Europe again of the consumption of the goods produced by the enslaved (Williams 1994; Rodney 1974; Page 1997).

With regard to the rise of the interstate system, in a narrow sense, history textbooks also tell us that what became known as Western Europe emerged after 30 years of religious wars waged by a group who later became known as Protestants against the dominance of the Roman Catholic church, ruled from Rome (Palmer and Colton 1978).

These religious wars gave rise not only to Protestantism and Catholicism as we know them now, but also to the Peace of Westphalia in 1648. The Peace of Westphalia was signed between states that now form Germany, Spain, France, Sweden and the Netherlands. In a nutshell, the Peace of Westphalia led Spain to end the 80 years of hostility towards the Dutch known as the Eighty Years' War (1568–1648) and to recognize the Dutch Republic as a sovereign state. The Peace of Westphalia in turn gave rise to religious states, led by Protestant or Catholic monarchs. It also brought a formal separation of the Dutch Republic from the Holy Roman Empire. In other words, by adopting Protestantism as their religion, the monarchs of England, the Netherlands and parts of Germany turned their states into Protestant states; similarly, states whose monarchs maintained Catholicism as the dominant religion, such as France, Italy and Spain, became Catholic states. Discrimination became common in these 'religious' states against those who adhered to other religions.

Equally important to note is that the Peace of Westphalia set the parameters for competition and cooperation within European statecraft, of which more below. These in turn formed the basis of European sovereign states and the related interstate systems. Essentially, the process of the formation of Catholic and Protestant states went hand in hand with the institutionalization of the Atlantic 'slave' trade and slavery.

THE AGE OF BANDITRY (1492–1648)

We have noted above that the Atlantic 'slave' trade and slavery gave rise to an international division of labour in which Europe, Africa and the Caribbean and the Americas each played their separate roles. As we see below, Africa never graduated from the age of banditry; abduction and the captivity of vulnerable peoples was not restricted to any specific ethnic group or nationality; those who abducted others could also become victims of abduction. For the moment it is necessary to note that there appears to be 'consensus' that the international division of labour around the Atlantic slavery that emerged after 1500 was influenced by the arrival of Columbus in the Americas.

The reasons for the voyages of Columbus in 1492 and of Vasco da Gama in 1498 have been long debated. These events were not accidental. After all, Columbus 'discovered' America because he went in search of markets and gold in East Asia. That happened when a growing bullion shortage and the consequent rise in the Afro-Eurasian world market price of gold made such an enterprise attractive and potentially profitable (which it turned out to be). 'Recall that Columbus was Genovese, first offering his service to Portugal to open a new route to the Orient, and only later accepting Spanish patronage' (Frank 1998: 56–7).

Let us stay with the issue of gold supplies in the Afro-Eurasian world market for a moment and see how Africa fits into the European 'discoveries' equation.

Until a new international division of labour took shape in the world economy after 1500, Africa had been a supplier to the global economy of gold, amongst others things. The bulk of the gold came from West Africa:

> which exported perhaps some 50 tons in the sixteenth century and nearly 100 tons, or a ton a year, in the seventeenth century. This gold export declined to 60 tons in the eighteenth century, before it ceased near the end of the century ... Other supplies of gold came from Nubia, which exported gold via Egypt to Constantinople/Istanbul and from Ethiopia to Egypt, the Red Sea, and India. Zimbabwe, which for a millennium had been an important source of gold for the world, reached its peak production of one ton during the fifteenth century. (Frank 1998: 149–50)

The essence of the 'age of banditry' was that those who were enslaving others could also be enslaved by others (Davis 2003). There was no clear legal framework and regulatory mechanism of what later became known as the transatlantic slave trade and the practice of chattel slavery. This is why the infamous debate between Bartolemé de Las Casas (1484–1566) and Ginés de Sepúlveda (1494–1573) in the School of Salamanca in the 1550s about the religiosity of native Americans should be analysed in a broader context than that of mere religious discourse.

The debate is well known and should not detain us here; however, for the record, let us re-state it briefly. Sepúlveda argued that indigenous peoples of the Americas had no souls and therefore were not humans and could be enslaved without sin being committed in the eyes of God; Las Casas argued that they were savages with souls, that is, though culturally inferior and childlike, they were ultimately humans, to be Christianized rather than enslaved. It is true, as Grosfoguel and Mielants have argued, that the two arguments represent the initial formal articulation of the two forms of racism that continued for the next five centuries. Sepúlveda represented a biological racist discourse; Las Casas a cultural racist discourse.

Las Casas argued that 'Indians' should be incorporated in the *encomienda* (a form of semi-feudal coerced labour) and called for Africans to replace them as slaves in the plantations. After all, Africans were characterized by Las Casas as not only 'people without religion' but also 'people without soul' (Grosfoguel and Mielants 2006: 3). Viewed in the context of religion, the debate was essentially about what constitutes a 'sin'. In plain language Las Casas and Sepúlveda wanted to satisfy themselves about whether the subjects of the King of Spain, whom they represented, might live with their consciences after they had killed people. For this to be possible, other people had to be dehumanized, and race had to become a major organizing principle of slavery.

We take the issue of religion and race a step further and argue that the absence of a clear legal framework and regulatory mechanism for chattel slavery formed the basis for the debate between Las Casas and Sepúlveda about whether Mexican Indians should be enslaved or not.

But, as is now acknowledged, the native 'Indians' did not need to be enslaved; according to Alfred Crosby, 'ecological imperialism' conquered the native population in the Americas. The germs that the Europeans brought with them were by far their most powerful weapons of conquest; they 'were most devastating in the New World, whose population had no immunities to the disease germs that Europeans brought with them' (Frank 1998: 58).

Neither were the territories where slavery was practised, especially the Americas, secure. For this reason several territories changed hands in the period:

> The spread of sugar cultivation in the 1600s stimulated the expansion of the Atlantic slave trade dramatically. After sugar production became successful in Brazil, the Dutch sought to

dominate the industry by capturing northern Brazil in 1630, which got them started in the traffic. Although the Portuguese regained all of Brazil a few decades later, the Dutch remained active in the slave trade. Some of the planters who had cooperated with the Dutch fled Brazil and settled in the Caribbean, where they helped to establish sugarcane cultivation. (Postma 2003: 12)

The Dutch took over Sint Maarten in 1631 and made it a property of the West Indies Company. Two years later the Spaniards drove the Dutch from Sint Maarten and took it over. In 1634 the Dutch drove the Spaniards out of Curaçao and made it a Dutch possession; Sint Eustatius, Bonaire and Aruba became Dutch possessions in 1635, to be followed by Saba in 1640 (Goslinga 1985). Viewed in this context, Atlantic slavery was a constituent part of the Eighty Years' War.

We return to this below. For the moment, suffice it to say that it is also within the context of the age of banditry that we should assess the following observation:

In Mexico, Colombia, Bolivia, Peru, and Chile slaves were found in the higher occupations from the very beginning of Spanish colonization. An uncertain number, perhaps a few hundred, were even assistants to the conquistadors in expeditions into new territories and enjoyed the spoils of conquest. Some slave soldiers became free [at the expense of native populations], some rose to be conquistadors, and some became slaveholders themselves. By the 1570s it was no longer possible [for Africans] to gain entry into the ruling elites by accomplishing great military feats. (Fogel 1989: 42)

In other words some of the enslaved Africans themselves became instruments of conquest; but their black skins betrayed them, so after conquest they had to revert to the roles assigned to them in the international division of labour, with race as the organizing principle of slavery.

Not only were the rules between nations unclear with regard to slavery; so were the rules governing citizens. A case in point is that of a Dutch captain who captured a Portuguese ship with some 130 African captives and commandeered it, landing at the Dutch seaport of Middleburg in November 1596.

At first the African captives were kept in their '*vrije lyberteyt*' ('natural liberty'), because they were baptized Christians. The conventional wisdom then was that Christians no longer enslaved other Christians. Thus, it is recorded in the minutes of Middelburg:

> [t]hat many Moors were deposited here on ships from Guinea, almost certainly a hundred, men as well as women and children, and for this reason they do not belong to someone, nor can they be sold as slaves, but they have to be put in their natural liberty, without anyone laying claim to the ownership of these people. (Willemsen 2006a)

The Portuguese ship-owner and the captain of the ship, who were no longer able to capitalize on their 'cargo', did not take this lying down. Twice they appealed to the States of Zeeland to transfer their 'goods' to the West Indies. The first appeal was rejected, but the second was more successful. It was ordered that the shipowner (a certain Pieter van der Haegen) was authorized to do '*soe hy 't verstaet*' ('as he pleases') – as is the case with any cargo.

But what became of the Africans on board the ship? This question has also been posed by Dienke Hondius:

> Of such a large group entering the small town of Middelburg, one expects to find some historical traces of them. The Leiden historian Pieter Emmer suggests that 'a large part of the slaves will no doubt have been transported directly to the market in Antwerp, where slaves were regularly traded'. However, there is no indication of this at all. It is certain that there were more Africans in Antwerp, but an organized trip of a group of Africans, or an agreement between traders from Zeeland and Antwerp are both highly unlikely. The city of Antwerp could not be reached at that time because the Schelde River was already closed off and the Antwerp Exchange was no longer active. Some of the Africans may have reached Antwerp but not the whole group. (Hondius 2009: 35–6)

The bottom line is that at that point in time there were no clear rules that regulated what later became known as the transatlantic 'slave' trade and slavery. With regard to Africa some states, such as Asante and Dahomey, emerged in the eighteenth century as a consequence of the Atlantic 'slave' trade; on the whole Africa remained trapped in the banditry phase, whereas Europe graduated from the banditry phase after the Peace of Westphalia.

Between 1500 and 1600 the majority of African captives transported across the Atlantic for enslavement were transported by the Portuguese or on Portuguese ships (266,100), followed by Britain (2,000) (see Table 2.1). However between 1600 and 1650 the Netherlands replaced Britain as the second major transatlantic transporter; the figures for this period are as follows: Portugal (439,500), Netherlands (39,900) and Britain (23,000). The smaller countries transported more captives than the larger ones in the first 50 years of the seventeenth century. As we see below, this changed after the Peace of Westphalia (1648) as European states became more delineated. The figures for 1651–75 were Britain 115,200; France 5,900; Netherlands 59,500; Denmark 200; Portugal 53,700.

Whereas chattel slavery became regulated under European states, in Africa banditry continued, with the forcible capture and abduction of Africans, their imprisonment in European dungeons in Africa, and their forced transportation to the Caribbean and the Americas; this was done by Europeans for the sole purpose of enslavement between the sixteenth and the twentieth centuries. In plain language, in the age of banditry every African of whatever nationality or ethnicity and status might be forcibly captured, abducted and transported for enslavement (Rodney 1974; Davidson 1980). The linguistic variety of captives who arrived at the other side of the Atlantic attests to this (Wooding 1972; Martinus 1996).

Thus, as we see below, whereas banditry informed African participation in the 'slave' trade from the fifteenth to the nineteenth centuries, sovereignty and citizenship informed European participation in the slave trade and slavery after 1648. In other words, European sovereign nations had to decide whether to participate in Atlantic slavery or not because chattel slavery required sovereign state backing and enforcement, though slavery preceded the rise of the European sovereignty and world order.

The roles played by states in slavery include the forced withdrawal of Denmark from the 'slave' trade and slavery at an early stage, and British initiatives to abolish the trade and slavery (Wallerstein 1982). Viewed in this context the Peace of Westphalia and the rise of the European world order had a lasting impact on the rest of the world beyond the geographical location of Europe in three important ways: sovereignty, citizenship and science. Let us take these issues in turn.

SOVEREIGNTY AND CHATTEL SLAVERY (1648-1789)

If the period between 1492 and the Peace of Westphalia (1648), including the Thirty Years' War (1618-48), can be characterized as the age of banditry in relation to chattel slavery, the period between the Peace of Westphalia and the outbreak of the French Revolution in 1789 can be characterized as the age of sovereignty. Though territorial integrity of peoples has been part of human history generally, the Westphalia 'sovereignty', signed by the Netherlands, France, Germany and others, added another dimension.

At one level, it gave rise to the mutual recognition of the signatories of the Treaty of Westphalia. Following this, reciprocal recognition became fundamental to the legitimacy of sovereignty. Once one major European country recognized the existence of another, other nations were likely to fall in line or form alliances. Important to note is that one of the constituent components of sovereignty is the monopolization of violence by the state. Thus at another level the Peace of Westphalia gave rise to the monopolization of violence; the state demanded the exclusive authority to intervene coercively in the activities within its territory. In fact the architecture of the Atlantic 'slave trade' and slavery overlaps with the formation and consolidation of nation states in Europe.

For the 'outside world', the importance of the Peace of Westphalia lay not in the reciprocal recognition of the sovereignty of the signatories, but rather in the non-recognition of the sovereignty of 'others'. With regard to chattel slavery, the period between the Peace of Westphalia and the French Revolution was mediated by the Treaty of Breda (1667), the Peace of Ryswick (1697) and the Peace of Utrecht (1713).

For our current purposes, we delineate four constituent components of sovereignty relevant to addressing the issue of chattel slavery; *territorial control, nationalism, international relations and emigration.*

The first is *territorial control*. The demarcation of borders and territories and the reciprocal recognition of each other's borders by the warring factions, who constituted themselves as monarchs, facilitated the end of the Thirty Years' religious wars and gave rise to the Westphalia sovereignty (see the Avalon Project, Yale Law School 2010, www.yale.edu/lawweb/avalon/). This complicated the regulation of chattel slavery, which required the control of given territories and the recognition of other enslaving nations:

The bitter commercial warfare of the second half of the seventeenth century between England and Holland represented an effort on the part of England to break the commercial net the Dutch had woven about England and her colonies. 'What we want,' said [General George] Monck with military bluntness, 'is more of the trade the Dutch now have.' Whether it was nominal peace or actual war, a sort of private war was maintained, for thirty years, between the Dutch West India Company and the Royal African Company. (Williams 1994: 40)

In practice however territorial control required the recognition of the sovereignty of those involved (in Europe) and the *non-recognition* of the sovereignty of those not involved (in Africa, the Caribbean, the Americas and elsewhere).

Territorial control also made it possible for the state to mobilize natural and human resources within national territories, which in turn made the measurement of the wealth of individuals on the one hand, and the wealth of nations on the other, more visible (Smith 1977). The share of slavery in the economies also became visible and measurable. Thus we are informed that both the price the Europeans paid each other for captives in Africa and the number of captives doubled after the Peace of Ryswick in 1697 (Wallerstein 1986: 104).

The Peace of Ryswick, signed on 30 October 1697 at Ryswick near The Hague by England, Holland, Germany and Spain on the one hand and France on the other, terminated the sanguinary struggle which had begun in 1688. England did not disguise its interests in this period:

> The keystone of this mercantilist arch was the Navigation Laws. 'English measures designed for English ends.' The Navigation Laws were aimed at the Dutch, 'the foster fathers' as Andrews called them, of the early British colonies, who supplied credit, delivered goods, purchased colonial produce and transported it to Europe, all at more attractive rates than the British could offer in open market. But the laws were aimed also at the Scots and Irish and Scotland's attempt to set up an independent African Company aroused great fears in England and was largely responsible for the Act of Union in 1707. (Williams 1994: 56)

The Peace of Utrecht superseded the Peace of Ryswick and strengthened the Westphalia sovereignty. If the Treaty of Westphalia had paved the way for the Dutch and other European nations to delineate the boundaries of nationhood and sovereignty, the Treaty of Utrecht (1713) reduced the powers of Spain over the Dutch and affirmed the latter's sovereignty by emphasizing balance of power. Textbooks tell us that the Treaty of Utrecht was a series of treaties concluded between France, Great Britain, Portugal, Prussia, Savoy and Holland in 1713 and 1715, which ended the War of the Spanish Succession. It should be noted however that the Treaty of Utrecht was not just a European affair. The treaty led France to cede Newfoundland, Acadia or Nova Scotia, the district around Hudson Bay, and St Kitts to Great Britain, which had conquered them. The treaty also made it possible for Great Britain to acquire Gibraltar and Minorca from Spain, and gain the monopoly of the 'slave' trade with Spanish America, in an agreement known as the Asiento (Elliot 2006).

In other words the Peace of Utrecht took the issue of sovereignty one step further than reciprocal recognition. With territorial control assured, the involvement of the state in the 'slave' trade and slavery became important. For instance,

> [i]n the second half of the eighteenth century, the French government offered bounties to slave ships leaving France for Africa, and made an additional payment for every slave they landed in the French West Indies. This concern is understandable when it is realized that ... sugar was the largest single item imported into England in the eighteenth century. (Hopkins, quoted here from Wallerstein 1986: 105)

This demonstrates the active participation of the French state in the Atlantic slavery, in providing a subsidy for the hunters of captives, traders in captives and enslavers. Overall Britain was the second major trader and transporter of African captives after Portugal. But France made major advances and bypassed the Netherlands between 1700 and 1800. Available data indicate that France transported 34,100 African captives between 1676 and 1700. This figure jumped to 106,300 between 1701 and 1725, then to 256,900 between 1726 and 1750, then to 321,500 between 1751 and 1775; between 1776 and 1800 the figure stood at 419,500.

The French revolution interrupted this process; thus between 1801 and 1825 the figure declined to 217,900, then to 94,100 between 1826 and 1850, and then to 3,200 between 1851 and 1867. By the time France ended its share in the slave trade in 1867, following its official declaration of abolition in 1848, it had transported 1,456,400 African captives across the Atlantic Ocean. That is equivalent to 13.2 per cent of African captives between the sixteenth and nineteenth centuries.

However, countries that transported captives did not necessarily use them as slaves. Recall that the Asiento gave Britain increased power to supply African captives to Spanish-controlled territories in the Americas after the Peace of Utrecht. Between 1701 and 1725 Britain transported 380,900 African captives; this jumped to 490,500 between 1726 and 1750 and to 859,100 between 1751 and 1775; it declined to 741,300 between 1776 and 1800, perhaps due to American independence, and declined further to 257,000 between 1801 and 1825. So we should make a distinction between the transportation of captives and their end use as slaves. Though Spain made use of enslaved African labour, evidence suggests that it did not transport African captives between 1500 and 1750.

Available figures suggest that Spain transported around 1,000 African captives between 1751 and 1775; this jumped to 8,600 between 1776 and 1800, then to 204,800 between 1801 and 1825 and reached a peak of 279,200 between 1826 and 1850, before it declined to 23,400 between 1851 and 1867. By 1867 Spain had formally transported 517,000 African captives across the Atlantic; this constitutes about 4.7 per cent of African captives transported across the Atlantic by seven European nations between 1500 and 1867. On the one hand this is a consequence of the way in which sovereignty had been constructed in the period before the Peace of Westphalia, rather than of the actual participation of Spain; especially when it is considered that Spain occupied the Netherlands for a while. On the other hand this suggests that Spain started transporting more captives after the legal abolition of the Atlantic 'slave' trade by Britain in 1807.

Neither did Britain's expansion prevent France from increasing its share. Thus:

> England's supremacy was the result of the relatively quick pace of her commercial expansion and was not brought about by an absolute decline in French commerce with West Africa ... Indeed, the tempo of French activity in West Africa actually increased after 1763, following Choueul's efforts to develop Africa to compensate for the loss of Canada, and to free the French West Indies from dependence on British ships for supplies of slaves. (Hopkins, quoted here from Wallerstein 1986: 105)

This brings us to the second component of sovereignty, namely, *nationalism*. Recall that the Peace of Westphalia set the parameters for competition and cooperation among the signatories. Territorial control and mobilization of people and resources facilitated notions of belonging. Those within national boundaries differentiated themselves from people outside their borders – 'us' and 'them'. On the one hand the process within Europe of mobilizing the 'us' within territories against the 'them' outside them gave rise to what was later to be called nationalism and racial consciousness (Anderson 1983; Gellner 1983). But Columbus, who would be classified today as Italian, was commissioned to undertake his historic mission by a Spanish King, before the emergence of national sovereignty and nationalism proper. In this vein, there are parts of the narrative that are distinctly European in nature, because the narrative is not located in individual countries alone; it derives, firstly, from a culture of the monopoly of law and force or the means of coercion, and secondly, from the desire for internal unity, homogeneity and legal sovereignty (Palmer and Colton 1978).

On the other hand those within the borders who did not subscribe to the conditions within the new boundaries resorted to the maintenance of their physical space, identities and culture, which became known as ethnonationalism (Smith 1986; Muller 2008). In the words of Muller, '[t]he core of the ethnonationalist idea is that nations are defined by a shared heritage, which usually includes a common language, a common faith, and a common ethnic ancestry' (Muller 2008: 20). As we see below, this in turn gave a European character to science and research on the 'slave' trade and slavery despite appeals to, and the appearance of, universalism. Underlying this was the self-proclaimed superiority of the European man in relation to Africans.

With regard to the Netherlands, the self-proclaimed superiority of the Dutchman in relation to other peoples went hand in hand with the chauvinism of Dutch nationals in relation to other European nationals. Thus, in comparing the humanity of Dutch people and their treatment of African captives in relation to other Europeans, the Dutch 'slave' trader, Willem Bosman, made the following notes in the seventeenth century:

> You will really wonder to see how these slaves live on board, for though their number sometimes amounts to six or seven hundred, yet by the careful management of our masters of ships they are so regulated that it seems incredible. And in this particular our

nation exceeds all other Europeans; for as the French, Portuguese, and English slave-ships are always foul and stinking, on the contrary ours are for the most part clean and neat. (Bosman, in Postma 2003: 126)

This observation and statement gives an insight into how the 'slave' trade was designed and planned from the Netherlands and Europe. The statement also suggests that the Dutch imagined that they treated their captives better than the French, Portuguese and English, the assumption being that it was legitimate to enslave Africans provided that they were treated with Dutch care. The paradox is that despite this attitude towards other European 'slave' traders, Bosman also recorded that when a 'slave revolt' occurred on a Dutch ship, the Dutch sailors were rescued by French and English sailors. In other words, though the European nations competed among themselves, when it came to their engagement with Africans, Europeans cooperated with each other (Nimako 1991).

Recall that at the time Africans were considered by European enslavers to be subhuman. Thus in his manual on how Dutch enslavers working for the West Indies Company (WIC) should interact with Africans, including the provision of items such as guns and alcohol necessary to obtain captives, Bosman gave the following advice to Dutch workers on the WIC ships:

Captains should carefully watch out for the thieving of the Negroes, in order that not too much gets stolen. I say 'too much', since it is almost impossible to escape theft completely; at least I have never heard of such a situation. Even the rowers hired by the captain will try to steal. For this reason he must watch everyone, since theft seems to be an inherited trait of the people there. (Bosman, in Postma 2003: 138)

The implications of this are that in fostering slavery outside Europe, race became the organizing principle and reinforced nationalism.

The period between 1762 and 1790 also saw several major political upheavals in France, the Netherlands, St Dominique/Haiti, the British North American colonies and the United States of America, India, and elsewhere, as well as the technological beginnings of what has been called the 'industrial revolution' (Frank 1998: 251).

Widespread European warfare disrupted Atlantic commerce in 1690–1715 and again in 1740–63. French and Dutch support for the Americans during their Revolutionary War (1775–83) virtually halted the slave trade of these two countries. The French Revolutionary Wars (1792–1815) did not interrupt the slave trade but changed the relative commercial balance among nations, increasing the power of Britain in the long run. (Postma 2003: 16)

Britain had earlier supported Portugal in its bid to separate from Spain in the 1640s. But when Haiti sought independence, all the European slave-trading nations and the United States of America cooperated against it. Haiti stood alone as an island in a sea of slave-trading nations: this should not be viewed in the context of interstate conflicts; it should be viewed in the context of race as the organizing principle of the Atlantic slavery.

The third component of sovereignty was modern *international relations*, born out of the Peace of Westphalia. The consolidation of territories and the recognition of each other's territories laid the foundations of modern European international relations, trade and law. We speak of European international relations because the recognition of European territories by Europeans did not imply the recognition of non-European territories by European explorers, travellers and emigrants. On the contrary, as we see below, European citizens placed flags on non-European territories to symbolize the extension of European sovereignty. But this did not imply that foreign nations or peoples recognized and gave consent to European flags and laws. However, it did imply that European states could hold slaves in foreign lands that had been expropriated, though they could not hold slaves on their home territories. This constituted the 'free soil ideology', which we expand on below.

These explorations gave rise not only to chattel slavery, but also to the financial system that facilitated the 'slave' trade and kept slavery afloat, of which more below.

This brings us to the fourth and last component of our discussion of sovereignty, namely, *emigration*. Sovereignty highlights emigration and immigration and delineates who belongs to a nation and who does not. Sovereignty also regulates who comes and goes out of a country. Since an enslaved population works under coercion without consent and contract and thus requires supervision, the transportation of African captives and their enslavement required the emigration of Europeans to supervise the enslaved.

Europe's newfound sources of income and wealth generated some increase in its own production, which also supported some growth of population. That began to recover from the disastrous fourteenth-century decline in the fifteenth century, and for the next two and a half centuries Europe's population grew at an average of about 0.3 per cent a year, to double from 60 or more in 1500 to 130 or 140 million in 1750. (Frank 1998: 75)

Part of the population growth was absorbed by emigration to the 'New World'. As we have seen, conducting the 'slave' trade and slavery on foreign soils, especially Africa and the Americas, required European citizens to be on the spot. To this effect they went as seamen, soldiers, plantation owners and supervisors, doctors, researchers, and last but not least, as spouses and wives of men (Verwey-Jonker 1983: 17). It has been estimated that 50 million people emigrated from Europe to the Americas in less than a century, and the European population still registered an increase (Palmer and Colton 1978; Postma 2003).

The arrival of Columbus in the Americas in 1492, European encounters with non-European peoples, and the emigration of Europeans that ensued not only strengthened European national and racial consciousness; it also violated both the territorial integrity and the humanity of other peoples.

Equally important to note is that from the point of view of epistemology, the emigration of Europeans to the Americas at this point in time has given rise to two broad recurrent notions that tend to serve as a backdrop to the discussion of the transatlantic 'slave' trade and slavery, namely, the notions of European *expansion* and of *colonization*. It is taken for granted that the rise of nation states in Europe and their extension and expansion to other regions in the world formed the basis of a process that is referred to by some authors as European expansion (Hartog 1961; Paquette and Engerman 1996; Emmer and Mörner 1992), and by others as conquest and colonization (Rodney 1974; Davidson 1992; Dussel 1985; Mignolo 2007). In turn, the expansion and extension or conquest and colonization found their expression in the construction of 'new' nations and new national borders, the introduction of European languages in other societies, and the introduction of administrative structures and cultures to mirror specific European countries (Amin 1974; Bernal 1987; Chomsky 1993; Nimako 1991; Willemsen 1980 and 2006a).

Table 2.1 Transportation of African Captives by Nationality of Carrier (thousands)

	Britain	France	Spain	Netherlands	USA and Br. Carib.	Denmark	Portugal and Brazil	All nations	Annual volume
1519–1600	2.0						264.1	266.1	3.3
1601–1650	23.0			39.9			439.5	502.4	4.1
1651–1675	115.2	5.9		59.5			53.7	234.5	9.4
1676–1700	243.3	34.1		97.4			161.1	551.3	22.1
1701–1725	380.9	106.3		74.5	11.0	15.4	378.3	967.7	38.7
1726–1750	490.5	253.9		76.4	44.5	16.7	405.6	1,278.5	51.2
1751–1775	859.1	321.5	1.0	118.2	89.1	7.6	472.9	1,875.2	75.0
1776–1800	741.3	419.5	8.6	34.2	54.3	13.4	626.2	1,914.5	76.6
1801–1825	257.0	217.9	204.8	1.3	81.1	30.4	871.6	1,644.2	65.8
1826–1850		94.1	279.2			10.5	1,247.7	1,621.0	64.8
1851–1867		3.2	23.4			.02	154.2	180.8	10.6
All Years	3,112.3	1,456.4	517	501.4	280	94.2	5,074.9	11,036.2	30.4
Percentage	28.2%	13.2%	4.7%	4.5%	2.5%	0.9%	46.0%	100.0%	

Source: This table is taken from Johannes Postma (2003) Table 3.1, page 36; sourced from David Eltis, 'The Volume and Structure of the Transatlantic Slave Trade: A Reassessment', *William and Mary Quarterly*, 58(1) (January 2001): 17–31.

Note: The original heading of Postma's table is 'Exports of Slaves from Africa by Nationality of Carrier'; owing to our conceptual innovations we have replaced 'Exports of Slaves from Africa' with 'Transportation of African Captives'.

It is now common for people to speak of the Dutch Antilles, of Spanish America, of Anglophone, Francophone, and Portuguese Africa. Viewed in this context, the notions of European expansion and modernity on the one hand and of the colonization and subjugation of others on the other are two sides of the same coin in modern history (Mignolo 2007; Dussel 1985). This phase in human history, also referred to as the 'modern world', is usually considered to have begun at around the end of the fifteenth century (Abu-Lughod 1989; Davidson 1980; Frank 1978; Wallerstein 1974).

Despite these broad generalizations it should be noted that the notion of European expansion can also be misleading because not all European nations could, or did, expand. Even among those nations that might have expanded, some, such as Denmark were forced by more powerful Europeans states, such as Britain, to drop out. The Netherlands 'which tried for some time to stay on by maintaining the slave-trade, was eventually forced to transfer her forts to Great Britain' (Wallerstein 1982).

Behind these systemic and structural changes were concrete developments that affected numerous peoples of great diversity. Among the processes that were set in motion was the appropriation of land, whose extreme form was the extermination of what is referred to as the indigenous population (Wolf 1982); and the exploitation of labour, whose extreme form is chattel slavery (Fogel 1989; Williams 1994). These in turn gave rise to the international division of labour we have referred to above and to a new form of race, ethnic, class and gender relations in various regions of the world (Hoetink 1973; Moitt 2001; Small 1994a).

In the context of broader historical and political discourse European emigration to the Western hemisphere led to the notion of the West, from which the idea of the Western world later emerged: Europe and its descendants across the Atlantic Ocean. Chattel slavery in turn gave rise to the notion of an African diaspora. Viewed in this context, the Atlantic 'slave' trade and slavery should not be studied as a historical accident but rather as an extension of the formation of nation states in Europe.

CITIZENSHIP, SLAVERY AND THE 'FREE SOIL IDEOLOGY'

European-led chattel slavery became a total institution with or through the maturity of citizenship. Recalling the events that gave rise to what became known as the Western world or Euro-America, Huntington writes that for a century and a half after the emergence of the modern international system with the Peace of Westphalia (1648),

> the conflicts of the Western world were largely among princes – emperors, absolute monarchs and constitutional monarchs attempting to expand their bureaucracies, their armies, their mercantilist economic strength, and, most important, the territory they ruled. In the process they created nation states, and beginning with the French Revolution the principal lines of conflict were between nations rather than princes. In 1793, as R.R. Palmer put it, 'The wars of kings were over; the wars of peoples had begun.'
> (Huntington 1993: 22–3)

In other words, citizens also became stakeholders in states and national conflicts after the French Revolution.

Perhaps Huntington should have extended his observations and analysis to include the fact that the wars of European kings were extended to engulf the rest of the world before 'the wars of peoples had begun'; the religious wars went hand in hand with attempts and efforts to expand international trade to Asia.

> Like the Ming [in China] and the English, the Spanish state experienced financial difficulties to maintain sufficient armed forces, when its revenues declined first because of the decline in the value of silver due to overproduction and then due to the sudden shortage when American silver mines cut production and remittances in the 1630s ... When confronted with threats to its sovereignty by the Portuguese to the west and the Catalans to the east, Madrid gave priority to the challenge from the Catalans, who were supported by their French neighbors, which led to the sacrifice of its domination over Portugal. The authoritative historian of Spain J.H. Elliot in his oft-cited article on 'the Decline of Spain' dated it 'from the end of the 1640 [when] Spain and Spain's international power were visibly crumbling.'
> (Frank 1998: 245)

Frank also notes that:

> Portugal signed its first commercial treaty in 1642. It was the first of the three forerunners (the others were in 1654 and 1667) of the Treaty of Methuen of 1703, which cemented the protection Portugal now sought and accepted – at a price – from

Britain. Portugal forced Dutch capital out of its sugar plantations in Portuguese Brazil after 1640, so the Dutch went to British Barbados, which they converted into a sugar plantation in turn ... The Dutch VOC [East India Company] exports, mostly silver, to Asia were also comparatively low in 1640 ... The sudden decline in silver production around 1640 that these market forces generated then pulled the rug out from under the Spanish economy entirely. (Frank 1998: 245–6)

It should be noted that the driving forces behind these economic activities, sugar and silver production, was enslaved African labour. In Barbados:

Dutch merchants saw the potential of Barbados as a market for slaves and sugar-making. By financing sugar planters, these merchants expected a derived demand for slaves which the English could not supply themselves as they had no secure slave-trading base on the West African coast. As leading slave traders they desired to replace [European] indentured servants with [African] slaves everywhere they could. Being in large part Jewish, many Dutch merchants in Barbados were not allowed, by [English] law and custom, to contract white servants – the result of the exportation of English anti-semitism to the colony. Logically, therefore, they conceived indentured servitude as inconsistent with their New World economic and social interest. (Beckles 1990: 20–1)

Thus, operating largely from Pernambuco in the north-east of Brazil, Dutch merchants monopolized the Barbados slave market for about 20 years (Beckles 1990: 30).

The implications of the forgoing discussion are that after the European monarchs had settled part of their wars amongst themselves they turned their attention to the wars with the outside world. Thus the wars of the peoples were both wars between Europeans and wars against non-Europeans. With regard to the Netherlands, Karel Davids observes that:

[t]he origins of arms manufacture in the Netherlands can be traced back to at least the early Middle Ages. However, the transition from small-scale fabrication to large production in this industry did not begin until about 1600. The immediate cause of the expansion was the outbreak of the Revolt [against Spain].

Lots of weapons were needed to arm the soldiers, ships and fortified positions that were used to defend the newly-proclaimed independence of the United Provinces and to lend protection to merchantmen and vessels equipped by trading companies to sail to Asia, Africa and the West-Indies. Once the inland arms industry had begun to grow, it also developed export outlets itself. The Dutch Republic thus became both an importer and exporter of arms. By the 1620s, bronze cannon was sold to Morocco and Muscovy and large amounts of small arms, armour and powder found their way to Denmark, Sweden, France, Italy and Germany. (Davids 2008: 146–7)

Chattel slavery, which could be enforced only by perpetually waging war on the enslaved, became part and parcel of the 'wars of peoples'. In turn, since race was the main organizing principle of chattel slavery, the 'wars of peoples' also became racialized wars, in the sense that one of the key elements of citizenship is to determine who should be included in a nation and who should be excluded. Citizenship was sharpened after the French revolution with the claims for more liberty, equality and fraternity. In the words of Wallerstein:

To be a citizen meant to have the right to participate, on an equal level with all other citizens, in the basic decisions of the state. To be a citizen meant that there were no persons with statuses higher than that of citizen (such as aristocrats). To be a citizen meant that everyone was being accepted as a rational person, capable of political decision. The logical consequence of the concept of citizen was universal suffrage. And as we know, the political history of the following 150 years was one of steady expansion of suffrage in country after country. (Wallerstein 2004: 51)

Recall that to consolidate and defend the territorial gains from the Peace of Westphalia, the ruling groups in Europe needed to mobilize natural and human resources. To this effect, monarchs and princes became intertwined through intermarriage and other interests. But citizens made claims on the ruling group. As a trade-off, European citizens gained more freedom at the expense of other peoples, hence making Europe rhetorically a 'free soil'.

Whether by coincidence or not, it was three important slave-trading nations, England, France and the Netherlands, which were the first countries in north-west Europe in which the notion of civil liberty started to develop, around 1500. This was exemplified in terminating the servitude of the domestic populations, and in the idea that there was no place for slaves in their respective countries. The decision of the Middleburg administrators in 1596 that led to the immediate release of a shipload of Africans arriving in the city reminds us of the doctrine of 'free soil' or 'free air'. As we noted above, the Africans had reached Middleburg on a ship seized from the Portuguese. At first they were freed, as baptized Christians, although they were later delivered into slavery when the second appeal of the Portuguese was granted (Willemsen 2006a; Hondius 2009).

So it was not always clear how to deal with slavery on Dutch soil. It should also be mentioned that enslavers quite regularly brought slaves, their 'human capital', from Suriname and Curaçao to the Netherlands. Landing on Dutch soil did not automatically give them their freedom. A bill from the Dutch Parliament, dated 23 May 1776, 'Concerning the Freedom of Negroes and other Slaves brought over from the colonies', indicated this in no uncertain terms.

It was only in 1838 that slavery on Dutch territory was officially abolished. Article 2 of the Civil Code states: 'All those residing in the states' territory are free and entitled to their civil rights. Slavery and all other personal servitudes of whatever kind or known by whatever name are not tolerated in the Kingdom' (Willemsen 2006a: 36).

Matters were just as complicated in England. Although a judicial verdict dating from 1569 stated that 'England was too pure an Air for Slaves to breathe in', this was not always enforced and the pendulum swung both ways. In 1765, this verdict was confirmed by lawyer William Blackstone, who wrote: 'And this spirit of liberty is so deeply implanted in our constitution, and rooted even in our very soil, that a slave or a Negro, the moment he lands in England, falls under the protection of the laws and so far becomes a freeman.'

But through their West Indian lobby, slave owners continued to insist in several lawsuits that the enslaved were their personal property and could not become free simply by treading on English soil. Public opinion, however, took the view 'that Black Slaves, brought into England, and baptised, are free from Slavery, though not from common Service; that is, they are free from being bought and sold'.

The relationship between the notion of 'free soil', state law, the enslavers and the public came to the fore in the case of James Somerset (see Willemsen 2006a for more details; also Walvin 1973; Shyllon 1977).

The narrative of the Somerset case is as follows. In October 1769, an enslaved African called Somerset arrived in England with his enslaver from Virginia. There he became acquainted with other black people from London; he even became good friends with some prominent white people. In August 1771, he was baptized in the church of St Andrew, Holborn, and chose 'James' as his Christian name. Within the Black community it was said that baptism and Christianization would entail freedom for an enslaved African – or at any rate would be of great help in a request to change his legal status. Shortly thereafter, James Somerset escaped. But on 26 November 1771 he was captured, to be shipped off to Jamaica. Some of those who sympathized with the fate of the enslaved, however, prevented this from happening, and the captain of the ship that was to transport Somerset was summoned for imprisoning Somerset on his vessel. The verdict of the court, presided over by the influential parliamentarian and famous lawyer Lord Mansfield, was that Somerset could not be forced to leave England. The blacks who attended the verdict screamed with joy, because they thought that Somerset's release would automatically result in the liberation of all blacks in England. They all rose and bowed their heads in respect for the court. A few days later, more than 200 black people assembled in a public house in Westminster and paid five shillings each to be able to celebrate with Somerset, and to dance and drink to Lord Mansfield's health.

The news of the verdict crossed the ocean and gave North America cause for protest against England: if Mansfield had pronounced slavery illegal in England, it implied that slavery was also illegal in America, since English law superseded local laws. According to Blumrosen and Blumrosen (2005), this matter sparked the American War of Independence and even the American Civil War which – as is well-known – was about halting the expansion of slavery in the new US territories.

Lord Mansfield's verdict, however, did not mean that slavery in England was abolished (Shyllon 1977). The decree was formulated in such a way that it did not go beyond the conclusion that a master does not have the right to coerce an enslaved person into going to another country. Though almost everybody believed that slavery had been pronounced illegal by Mansfield, it survived in England long after the Somerset case; it was not officially abolished until 1833, when Parliament legislated for the entire British Empire. (Many enslavers got round the law by kidnapping their escaped enslaved and transferring them to plantations in the Caribbean.)

An incident similar to the case in Middleburg took place in 1571 in Bordeaux. James has recorded that '[u]p to 1716 every Negro slave who touched French soil was free, and after an interval of fifty years another decree in 1762 reaffirmed this'. (James 1980: 40). As in England, several cases went to court in France on the issue of whether an enslaved person might obtain his freedom by setting foot on French soil. In 1777, it was stipulated that enslaved and free black people were not permitted to enter France. This regulation was cancelled in 1848, when slavery was abolished in the French colonies.

With regard to the Netherlands, four political and social events took place in 1795 that are relevant to the discussion of citizenship and slavery.

The first was the emergence of the Batavian Republic, in which the Dutch state became a vassal state of France under Napoleonic occupation. This set in motion a struggle for the survival of the Dutch state itself. During the French period (1795–1813), the Netherlands was governed by the French or by Francophile Dutchmen.

The second event was the spread of the concepts of freedom, equality and fraternity, which began to resonate beyond French borders.

The Napoleonic occupation of the Netherlands from 1795 to 1813 resulted in a Unitarian state and a modernized state apparatus, legalized by the 1815 constitution. All citizens were to be subjected to the same system of justice and received equal rights, although the large 'Nederlands Hervormed Kerk' (Dutch Reformed Church) took up a privileged position while the Roman Catholic Church took second place. (Buiting 1990: 58)

We return to this in Chapter 5. For the moment suffice it to say that the French declaration of liberty, dating from 1794, was not adopted by the Dutch. The institution of slavery simply continued to exist under the Batavian Republic. As far as the Dutch were concerned, the ideology of liberty and equality was limited to Europeans and did not apply to their fellow black people, though this had been, for a short while, the case in France.

The third of these events was the Haitian revolution, the first and only successful revolt by the enslaved, resulting in the first republic led by people of African descent in the 'New World'. This constituted a watershed moment for Africans in the New World. It also caused shock waves throughout the Caribbean slavery societies. James has argued that the French and Haitian revolutions were intertwined:

> While the French bourgeoisie led the assault on the absolute monarch at home, the planters followed suit in the colonies. And, as in France, the geographical divisions of San Domingo [Haiti] and their historical development shaped the revolutionary movement and the coming insurrection of the slaves ... Rejected in France, humiliated at home, the Mulattoes organized a revolt. It was the quarrel between bourgeoisie and monarchy that brought the Paris masses on the political stage. It was the quarrel between whites and Mulattoes that woke the sleeping slaves. (James 1980: 58; and 73)

In addition to this, the Haitian revolution also formed part of a broader competition between Britain and France for the survival of their states and empires. Just as France had supported the American revolutionary wars, so Britain had supported the Haitian revolt, but not to its conclusion (James 1980: 53).

As will become clear in Chapter 3, after the loss of America, Britain shifted its attention to India, and propagated the abolition of the slave trade. Thus, just as the French and Haitian revolutions were intertwined, so was chattel slavery intertwined with the development of the world economy.

The fourth event was the slave rebellion on Curaçao under the command of Tula. This uprising took place on 17 August 1795, while the Haitian revolution was still taking place. Legend has it that Tula was born in Europe to African parents and spent his adolescent years travelling with his enslaver throughout Europe and in part of Africa. In Portugal, he graduated from the nautical college. By the time he arrived in Curaçao, Tula had become a so-called man of letters: he spoke various European and African languages and was an effective herb doctor. Tula was also a man of the Bible: he knew it by heart. Wherever he went, he took his Bible with him. When his enslaver left for Santo Domingo, Tula had the time and the opportunity to take care of the enslaved on Curaçao. He visited many plantations to convert and help them. In 1789, he founded the Unie van Slaven (Union of Slaves). Its aim was to promote liberty and equality for the enslaved. All enslavers were informed of its formation, and in October 1789 a conference took place between the Union and the enslavers. Tula and his fellow combatants demanded better working and living conditions. As a result, rations were upgraded slightly and the working day was cut by half an hour (Willemsen 2006a; do Rego and Janga 2009).

We return to these political and social events below. For the moment suffice it to say that underlying the political and religious developments of the Peace of Westphalia, the Peace of Ryswick, the Peace of Utrecht, and the French Revolution was an economic system that was woven into society and involved business, the state and citizens. In the Netherlands, the Dutch East India Company (VOC) led the way for Dutch international trade. It is worth recounting this, because the response of the Dutch state and citizens to post-Columbus expeditions can be illustrated by the formation of the VOC in Asia and later the West Indies Company (WIC) in the Caribbean and the Americas.

It is likely that the decision to set up the VOC benefited from espionage:

> Espionage trips to Portugal and Portuguese trading posts in Asia by enterprising Dutchmen like Jan Huigen van Linschoten and the De Houtman brothers, which yielded a vast amount of information in the form of rutters and charts, were a vital part in the early phase of ocean shipping in the 1590s. During the first Dutch voyage to the East Indies around 1600, a few Englishmen lent their service as pilots. (Davids 2008: 232–3)

The rise of the VOC gives us insight into the development of statecraft, business and citizenship. With regard to the VOC, there is no need for us to reinvent the wheel; a plaque at the University of Amsterdam gives us a good insight into the operations of the VOC from East India House, the headquarters of the company at the time, and some of the activities that went on there. The university provides this information to show us the historical significance of the buildings, which now house parts of the administration and research institute of the departments of anthropology, communication sciences, political science, and sociology. We therefore take the liberty of reproducing the following account as it appears on the plaque:

> In April 1603, the Amsterdam Chamber of the United East India Company (known in Dutch as the VOC) rented a part of the building housing the city's arsenal. Two years later it was able to rent the entire building on the Kloveniersburgwal. On the ground floor was the slaughterhouse, where hundreds of oxen [were] slaughtered annually. The meat was then pickled and used on the long ocean voyages to Asia.

The state had interest in this enterprise because we are further informed that:

> In 1606 a new wing was built. The bookkeepers and the *tax collectors* had their offices there and the directors had their meeting room. At the head of the Company stood the Gentlemen of Seventeen who met for a couple of week[s] every spring and autumn. These meetings were held for two consecutive years in Middleburg in Zeeland, then for six years in Amsterdam. (Emphasis added)

We are told that

> [t]he Asian trade increased steadily after the Company was set up in 1602, and more space was constantly needed. In 1634 another wing was added to the building. This created an enclosed inner courtyard. The last building extension was completed in 1661. The United East India Company bought the complex in 1772.

International trade became a total system:

> The directors held their meetings seated round a large oval table. The secretary prepared the agenda and took minutes. We are well informed about the matters addressed, because the reports have been preserved. The gentlemen discussed the building of new ships and the auctioning of pepper, spices and other Asian products. They talked about outlay and profits.
>
> They pondered over the reports from Batavia [Indonesia] and other VOC settlements. The members from the five committees reported on their activities. The gentlemen known as the Heren van de Equipage would give an account of their inspection of the boats lying in the roadside off the island of Texel. This was the point of departure and destination for the vessels of the Dutch East India Company.

But this does not tell us the goods that were traded. The information on the plaque informs us of the auction of pepper, spices and other Asian products; but we are not given any information about the goods the Dutch sold in Asia in order to obtain the Asian products. For this we have to turn to other sources. According to Frank, Das Gupta and Pearson have noted that in 1615, only six per cent of the value of cargo exported by the Dutch East India

Company was in goods, and 94 per cent was in bullion. Prakash notes that 'over the sixty years from 1660 to 1720, precious metals made up on the average 87 per cent of VOC imports into Asia ... Most European exports were of metal and metal products' (Frank 1998: 74). We return to this in Chapter 3.

With regard to employment and the population at large, the plaque informs us that:

> [t]wice a year, sometimes more often, town criers would parade the city streets announcing that new personnel were to be hired for the ships. Hundreds came for the jobs, thronging before the gateway in Oude Hoogstraat, hoping to be taken on as a sailor or soldier. After a long wait, they would appear before the directors in the board room. They would be asked about their experience and background; they would be assessed on the spot. In this way about 500,000 employees were taken on by the Company up until 1795.

As we see below, the experience of setting up the VOC as a business, acquiring state support for it, and involving and recruiting citizens to strengthen the venture were all applied in constructing, supporting and strengthening the WIC when Holland entered the Atlantic 'slave' trade and slavery in a systematic way; this provided a model for what later became known as the joint-stock company.

Legêne and Waaldijk have noted that:

> [t]he Dutch East Indies Company (VOC) had operated in the Indonesian archipelago since the seventeenth century. Basically, it was a merchant company within an extensive monopoly charter. After 1813, the company was not reinstated. Instead, the Dutch introduced direct territorial rule, in line with the transformation of the federal Dutch Republic into a unitary nation-state. In the course of the nineteenth century, the Dutch extended their rule over the entire Indonesian archipelago, incorporating the peoples of Indonesia in a series of colonial wars. Simultaneously, they introduced forced labour and large-scale exploitation of natural resources. After the 1860s, free enterprise was allowed in, and a growing number of colonial entrepreneurs and officials with their families settled in Indonesia. However, it was only towards the end of the nineteenth century that the Dutch introduced a more intensive and 'enlightened' mode of colonial rule, which they named the 'Ethical Policy'. It sought to achieve political

commitment to the colonial system among the Dutch and the Indonesian population. On both sides of colonial rule, ever more people had to participate in the implementation of colonial rule, under the guidance of an elite of politicians and administrators. (Legêne and Waaldijk 2007: 189)

In other words entrepreneurs, the state and sections of the population all became involved in the various economic activities of the VOC and the WIC.

But the 'slave' trade and chattel slavery is not an ordinary business. It requires the active support of rulers, the state and its citizens. As Postma has noted:

> Transporting slaves across the Atlantic was an expensive enterprise. Including the time needed to outfit a ship [i.e. design and planning], slave voyages [from Europe to Africa to the Americas and back to Europe] often lasted more than a year. Shipping a large group of *unwilling passengers* who might revolt at any opportunity required a crew twice the size needed for a regular commercial ship. (Postma 2003: 57–8; emphasis added)

From the point of view of state construction, the recruitment of crew creates employment and ties the interests of the workers to the interests of 'slave' traders. This had a multiplier effect on other sectors of the economy and society. 'Insurance tended to be quite high to cover the value of the ship, merchandise, and human cargo. Large quantities of food and other provisions, mostly for the Middle Passage, had to be purchased and boarded' (Postma 2003: 57–8).

With regard to the role of the state in enslavement, '[s]everal permits had to be purchased and kept aboard to provide *legitimacy* and protection for the voyage, and numerous other duties and fees had to be paid at every port of call' (Postma 2003: 57–8; emphasis added). We emphasize the word *legitimacy* because it refers to agreements between European slave-trading nations; it has little to do with the captives in question. Slavery required the active involvement of the state. On the ground:

> [b]roker and pilot fees and customary presents to prominent African rulers and merchants had to be paid. Wages for carriers and boatmen who transported slaves and provisions, fees for auctioneers and announcers, as well as duties to officials, churches, and funds for the poor were collected at many ports

in the Americas. Individually, these fees may have been modest, but together they added up to a considerable expense (Postma 2003: 57–8)

In summary, Atlantic slavery evolved from banditry to a total system. The needs of monarchs to mobilize human resources galvanized the populations to seek their share in the wealth of nations and more freedom. European citizens represented and spoke for their nations. The most concrete and durable expression of this was in France, culminating in the French Revolution. Thus as European citizens became free, non-European citizens who were in contact with Europeans overseas became less free. This was reflected in the pursuit of knowledge, a subject to which we now turn.

SCIENCE AND CHATTEL SLAVERY

If sovereignty gave rise to nation states, the interaction between rulers of nations and subjects gave rise to citizenship. Citizenship fostered freedom; freedom fostered education. Education gave rise to the emergence of scientific communities. Members of the scientific communities became commentators on social, political, economic and cultural development, including chattel slavery. We owe much of our knowledge of the past to those scientific communities. With regard to chattel slavery the debate between Las Casas and Supúldeva led the way.

Recall that the emigration of Europeans to the Americas at this point in time had given rise to two broad recurrent notions that have tended to serve as a backdrop to the discussion of transatlantic slavery, namely *expansion* and *colonization*. This has affected disciplines, frameworks, theories and concepts in the field of study. But the politico-military and the religious context of the emergence of a European scientific community should not be overlooked. Mignolo has noted that:

[i]n eighteenth-century Europe, the movement toward secularization brought with it a radical transformation of the frame of mind and the organization of knowledge, the disciplines and the institutions (e.g. the university). The Kantian–Humboldtian model displaced the goals and the format of the Renaissance university and instead promoted the secularization of the university founded on secular science (from Galileo to

Newton) and on secular philosophy, and both declared war against Christian theology. (Mignolo 2009: 6)

In short, science began to supplant religion and tradition. The belief in science was coupled with the belief in modernity, progress, democracy, nationalism, citizenship and inalienable rights. A new delineation of the races, based on the theological dogma of the superiority of the white Christian, emerged in scientific and philosophical language.

Phrenologists suggested that biological superiority could be proved, and set out to do so with the ample number of bodies and skulls that were collected throughout the colonies. Separate schools of thought on the origins of mankind began to emerge in contrast to the single-race theory of human origins, which had a religious underpinning in the biblical story of Adam and Eve. Separate creationist theories suggesting that humans had evolved from separate races or species were increasingly popular in the eighteenth century. One of the first theorists to posit the theory of separate races was the Swedish botanist Carolus Linnaeus, who was celebrated in the Netherlands. Linnaeus's hierarchy of humankind included a description of characteristics of each separate species. For example, Linnaeus described Homo Africanus as 'cunning, lazy and lustful' (Haller 1995).

In the context of slavery, apart from the classification of people into free persons and slaves, Johann Friedrich Blumenbach, a German anthropologist and physiologist, also developed a racial classification system that defined the nature and characteristics of separate species based on craniometry and phrenology. Blumenbach's work had a tremendous impact on biologists and human anatomists who were interested in the separation of the species (Haller 1995).

We can see evidence of this trend in the work of Charles Darwin. Darwin's descriptions of so called 'savages' and 'primitive' people as he travelled aboard the Beagle is often denigrating and reflects a cultural racism in which an evolutionary scale is introduced to describe the measure of civilized behaviour. In his encounters, Darwin graded humans using his own scale of morality, behaviour and civilization; in short, in terms of their similarity to the British ideal. Upon first seeing the Fuegians, he describes the difference between the Fuegians and Europeans as similar to the difference between a 'wild and domesticated animal' and he states, 'surely no lower grade of man could be found'. He later states that civilization as a goal is to be built on the 'instincts of wisdom and virtue' already inherent in the white races (Darwin 1996; Desmond and Moore 2009).

In other words scientific communities made it their task to describe, analyse and explain the world around them and beyond (Gossett 1965; Gould 1996). Among other things, in the process, they measured, standardized, classified and produced evidence to support the objects of their studies, including slavery and chattel slavery. With regard to Africa and slavery, stories brought to Europe by travellers and 'slave' hunters informed intellectual discourse.

In addition to this it is important to note that the sources of narratives vary: they may be official, unofficial or academic. Narratives can also overlap and contradict. Official records can form the basis of the framework and guidelines for non-official actions. The records of non-official actions can form the basis for academic narratives and literature. In the Dutch context, the activities of the West Indies Company formed the dominant framework within which enslavers operated. In turn the notes and records of enslavers, and the opinions expressed in such records, formed the basis for academic literature. A case in point is the liquidation of the WIC, which some academics later incorrectly quoted as evidence that Dutch Atlantic slavery was unprofitable for the Netherlands (see below).

With regard to the culture of scholarship that emerged to support the self-proclaimed superiority of the European man, Amina Mama has noted that '[f]or centuries Africa has occupied a peculiar place in Western mythology, a dark land of fables and fantasies, the antithesis of Western civilization, enlightenment and reason' (Mama 2005: 104). This phenomenon is best encapsulated in the following passage by Lewis Gordon:

> In all, by now the portrait of the organizing schema is evident. Although Africans as an ascription of people from the southern shores of the Mediterranean Sea downward was used in the Middle Ages, the African as black emerged in the modern world, and with that the logic of the difference from those who designated the black as such and the correlated, continental difference of European and white. The move from Christendom and the land of heathens resulted in those of Europe and whites versus the African and the blacks, and then the Indians and the Asiatics. Along the way, many of the South Pacific Peoples and those in the islands of the Indian Ocean were also brought into the schema, although with a separation of black from African. Thus

we have it: the emergence of the black, a being mostly associated with the African but not necessarily such since also associated with, for example, the Australian Aboriginal. And there is the African, which mostly means the black, although by the fifteenth century fall of the Moors there were many descendants from the northern other side of the Mediterranean, whether by slavery or earlier Greek and Roman colonial rule, whose identity became African but certainly not black. These developments offered, as well, practices of justification and legitimation with their own naturalism culminating in what we could call modern naturalistic anthropology. (Gordon 2009)

One of the grounds for enslavement was the denial of the humanity of the enslaved. This in turn was tied to the denial of the history of some peoples (Wolf 1982). This is compounded by the fact that some scholars have studied (and still do study) humanity not in and of itself, but in relation to other things. Perhaps influenced by the tales of European explorers, Adam Smith viewed humanity in relation to material things. This led him to observe of 'the very meanest person in a civilized country' that:

> [c]ompared, indeed, with the more extravagant luxury of the great, his accommodation must no doubt appear extremely simple and easy; and yet it may be true, perhaps, that the accommodation of a *European prince* does not always so much exceed that of an industrious and frugal peasant as the accommodation of the latter exceeds that of many an African King, the absolute master of the lives and liberties of ten thousand *naked savages*. (Smith 1977: 117; emphasis added)

In everyday language, what Adam Smith was saying was that the worth of a human being was in his or her material wealth; so was the 'worth of nations'. Smith seemed not to be speaking for Britain but rather speaking for Europeans of his time. The story of Hegel's 'dismissal of Africa's historicity and diminution of its humanity' has been told in several places, but for our present purposes, we cannot do otherwise but to repeat it here. According to Hegel:

> [a]nyone who wishes to study the most terrible manifestations of human nature will find them in Africa. The earliest reports concerning the continent tell us precisely the same, and it has no history in the true sense of the word. We shall therefore leave

Africa at this point, and it need not be mentioned again. For it is an unhistorical continent, with no movement or development of its own ... What we understand as Africa proper is that unhistorical and undeveloped land ... which had to be mentioned before we cross the threshold of world history itself (Hegel, quoted here in Magubane 2006: 62)

Clearly, for Hegel, what he did not know did not exist. Of course, behind Hegel's ideas and those of other philosophers, was a commercial system that had become advantageous to certain European countries, and which certainly did exist.

In the material real world the transatlantic 'slave' trade and slavery took place between the sixteenth and the twentieth centuries. This process became institutionalized and involved the abduction of *some Africans*, holding them in captivity, and forcibly transporting them to the Caribbean and the Americas to work under coercion without contract, consent or pay, so that the goods the enslaved produced could be transported to Europe and elsewhere for consumption (Fogel 1989). We speak here of *some Africans* because in the context of the 'science' of slavery, namely, designing, planning, classification, standardization and measurement, not all Africans were eligible for enslavement according to the criteria that were set up by the European enslavers. Generally babies, those more than about 35 years of age, the sick and invalids were exempted. It was also the case that women were less likely to be abducted than men, though of course very large numbers of women were still kidnapped. However Africans of all ages and physical condition who lived in the Caribbean and the Americas in the age of the Atlantic slavery were or could be classified as slaves by those who held them in captivity.

From the point of view of the enslavers, slavery was a means to an end. The *means* was to coerce the African captives to work without contract, consent and pay in order to produce specifically assigned goods; the *end* was the consumption in Europe of the goods produced by the enslaved.

It is worth emphasizing the relationship between the means and the end because it influences the place given to the phenomenon of slavery in European history. Since slavery was a means to an end, the study of slavery could be treated as an appendix to the Dutch and European master narrative; and in a way, that is how it has been treated.

This brings us to the notion of 'enslaved'. Whereas those who enslave others may classify their subjects as 'slaves', those who are enslaved do not necessarily accept this status. The term 'enslaved' is preferred when describing those who are being treated as slaves by those who hold them in captivity. Here too, it must be said that what makes slavery distinctive is not force per se, but power and the legal framework, and their reproduction. The power and the legal framework that sustained Atlantic slavery were the Westphalia sovereignty and state. This brings us to the notion of 'chattel slavery'. According to Lovejoy, chattel slavery's

> special characteristics included the idea that slaves were property; that they were outsiders who were alien by origin or who had been denied their heritage ... that coercion could be used at will; that their labour power was at the complete disposal of the master; that they did not have the right to their own sexuality and, by extension, to their own reproductive capacities; and that the slave status was inherited unless provision was made to ameliorate that status. (Quoted here from Postma 2003)

This definition is apparently the description of what actually happened; in this definition the word *alien* is used instead of *race*. We have already noted that one of the organizing principles of chattel slavery was race.

Before the advent of chattel slavery, various forms of servitude were considered as an extension or a product of war, predominantly between neighbouring peoples. What the notions of vassals, pawns, indentured servants and serfs have in common is that there is an element of 'contract and consent'. Chattel slavery changed that. This makes putting vassals, pawns, indentured servants and serfs on the same continuum as slaves and chattel slavery problematic (see Postma 2003).

One of the curious things about the transatlantic 'slave' trade and slavery is that there is no evidence to suggest that the victims of abduction were slaves before they were abducted. Yet career historians of the field have maintained the notion of a 'slave' trade for centuries. For clarification, Atlantic slavery refers to the actual enslavement of Africans forcibly transported to the Caribbean and the Americas for the sole purpose of enslavement by Europeans.

Our distinction between the transatlantic 'slave' trade and Atlantic slavery is of added significance because unlike Britain, which was involved in the abolition and the suppression of the transatlantic 'slave' trade and Atlantic slavery, the Dutch were not involved in the abolition and the suppression of the transatlantic slave trade. The implications of this for the Dutch master narrative should not be underestimated. In practice, it means that, unlike Britain, which has national heroes like Wilberforce, the Netherlands has no visible national abolition heroes. This gives rise to different national intellectual traditions. Whereas the British put emphasis on abolition, the Dutch put emphasis on the 'slave' trade (Dantzig 1968; Postma 1990; Emmer 2000; den Heijer 1997) and downplay slavery and racism (Essed and Nimako 2006).

On the notion of the institution of slavery, career historians have done sufficient work on the Atlantic 'slave' trade to enable us, the non-historians, to question the narratives that accompany some of their work. This includes reflecting on concepts such as 'slave' and 'trade' and notions of cooperation that underpin the study of what is known as the transatlantic 'slave trade'. The concept of 'slave trade' may make sense to Europeans; it does not necessarily make sense to Africans.

The concept of the 'slave trade' suggests that the victims of enslavement were slaves before their captivity and forcible transportation to the Americas. But there was no permanent African slave-trading class. Everybody could be enslaved in that part of Africa where the banditry of abduction and captivity took place. In fact some of the so-called kings and rulers who participated in the 'slave' trade rose to their status because of the gifts and bribes they received from the Europeans in the form of guns (perhaps for their own security from being victims of abduction). Whether you use persuasion or force to overpower another person is another matter (Postma 2003: 13–14). The instrument and institutions of power may change, but its fundamentals remain the same.

But where does 'trade' fit in? To this, Postma, like many historians on the subject, informs his readers that the Atlantic slave trade was a cooperative effort. In the section of his book *The Atlantic Slave Trade* (2003) on the 'Institutions and Methods of Slaving', Postma states:

> The Atlantic slave trade was a *cooperative* venture between European and African merchants and their respective rulers. With few exceptions, Africans were responsible for enslavement and transportation to coastal outlets. Europeans provided the ships, the capital, and the commercial organization to transport the slaves across the Atlantic and sell them at American destinations. (Postma 2003: 13–14; emphasis added)

This is a discussion above the heads of the victims. Contrary to Postma, we argue that nobody gave her/himself up voluntarily to be enslaved. The victims of enslavement in the Americas were captives in Africa.

In the same book Postma had noted that:

> [w]hen the Portuguese explored the African coast during the fifteenth century, they frequently captured Africans. Ten Africans were taken from the Mauritanian coast in 1441, and 240 were shipped to Lisbon three years later. As the Portuguese moved farther south to more populated areas, they discovered that Africans skillfully maneuvered their coastal vessels and defended themselves well against slave raids. Subsequently, the Portuguese decided to negotiate peace treaties with African rulers and trade with them. This became standard practice, and most slaves were purchased from African merchants and shipped to European markets. (Postma 2003: 5)

In fact it is not clear why Postma decided to include this section in his narrative, which is supposed to serve as a textbook, given the fact that the empirical foundation of his narrative was weak. Norman Klein rebuked such a claim more than three decades earlier. On the issue of so-called African merchants and rulers Klein has noted that:

> Both Ashanti and Dahomey began state formation more than 150 years after European powers had begun establishing themselves on the Guinea Coast. Among the Akan-speaking peoples, it was only 'the importation of firearms from the coast' toward the end of the seventeenth century, which made possible a combination of matriclan segments that had come under the leadership of Osei Tutu resulting in the formation of the Ashanti Confederacy. When the kingdom of Dahomey appeared on the coast in 1727 it was barely a century old. In other words, both Ashanti and Dahomey inaugurated their careers as 'state' societies with a direct and immediate economic dependence on the European powers. The guns and powder necessary for the maintenance of state armies waging almost continuous warfare and slave-raiding had to come from overseas, or at least across the Sahara. (Klein 1969: 88)

Let us take Klein's observations a step further. First, the process of enslaving suggests that the victims were once free people. However the notion of slave trade suggests that the victims of slavery were slaves before they were 'traded'. This raises the following question: Why were people who were not slaves classified as slaves in historical literature before they were enslaved? What is the difference between capture, captivity, abduction, slaves and enslaved?

Secondly, no matter which way one approaches this problem or, for that matter, no matter who does the enslaving, power is crucial. You need to overpower someone before you can abduct the person. You also need to overpower the abducted person before you can enslave that person. The key to abduction was weaponry, which formed (and continues to form) the basis of the comparative advantage of the Europeans.

Of course the 'slave trade' would not have been possible without the 'collaboration' of some Africans. Indeed all human actions of matters of life and death, including slavery, require some response of the victim. But does that make a story or theory of collaboration or cooperation? (Robinson 1972). How then can we explain the fact that some of the enslaved agreed to whip others for the latter to work? Even in slavery many of the coercive practices are performed by other enslaved persons. Does that constitute cooperation or collaboration of sections of the enslaved? The idea of cooperation or collaboration has other implications because it is devoid of power relations and social formations. But despite evidence to the contrary, the concept of 'slave trade' has been maintained. We consider this a serious epistemological issue.

Over three decades ago Walter Rodney (1974) drew our attention to the use and misuse of the 'concept' of the transatlantic slave trade in the context of the transatlantic slavery system in historiography. Rodney noted that when the early Portuguese 'explorers' passed along the coast of Africa they did not record Africans sitting along the coast in chains waiting to be transported to the Americas for enslavement. What Rodney implied was a distinction between banditry, abduction, imprisonment and forceful transportation of individuals and groups in Africa on the one hand, and the enslavement of individuals and groups in the Americas on the other: a clear distinction is required between the transatlantic 'slave' trade and Atlantic slavery.

From the point of view of knowledge production, if the victims of abduction were not slaves, why have career historians come to classify this episode as the 'Atlantic slave trade'? Our contention is that the 'concept of slave trade' is anchored in some form of a collaboration theory; also it suggests that the victims of enslavement were slaves (in Africa) before they were enslaved (in the Americas).

In other words, the idea of the transatlantic slave trade suggests that slaves (as opposed to captives) were traded.

One of the key elements of collaboration theory is that 'it takes two to tango'. This implies that some form of African collaboration was required to initiate and sustain what became known in historiography as the transatlantic slave trade. If we take this reasoning to its logical conclusion, then no one can be brought to account for committing any crime, because even stealing from someone could be justified on the grounds that the victim of theft did not protect his/her property well. In the material real world however, no one around the Atlantic part of Africa was immune to this infamous transaction, recorded in history books as the slave trade. Thus, one could be a 'merchant' or 'ruler' today, and a captive tomorrow. The traces in the language, names, culture and arts of the descendants of Africans captives in the Americas testify to this (Wooding 1972; Martinus 1996).

This makes the idea that the 'slave' trade was a cooperative venture between European and African merchants devoid of power. The only constant factor in the slavery narrative is human vulnerability. Vulnerability explains why captives from certain regions predominated.

But as a definition (and a legal framework) it is unlikely that this particular form of slavery, namely, chattel slavery, will ever occur again, because the power relation and legal framework that underpinned the Westphalia sovereignty under which chattel slavery and colonialism flourished has been replaced by the sovereignty of the United Nations. The trajectory from the Peace of Westphalia (1648) to the United Nations (1945) was mediated through the First World War (1914–18) and the Second World War (1939–45). With regard to the First and Second World Wars, Muller has noted that

> [a] familiar and influential narrative of twentieth-century European history argues that nationalism twice led to war, in 1914 and then again in 1939. Thereafter, the story goes, Europeans concluded that nationalism was a danger and gradually abandoned it. In the postwar decades, western Europeans enmeshed themselves in a web of transnational institutions, culminating in the European Union (EU). (Muller 2008: 19)

This is only part of the narrative. There is another way of telling the story as a continuum. The First and Second World Wars were interruptions of the Westphalia consensus (Césaire 1972). These were when the Westphalia sovereignty consensus, namely, coordinated competition and cooperation, was broken. Recall that no European slave-trading nation supported the anti-slavery revolution in Haiti; but the Dutch and the French supported the American Revolutionary war. The height of the Westphalia consensus, after the abolition of the transatlantic 'slave' trade and slavery, was the Partition of Africa in 1884/85 in Berlin. Pope Alexander VI had attempted to partition the world outside Europe for Spain and Portugal without success in 1493. But with the Partition of Africa, the Westphalia sovereignty consensus succeeded in doing what the Vatican had failed to do. Though the United Nations has condemned it as a crime against humanity, it is likely that the legacy of chattel slavery will endure for centuries. As we have seen, one of the organizing principles of chattel slavery was race. Race and the memory of racial humiliation are instrumental in the discourse of chattel slavery. The question is whether to confront or circumvent them.

3
Chattel Slavery, Sugar and Salt

Some of the worst horrors of slavery find their expression in production processes; the horrors also tell us something about the art of slavery.

This chapter is devoted to the analysis of the primary purpose of the 'slave' trade and slavery by those who practised it, namely, the production of goods by the enslaved under the supervision of the enslavers. The enslaved chopped, planted, picked or harvested, carried, cooked, served, washed and cleaned, so that the enslavers on the plantations could pursue their non-menial activities – reading, writing, sport, and so on.

This entails repression and pacification on the part of the enslavers and active and passive resistance on the part of the enslaved.

Nobody gives him/herself up voluntarily to be enslaved. That is why the victims had to be captured and chained before they could be transported; that is why they had to be whipped and supervised in order to work. This is also why we use the concept of 'enslaved', instead of 'slave', whenever appropriate.

SLAVERY AND THE MAKING OF GLOBAL ECONOMY

We noted in Chapter 1 that many countries in Africa, Europe and the Americas acknowledge the place of the transatlantic slave trade and slavery in their histories during the past 400 years. In European historiography, this connection between the three regions became known as the Golden Triangle (Page 1997).

In the Golden Triangle we are told that Europeans sold goods to Africans in exchange for people; the people were shipped to the Caribbean and the Americas to produce goods which were in turn sent to Europe for consumption. What is less emphasized is that some of the goods that arrived in Europe were re-shipped to Asia in exchange for manufactured goods.

It has been noted that:

[i]n the seventeenth and eighteenth century, about 70 per cent of the American production of silver arrived in Europe, and 40 per cent of that was shipped on to Asia ... others suggest that most of the silver that did not arrive in Europe was not retained in the Americas, but was shipped to Asia across the Pacific instead. (Frank 1998: 143)

Viewed in this context the so-called Golden Triangle was a subsystem in a global world economic system. We should thus extend the Atlantic world narrative to include that of Asia. Indeed, both Columbus and Vasco da Gama were looking for alternative routes to Asia, which landed the former in the Americas and the latter in Africa. In other words the functioning and success of Atlantic world trade makes sense only in relation to the Asian world. Thus from the perspective of a global world economy, the story of the Atlantic slavery should start with some knowledge of the Asian world. Recent studies by Arrighi (1994; 2006), Pomeranz (2000) and Frank (1998) have given us added insights into the role of Asia in the world economy before Europe got the upper hand. The richest of these studies is the work of Frank, to which we therefore make extensive reference, while not altogether ignoring the others.

Our understanding of Frank's major concern in his book, *ReOrient: Global Economy in the Asian Age* (1998), is to demonstrate that between 1500 and 1800 the Asian world was far more important and dominant in the world economy than the European and Atlantic worlds. However, Europe's success in dominating the Atlantic world and making the latter an extension of the European world made it possible for Europe to compete effectively with Asia, and later to colonize it.

There are other reasons to speak of the emergence of European world order in relation to the development of chattel slavery. Developments that took place in one centre had a spin-off effect on other areas, which could rival or take over from the original centre. A case in point is the development of financial centres. As Venice and Bruges constituted the two largest financial centres in Europe at the beginning of the fifteenth century, the decline of one, Venice, led to the rise of the other, Bruges. In turn the decline of Bruges led to the rise of Antwerp. Antwerp was replaced by Amsterdam as the financial centre of Europe and later London replaced Amsterdam (Spufford 2006: 144).

In 1636, according to Spufford, within Europe, 40 per cent of all European imports came from the Baltic, and only 15 per cent came from the British Isles. Certain essential commodities were transported in each direction. 'Salt, herring, wine, textiles and assorted colonial goods [much of them produced by enslaved labour] were shipped from the Netherlands into the Baltic, whilst rye, wheat and other grains, wood and iron were carried on the return journeys.' Spufford also informs us that trade between the Netherlands and the Baltic was an unbalanced one. At the same time, there was also a striking imbalance between South and North Holland. According to Spufford, there was:

> [m]assive outflow of southern coin to the Republic, nearly as great as that from the Republic to the Baltic. Between 1612 and 1675 the Habsburgs had some 200 million guilders worth of silver *patacon* and *ducaton* minted in the southern Low Countries, a large part of which circulated in the north. (Spufford 2006: 163)

We extend this insight into Dutch trade in Europe to look at the role Atlantic slavery played in Dutch trade. With regard to why both Columbus and Vasco da Gama were looking for a route to Asia, we note that the successes of Venice and Genoa in the world economy was based on their relationship with Asian suppliers and their ability to sell Asian products to the European market. This trade set the stage for European expansion into other arenas, namely around the tip of Africa to India and, in search of a new route to India, across the Atlantic to the Americas (Frank 1998). Columbus's voyage and subsequent 'discovery' of America was prompted by the search for an alternative route to the East. As Frank states: 'a growing bullion shortage and the consequent rise in the Afro-Eurasian world market price of gold made such an enterprise attractive and potentially profitable (which it turned out to be)' (Frank 1998: 56–7).

What we can summarize from these events is the following. The worldwide economy began to emerge at the onset of international trade in the sixteenth century. This signified the rise of a global division of labour and multilateral trade, 'whose roots in Afro-Eurasia extended back for millennia' (Frank 1998: 52–3). This global economic structure stimulated European expansion and interest in new passageways to the East, eventually leading to the 'discovery' of the Americas and their subsequent incorporation into the existing system. Also as Frank states, 'the incorporation into this Old [Afro-Eurasia] World economy of the New [Atlantic] World in the Americas and their contribution to the world's stocks and flows of money certainly gave economic activity and trade a new boost from the sixteenth century onward' (Frank 1998: 56). Asia was then, as it is now, 'the world factory', where the action was. Asian, especially Chinese and Indian, production, competitiveness and trade dominated the world economy. China produced and exported silk, ceramics, some gold, copper cash, and later tea. India produced and exported cotton textiles and silk textiles. European nations sought to trade directly with Asia, without the intermediation of the Ottomans and Persia. This of course raises the question as to what Europe had to offer Asia in order to trade.

As we have noted most European exports were of metal and metal products, silver and gold bullion. These products were used to offset trade deficits with other lands. This of course excluded the Americas and Africa, where exploitation of the local population and land allowed Europeans to extract more than they gave (Frank 1998: 74).

In 1615, 94 per cent of the value of exports by the Dutch East India Company consisted of bullion. From 1660 to 1720, silver and gold bullion constituted on average 87 per cent of Dutch East India Company exports to Asia (Frank 1998).

With regard to the Netherlands, according to Davids:

The total output of mints in the eighteenth century was vastly higher than in the Golden Age. Most of the coins struck in the United Provinces did not come into circulation at home, however, but were used as trade coins in international transactions, especially after about 1660. Between 1660 and 1750, nearly 20% of all coins struck in the Netherlands were exported to Asia alone. Mint production was to a large extent an export industry. The enormous outflow of mints was a deliberate consequence of the policy conducted by the States General, aimed at facilitating international trade by providing for an abundant supply of good coin with a stable silver or gold content. To realize this goal more effectively, the production capacity of the largest mints was after c.1670 enhanced and improved by increased mechanization, while the small, municipal mints were shut down in the 1690s after the conclusion of a generous compensation arrangement. (Davids 2008: 146)

After Columbus and Vasco da Gama led the way, the Portuguese and the Dutch stepped up their involvement in East Asia, seeking a role in the trade between China and other Asian countries. In addition, they also brought certain American crops to China, such as maize and tobacco; these exports were the product of enslaved African labour. Ultimately, the Chinese appetite for these products increased, as did the trade. As a result of the continued exportation of Chinese products to other areas, managed by Europeans, China became rich with silver bullion from Europe (Frank 1998: 128).

In short, the Europeans managed to position themselves as middlemen in trade between three major regions; Africa, Asia and the Americas. They were also the middlemen in some intra-Asian trade, whose profitability eventually came to surpass that of Europe's own trade with Asia (Frank 1998: 127).

As the profits from trade between Asian markets began to pour in, the Europeans started to use this money to offset trade imbalances in other regions. The selling and reselling of gold, silver and copper became essential to the financial dealings of the Dutch East India Company (Frank 1998: 135). Silver quickly became the standard of the world economy, although gold and copper were also perceived as currency. Enslaved labour played a significant role in the mining of silver in the Americas (Frank 1998: 139–40).

Eventually the trade imbalances took a toll. Unable to compete with the East, Europeans turned to the West (the Americas) and the South (Africa), where they could compete. But this competition depended on what Asia had to offer and was prepared to receive in return – silver. The need for silver to trade with Asia fuelled the exportation of silver from European slave colonies in the Americas and the enslavement of Africans. In this context Atlantic slavery was a means for Europe to buy goods from Asia.

In this equation, Africa's greatest disadvantage was the absence of an effective 'money economy'; cowries introduced in West Africa from the Indian Ocean by Europeans as a medium of exchange became worthless, since the same Europeans who introduced it as money refused to receive it as money from Africans; this was compounded by the introduction of alcohol and guns in Africa by Europeans to acquire captives. Thus for Africans, alcohol and guns became what germs had been for the native 'Indians' in the Americas. As Walter Rodney noted, under such conditions people could not lead ordinary lives (Rodney 1974).

We noted in Chapter 2 that in the international division of labour, the initiative, design and planning of the 'slave' trade and slavery were located in Europe. Thus while Africans tried to lead normal lives, the European states strove to thwart them. For instance, in 1751 the British Board of Trade ordered the governor of Cape Castle (on the coast of present Ghana) to stop cotton cultivation among the Fante people, arguing that:

> [t]he introduction of culture and industry among the Negroes [i.e. Ghanaians] is contrary to the known established policy of this country [i.e. Britain], there is no saying where this might stop, and that it might extend to tobacco, sugar and every other commodity which we now take from our [Caribbean and American slave] colonies and thereby the Africans, *who now support themselves by wars*, would become planters and their slaves be employed in the culture of these articles in Africa, which they are employed in in America. (Boahen 1966: 113; emphasis added)

This quotation contains more information than at first meets the eye. Firstly, this was clearly a man of power talking, someone who could stop Ghanaians from cultivating certain products and demand the supply of captives instead. Secondly, he mentions that Africans *now* support themselves by wars, which suggests that this had not always been the case. Nevertheless it was a strange logic on the part of the very Europeans who had initiated some of the wars to turn around and accuse Africans of 'supporting themselves by wars'. It is doubtful whether there would have been Africans left to be abducted and enslaved if they had actually been 'supporting themselves by wars'. The third assumption is that Africans 'would become planters and their slaves be employed in the culture of these articles in Africa, which they are employed in America'. Apparently the British official had 'naturalized' slavery to the extent that he assumed that slave labour was all that was required to produce certain goods. This in turn raises another question: if Africans had a need for slave labour, why would they be the sources of the supply of 'slave' labour elsewhere?

What is certain is that Ghanaian free labour was not allowed to produce certain goods in Ghana, but was transformed into enslaved labour and forced to produce elsewhere, including in Suriname. Thus, as we have noted in Chapter 2, despite intense competition amongst themselves, the European slave-trading nations cooperated and coordinated their activities, in the context of the Westphalia logic, to ensure a steady flow of captive people to be used as enslaved labour in the Americas.

In 1776, 25 years after the above statement was made by a British official, Britain's most important North American colony revolted against British rule and became known as the United

States of America. Here too, Asia, to which Britain turned for sugar cultivation, was called to the rescue. Whether intentionally or not, Britain's interest in abolishing the Atlantic 'slave' trade increased after it had lost the Unites States of America as its slave colony.

When the first consignments of sugar from Bengal started to arrive in Britain in 1793, Mr Randle Jackson informed his East India Company shareholders about the new orientation in the following words: 'It seemed as if Providence, when it took from us America, would not leave its favourite people without an ample substitute; or who should say that Providence had not taken from us one member, more seriously to impress us with the value of another?' (quoted in James 1980: 52).

Let us recapitulate. Asians were not interested in manufactured European products, only silver. Thus, Europeans focused on reselling precious metals between markets where the price fluctuated across the global economy and inserting themselves as middlemen in the intra-Asian trade. In the Dutch context, this goes some way towards explaining why the VOC was formed before the WIC. Viewed in the context of the Asian trade, the WIC was a means to an end, that of complementing the activities of the VOC; so was the 'slave' trade a means to an end, namely, slavery; in turn slavery was a means to an end, namely, the production and consumption of goods.

With regard to the world economy, the comparative advantage of Europeans was not in the production of goods, but in their capacity to travel around the world voluntarily in their own ships. The Dutch, in particular, had an advantage over other Europeans, as they were known to be good seafarers and shipbuilders, which helps to explain why the number of African captives transported to the Americas by the Dutch was greater than the number of Africans they actually enslaved.

Shipbuilding was reinforced by international trade. Davids has noted:

> True, the expansion of the Dutch shipping industry between the fifteenth and early eighteenth centuries was also due to a vast increase in capital stock and to organisational changes such as the use of the joint-stock company in the Asia trade. But it could never have established an international lead nor retained its primacy for so long, if it had not been for substantial advances in technology. (Davids 2008: 92)

Secondly, prior to the rise of silver in the global economy, it was impossible for one country or one power to dominate and control all markets at the same time or to extract profits in an efficient manner. The key to Europe's domination of markets was the steady supply of bullion from the colonies in the Americas – the only major commodity it was able to export was currency. And to do this, it was completely dependent on the enslaved labour in the Americas. Without the Caribbean and American slave colonies, Europe would never have been able to maintain its position as trading partner with Asian countries and middleman in intra-Asian trade (Frank 1998: 177–8).

In other words, whereas the VOC inserted itself in the already developed Asian market, the WIC specialized in the enslavement of Africans to produce goods that could be exchanged in Asia and support consumption at home and be re-exported abroad. Silver became the medium of exchange in Asia and sugar became the produce for consumption. Production from European slave colonies also had an impact on immediate neighbours. For example, as a result of Atlantic slavery, commodities that were produced in the Americas (e.g. cotton, coffee) and exported to Europe came to replace those that were produced in Turkey or the Middle East (Frank 1998: 272).

Another industry that benefited from slavery was tobacco. According to Davids, tobacco cultivation was introduced in the Netherlands in the seventeenth century by an immigrant from England.

> True, thanks to its location in the centre of the Dutch trading and shipping network tobacco processing for a long time enjoyed the benefit of easy access to supplies of raw materials and direct outlets to foreign markets as well. One of the principal assets of the Dutch tobacco processing industry since about 1650 was that it blended fine, relatively expensive tobaccos imported from Virginia and Maryland [produce by enslaved labour] with cheaper varieties cultivated at home, in the inland provinces of Gelderland and Utrecht. Much of the produce found its way to the Baltic region and the Rhineland. (Davids 2008: 192)

To conclude this section, it is clear that Asian production, competitiveness and trade dictated the world economy. In the Dutch context, this explains why the VOC was formed before the WIC.

The WIC was a means to an end, just as the 'slave' trade was a means to an end (slavery).

SLAVERY AND SUGAR

The importance of Atlantic slavery to the European economy moved in phases, depending at different times on a variety of commodities – silver, sugar, cotton, tobacco and other produce. However, in the Caribbean sugar has become the product most associated with Atlantic slavery (James 1980; Williams 1994; Dunn 1972; Beckles 1990; Moitt 2001; van Stipriaan 1993). Attempts to locate the origins of the relation between sugar production, slavery in general and African enslavement in particular have been sketchy. Some unsatisfactory accounts have been given in the context of Eurocentric frontier historiography. This historic account is concerned with both the frontier and chronology, because it starts with Europeans operating close to home and moving beyond their borders as they exhaust resources in Europe. This frontier historiography has been independently narrated by Fogel and Postma. According to Fogel,

> [s]ugar was introduced into the Levant in the seventh century by the Arabs. Europeans became familiar with it during the Crusades. Prior to that time honey was the only sweetening agent available to them. After taking over the Arab sugar industry in Palestine, the Normans and Venetians promoted the production of sugar in the Mediterranean islands of Cyprus, Crete, and Sicily. From the twelfth to the fifteenth centuries these colonies shipped sugar to all parts of Europe. Moreover, the sugar produced there was grown on plantations that utilized slave labour. While the slaves were primarily white, in these islands Europeans developed the institutional apparatus that was eventually applied to blacks. (Fogel 1989: 19–20)

This account is confirmed by Postma:

> During Europe's Middle Ages, sugar cultivation gradually spread from the Middle East to several Mediterranean islands. Because growing and processing sugar required a disciplined labor force, especially during the harvesting season, the use of forced labor became a virtual necessity.

Postma goes on to explain that the Iberians played a large role in sugar cultivation, as it took hold in many of the islands off the coast of Spain. The Spanish enslaved aboriginal people from the Canary Islands and transported them to the Madeiras for the express purpose of working on the sugar plantations. The Portuguese also actively shipped indentured labourers to the islands during the sixteenth century; but by the end of the century they had begun to enslave Africans for the purpose of sugar production.

> As the European taste for sugar increased, sugar cultivation spread and influenced the growing demand for slaves ... Forced labor became a necessity because the intense regimen required for harvesting sugarcane and toiling at the sugar mills had no appeal to workers who had a choice. (Postma 2003: 5)

Part of Postma's statement is speculative, exhibiting rationality with hindsight. This account does not tell us whose labour should be forced. The narrative also renders the role of economic incentives redundant. There are several dangerous occupations, including mining and military service, which people will not do if they have a choice. In short, this account suggests that the product, in this case sugar, dictated a certain form of labour, in this case forced labour, and by extension, slavery. If this assertion is true, then the following question should be answered: why then was slavery applied to produce goods other than sugar?

According to Fogel the demand for sugar in Europe grew rapidly. This led Spain and Portugal to expand their sugar production to the Iberian peninsula and the Iberian-owned islands off the coast of Africa. For the most part, enslaved Africans provided the labour for the expansion. Between 1451 and 1559, 130,000 Africans were brought to the islands, but only a tenth of this number were taken to the New World (Fogel 1989: 20).

This narrative is in line with Portuguese primary school textbooks. As we write (2010) a Portuguese school textbook states the following about the relationship between sugar and slavery:

> Portuguese presence in Black Africa. The climate in São Tomé is hot and damp and the soil is quite fertile. The Europeans, however, were deeply affected by tropical diseases, particularly malaria, and it was mainly thanks to the African slave labour that a dynamic sugar production was settled. The two archipelagos [S. Tomé and Cape Verde] became *entrepôts* of the slave trade. Slaves were

acquired in the African coast and thereafter re-exported to Europe and the American continent. (Quoted from Araujo and Maeso 2010: 17; original emphasis)

This is the climate thesis which Eric Williams challenged back in 1944 with regard to the Caribbean (Williams 1994). Furthermore the assumption underlying the above quotation is again that the Africans in question were slaves before they were captured and transported to be enslaved. As we have already argued, there is no evidence to support this assumption.

What is clear however is that Portuguese involvement in slavery in Africa was integrated into its trade networks. Spufford informs us that:

[i]n the fifteenth century merchants from Portugal were bringing in wine and sugar from their newly acquired Madeiras off the African coast. Just as cloth finishing sprang up because of the import of unfinished English cloth, so sugar refineries sprang up in the vicinity of Antwerp to cope with Madeira and Canaries sugar. Antwerp sugar refining was to expand yet further with the arrival of Caribbean sugar in the early sixteenth century. Hitherto European sugar refining had been concentrated in the vicinity of Venice, but Italian entrepreneurs, seeing the new opportunity, moved, with their capital, to Antwerp. Soon gold and ivory from the African mainland followed. From Lisbon the ivory reached Nuremberg where the ivory carving industry grew up, either via Antwerp and the Rhine and Main rivers, or since ivory was sufficiently valuable, by the long overland [route] across Spain and France. (Spufford 2006: 152)

As we see in the next section, plantation-based slave economies, like all economic systems, are subject to change. In the late 1500s, sugar and enslaved Africans were transported to the Americas, but by 1600, Brazil had become the largest exporter of sugar to Europe. In addition, sugar was being produced in Mexico, Peru, Cuba and Haiti. Even though the Old World colonies continued to produce sugar, their share of the market dropped significantly. Within 100 years, sugar production practically ceased in the islands off the coast of Spain and North Africa, as did the importation of slave labour to this area (Fogel 1989: 20). More importantly, once sugar production became located in the New World, Britain, France and the Netherlands also began to produce sugar. Britain began to produce sugar on the island of Barbados (Beckles 1990). Later, after wresting Jamaica from the Spanish in 1655, the British began to produce sugar there as well. During the 1700s, sugar production spread throughout the British Caribbean, surpassing the output of Brazil. By the beginning of the nineteenth century, sugar production from the British West Indies accounted for more than half of the sugar trade (Fogel 1989: 20–1).

In the French Caribbean, Haiti became the centre of sugar production, under the control of the French from the beginning of the seventeenth century until 1794, when the Haitians revolted. Shortly before the revolt, Haiti was exporting up to 86,000 tons of sugar per year. Including the other French territories in that area, total production in the French colonies was 125,000 tons (Fogel 1989: 20–1).

This should be placed within the broader context of state formation in Europe. The sudden decline in silver production around 1640 in the Spanish orbit generated market forces that entirely pulled the rug from beneath the Spanish economy (Frank 1998: 246). The Spanish crown had bitten off more in the Americas than it could chew.

Spain's share of the international sugar trade continued to diminish, unlike the shares of Britain and France, which grew larger as these countries came to dominate sugar production in the Caribbean. However, Spain re-emerged in the sugar trade in the nineteenth century through the development of plantations in Cuba and Puerto Rico.

The Dutch also became involved in sugar production in their colonies located along the northern central coast of South America. In 1787, the combined output of the Dutch and the Danish (on the island of St Croix) exceeded the amount of sugar exported by the Spanish colonies (Fogel 1989: 20–1).

Sugar production fuelled the enslavement of Africans in the Caribbean. In the British West Indies, more than two thirds of the enslaved were involved in some aspect of sugar production. Fogel estimates that approximately 40 per cent of the enslaved in Brazil were involved in sugar production and between 30 and 50 per cent in Spanish America. Second to sugar was mining, which constituted approximately 20 per cent of the enslaved labour in Brazil. The remaining enslaved Africans were forced to work in the production of other crops (e.g. coffee, tobacco) and a small number were servants or manual labourers (Fogel 1989: 20–1).

This much is known. But the question remains: why did Africans become the main source of enslaved labour? Should we take this interpretation of history at face value? No! The problem with this narrative is that it assumes that Europeans have always distinguished themselves as people and as a geographic entity; but this has not always been the case (Bernal 1987). Fogel argues that the extent of the Atlantic slave trade was determined by Europe's addiction to sugar. He estimates that between 60 and 70 per cent of all Africans who survived the middle passage ended up on one of Europe's sugar colonies (Fogel 1989: 18). This assessment puts the cart before the horse. It was slavery that made it possible for Europe to develop its 'sweet tooth', not the other way round.

Let us look at how this played out in Suriname.

SUGAR AND SURINAME

We noted in Chapter 2 that in the age of banditry the territories in which slavery was practised, especially the Americas, were not secure. For this reason several territories changed hands during the period, which culminated in the Treaty of Utrecht in 1713. Not only did the Dutch revolt against Spain; Portugal did so too. These conflicts on European soil proper had implications for the 'slave' trade and the territories where slavery was implemented and practised. In other words, some of the conflicts on European soil were tied to European slavery conflicts in the Atlantic. Thus in the context of competing claims to territories and colonies, it took about 50 years from the age of banditry to the Westphalia framework before the Dutch gained the legitimacy, in the context of Westphalia logic, to use Suriname as a sugar-producing colony.

> The spread of sugar cultivation in the 1600s stimulated the expansion of the Atlantic slave trade dramatically. After sugar production became successful in Brazil, the Dutch sought to dominate the industry by capturing northern Brazil in 1630, which got them started in the traffic. Although [with the help of the British] the Portuguese regained all of Brazil a few decades later, the Dutch remained active in the slave trade. Some of the planters who had cooperated with the Dutch fled Brazil and settled in the Caribbean, where they helped to establish sugarcane cultivation. (Postma 2003: 12)

In other words Suriname became the final destination of the Dutch for the production of sugar after they had been ejected from Portuguese Brazil.

It should be mentioned that small islands in the Antilles were also acquired for slavery. Just as the Atlantic world became complementary to the Asian world, so the Antilles islands became complementary to Suriname in a larger slavery project. Consequently the enslaved societies on the islands were very different from those in Suriname (Willemsen 2006a). This was because in these islands, the composition of the soil, drought and other climatological circumstances prevented the development of plantation economies in the conventional sense of the word. Therefore there were no large, labour-intensive agrarian enterprises on the islands manufacturing products for the world market with the help of enslaved labour. Insofar as one could speak of plantations, the production was principally aimed at the domestic market.

On Sint Maarten and Sint Eustatius, sugarcane and cotton were cultivated on a small scale, but the 'salt plantations' were far more important; both islands also produced some tobacco. Salt was extracted through the evaporation of sea water, and this heavy work was slavery-based and linked to the seasons. On Bonaire too, the enslaved primarily worked on salt domains belonging to the Dutch government. By the time slavery was abolished in 1863, the Dutch state 'owned' 92 per cent of the enslaved population in Bonaire (Zunder 2010).

With regard to salt, Davids has given us some insights into how external supplies and internal developments reinforced each other:

> The growth of demand for refined salts thanks to the expansion of herring fishing and the extension of dairy farming was not met by changes in technology, but by increased capital investment (more saltworks, more salt pan) and enhanced imports of raw salt from France, Portugal, Spain and South America. When salt refiners in Holland in the middle of the eighteenth century found their domestic markets threatened by outside competitors, they reacted by clamouring for protection. (Davids 2008: 142)

Salt, and the sources of its supply, has been of importance to the Dutch for some time. Apart from its use for conserving consumption goods, such as meat and fish, salt has also been important for Dutch international shipping, fishery and the export of herring. The outbreak of the Eighty Years' War with Spain led the Dutch to intensify their search for salt in Africa and the Caribbean. The first three Dutch ships from Vlissingen arrived in Panama in 1569. In 1590 several Dutch ships appeared in the Caribbean area in search of salt. Initially the Dutch were able to obtain salt from Punta de Araga, an island which is part of Venezuela. By 1600 more than 100 ships obtained salt from there annually. Since each ship carried an estimated 300 tons of salt, 30,000 tons were transported to the Netherlands each year (Cees Luckhardt November 2010; personal communication).

Aruba is a special case, since there were no plantations on that island. There, slavery was only introduced around the middle of the eighteenth century: it is alleged that no black enslaved lived permanently on Aruba (Willemsen 2006a). On this island, enslaved labour was mostly carried out within the household. Saba, the smallest of the West Indian islands, had a very small enslaved population working chiefly in patriarchal circumstances. The enslaved population spoke English like the white enslavers, and according to the State Committee presided over by J.C. Baud, the former minister of colonies (see Chapter 4), the enslaved (like those on Sint Eustatius) were 'very familiar with the ideas of white people, especially regarding emancipation'.

The situation was completely different on Curaçao, an island that the Dutch had acquired for purely strategic maritime reasons. Curaçao was not a plantation colony in the traditional sense of the word, but had evolved into an important slave market and slave depot. Here, the slave economy had a transit function: its aim was to import, 'season' and forward captives to plantations in other parts of the Caribbean. The island was also notorious for its active contraband of weapons and captives (Klooster 1997; Postma and Enthoven 2003).

> Cocoa was imported in the Dutch republic from Spanish America by way of Curaçao on a regular basis since the 1650s. Amsterdam quickly got the reputation as a centre of fine chocolate making ... Most of the cocoa beans which were brought to the ports of the Republic were in fact not processed in the Netherlands at all, but were re-exported to the Mediterranean, France, Germany and ... Spain. Not until the last decades of the eighteenth century, when the Dutch Guyanas [i.e. Suriname] meanwhile had grown into a major supplier of cocoa, did the scale of production increase by the spread of wind-powered chocolate mills, where roasted cocoa beans were ground to pieces by means of edge runners. The large clusters of these mills by then could be found

in Zeeland; Middleburg had thirteen chocolate mills in 1808. In coffee processing, the scaling-up of production started even later. While the imports of coffee from the East- and West-Indies already soared from the 1690s onwards, industrial processing of coffee remained a small-scale affair until the second half of the nineteenth century. (Davids 2008: 198)

Though Curaçao lacked a plantation economy, it did have some small-scale agricultural businesses for the domestic market. Maize, vegetables and fruit were produced, and the livestock consisted of goats, sheep, cows, pigs and some poultry. The owners of these territories could hardly be called planters, but rather dairymen and market gardeners. When times were difficult and the enslaver did not have the necessary means to sustain the enslaved, he gave his enslaved permission 'to go and work for a living' (Willemsen 2006a). Many of the enslaved worked as domestic slaves or were hired out by their enslavers as craftsmen and even as sailors. These economic and ecological realities impacted the composition of the population and the enslaver–enslaved relation. 'Coloured people' and the 'free black' population used to live on small parcels of land they rented from the owners, on the condition that they annually worked a number of days for the landowner without payment (the so-called *paga tera* system).

This brings us back to Suriname, a slavery-based plantation economy proper. One of the first acts was to put the enslaved to work to clear the land for the construction of plantations. The productivity of slavery-based plantations in the Dutch Caribbean was at its height in the seventeenth and the eighteenth centuries.

As can be seen in Table 3.1, in 1713 around 171 plantations were registered in Suriname. This grew to 294 plantations in 1745 and to 406 in 1770 and remained relatively stable till the end of the eighteenth century. In the nineteenth century the number of plantations fluctuated, but remained below 300.

It should be mentioned however that available data should be treated with care because they are indicative rather than authoritative. This can be observed in the discrepancy between the data on plantations provided by Zunder (2010) and that of van Stipriaan (1993) for 1854; Zunder's sources give us 256 plantations whereas van Stipriaan's give us 167 plantations. According to Zunder there were 707 slavery-based plantations in Suriname in 1827, but of these 143 had been abandoned, so the actual number of slavery-based plantations in operation was 564. This source indicates that slavery-based plantations were at their peak after the official abolition of the transatlantic 'slave' trade in Britain in 1807 (Sherwood 2007). We return to this point below. For the moment suffice it to say that the legal end of the slave trade made it possible for legally freed Africans to settle and produce goods, which were previously produced with enslaved labour. This in turn affected the plantation system elsewhere.

Table 3.1 Number of Plantations for Export in Suriname, 1713–1890

Year	Plantations
1713	171
1745	294
1770	406
1795	389
1812	383
1820	416
1825	346
1827	564
1836	294
1849	196
1854	256
1854	167
1860	256
1862	131
1890	86

Sources: Derveld and Heilbron 1993 (for 1820 and 1860); Zunder 2010 (for 1827 and 1854); van Stipriaan 1993 (all the rest).

Around 1820, there were no fewer than 416 plantations in Suriname producing coffee, sugar, cotton, and mixed crops; the number of plantations however declined to 256 in 1860, due partly to competition from West Africa, and finally to 64 in 1903 after the abolition of slavery in 1863 (Derveld and Heilbron 1993: 25; Willemsen 1980). On this score, the British official we quoted above understood how the global economy worked, because production in Africa competed with the slave-based economy of Suriname and the Caribbean.

Specifically, until the mid-eighteenth century sugar plantations dominated the economy. However as can be observed from Table 3.2, starting from 1745, coffee plantations emerged. Of the 294 plantations recorded in 1745, 154 (52 per cent) were sugar plantations and 140 (48 per cent) coffee plantations. In 1770, of the 406 plantations recorded, 295 (73 per cent) were coffee whereas

111 (27 per cent) were sugar. Of the 389 plantations recorded in 1795, 102 (26 per cent) were allocated to sugar; 248 (64 per cent) to coffee and 39 (10 per cent) to cotton. The figures for 1812 were sugar plantations, 100 (26 per cent), coffee plantations, 235 (61 per cent) and cotton plantations 48 (13 per cent). The balance was restored in favour of sugar after 1849. On the eve of the abolition of slavery, there were 131 plantations in Suriname, of which 86 (66 per cent) were devoted to sugar, 30 (23 per cent) to coffee, and 15 (11 per cent) to cotton.

Table 3.2 Number of Plantations for Export in Suriname, 1713–1890

Year	Sugar	Coffee	Cotton	Total
1713	171	n/a	n/a	171
1745	154	140	n/a	294
1770	111	295	n/a	406
1795	102	248	39	389
1812	100	235	48	383
1820	n/a	n/a	n/a	416
1825	95	178	73	346
1827	n/a	n/a	n/a	564
1836	105	137	52	294
1849	88	76	32	196
1854	n/a	n/a	n/a	256
1854	86	52	29	167
1860	n/a	n/a	n/a	256
1862	86	30	15	131
1890	14	n/a	n/a	86

Sources: Derveld and Heilbron 1993 (for 1820 and 1860); Zunder 2010 (for 1827 and 1854); van Stipriaan 1993 (all the rest).
Note: The 1890 total includes 72 cocoa plantations.

As Basil Davidson has made us understand, we will never know everything about the 'slave' trade and slavery; this is reflected in the gaps in the above data. But some of the implications of the evidence in the table above to the study and research on the slavery narrative in relation to sugar production should not be overlooked. The dynamics of the Atlantic economy centred around the demand for sugar (and other agrarian products) in Amsterdam and London, leading to the plantation system in the Caribbean territory.

Recall that in the above narrative, both Fogel and Postma advance a well-known slavery historiography that links the growth of demand for sugar in Europe with demand for African labour in the form of slavery. In fact it is difficult to sustain the narrative that the difficulty of producing sugar necessitated the application of slave labour. If this was true, then slave labour would not have applied in other less demanding work, including domestic services.

Given the significant gaps in the data, one of the ways to understand what went on in Suriname and the other Dutch colonies is to understand what went on in the Netherlands around the same epoch. After all, very many of the goods that the enslaved produced in the colonies were consumed in the metropole.

As can be observed from Table 3.2, it appears that demand for textiles by planters in Suriname gave rise initially to the import of textiles to Suriname and, later, to cotton production there. With regard to the expansion of the textile industry in the Netherlands, Davids relates that:

> [t]he second wave of expansion, which began after c.1710, was mainly based on an increased output of a cheaper variety of linen (*bont linen*), viz. many-coloured fabrics made of linen, or of a blend of linen with cotton, which were much in demand among planters in the Guyanas and the West-Indies. Linen yarn was obtained from Silesia, Flanders, Twente, cotton (through the VOC) from Asia. (Davids 2008: 132–3)

In the case of Suriname, sugar that was produced in Suriname was exported to the Netherlands for consumption, or for re-export. Thus whereas available data give us a window on plantations from 1713, the data on sugar exports from Suriname to the Netherlands date back to 1683. Specifically, in 1683, it is recorded that 1,736,250 kg of sugar was exported from Suriname to the Netherlands; this grew systematically to 4,632,900 kg in 1697 and declined to 3,465,00 kg in 1700. Thus, as can be seen in Table 3.3, between 1683 and 1700 around 54,000 tons of sugar was exported from Suriname to the Netherlands.

We noted above that coffee plantations followed sugar plantations.

> The productivity of sugar fields in one of the major supply regions of sugar, Surinam, stunningly increased from the 1790s onwards thanks to the rapid adoption of new varieties of sugar cane known as Bourbon or Otaheite cane. These were in 1789 introduced into Surinam from the nearby French colony of Martinique. Well before the close of the eighteenth century, moreover, Surinam saw the introduction of steam power into sugar processing. (Davids 2008: 245)

The data on plantations do not reveal coffee plantations until 1745; however data on imports reveal that 45 tons of coffee were exported from Suriname to the Netherlands between 1701 and 1725. This jumped to 26,000 tons between 1726 and 1750 and reached a peak of nearly 138,000 tons before it declined systematically to 30,000 tons between 1826 and 1850, and then to 3,000 tons between 1851 and 1863 (Zunder 2010).

Table 3.3 Sugar Imports from Suriname to the Netherlands

Years	Weight (kg)
1683–1700	53,558,270
1701–1725	141,631,793
1726–1750	193,763,050
1751–1775	172,719,090
1776–1800	148,088,980
1801–1825	221,629,442
1826–1850	379,437,900
1851–1863	202,820,088

Source: Computed from Zunder 2010 (see also van Stipriaan 1993).

The discrepancy between cocoa plantations and cocoa imports from Suriname is also evident. Available data on plantations do not feature cocoa plantations, but cocoa imports to the Netherlands from Suriname date back to 1726. The data indicate that nearly 2,000 tons of cocoa were imported to the Netherlands from Suriname between 1726 and 1750. This increased to nearly 7,000 tons between 1776 and 1800 and declined to around 3 tons between 1801 and 1850. Data on cotton imports to the Netherlands from Suriname date back to 1751; nearly 10,000 tons were imported between 1776 and 1800; it increased to a peak of 21 thousand tons between 1801 and 1825 and declined to around 17 thousand tons between 1826 and 1850. By the date of the abolition of slavery in 1863, the role of cotton in the Suriname slavery-based economy was negligible (Zunder 2010).

We should not lose sight of the fact that in the slavery literature, enslavers are referred to as planters. In the real world however they planted nothing; behind the plantations was enslaved labour. It is equally certain that the coordination and control of enslaved labour required active intervention in the social life of the enslaved, from the production process to reproduction and family life. These interventions still form part of the memories of descendants of the enslaved, of which more below.

Table 3.4 Coffee, Cotton and Cocoa Imports from Suriname to the Netherlands

Years	Coffee	Weight (kg) Cotton	Cocoa
1683–1700	n/a	n/a	n/a
1701–1725	45,857	n/a	n/a
1726–1750	26,574,897	n/a	1,893,175
1751–1775	130,592,434	928,963	3,141,749
1776–1800	137,933,488	9,759,551	6,581,717
1801–1825	75,716,252	21,042,204	1,492,688
1826–1850	30,845,524	16,450,611	1,037,247
1851–1863	3,401,606	4,255	2,506,875

Source: Computed from Zunder 2010 (see also van Stipriaan 1993).

Increasingly in Suriname, conventional use of water or labour by animals for the fabrication of sugar was being replaced by steam mills. Van Stipriaan states that the Surinamese sugar industry of that period ranked among the most technologically advanced in the Caribbean territory. In the 1820s, the average production of the Surinamese sugar plantations was among the largest of the region. According to van Stipriaan, it was even more remarkable that the colony proportionally surpassed the motherland: in 1855, 35 per cent of the plantation enterprises were already equipped with steam power, while in 1850 a mere 10 per cent of the industrial sources of energy in the Netherlands consisted of steam engines. To prevent Suriname from turning into 'a lifeless skeleton' due to the decrease of the enslaved population, emancipation had become a dire necessity.

We return to this below. For the moment, recall that the Dutch exported sugar from Brazil before they began exporting from Suriname. Thus sugar industries were established in the Netherlands before Suriname was acquired and transformed into a plantation colony (Postma 2003). The initial bloom of the sugar refineries in Amsterdam was largely dependent on the Brazilian sugar plantations' production. Suriname was the last Dutch conquest added to the WIC's patented territory in 1667. As can be seen in Table 3.5, the number of sugar refineries in and around Amsterdam in 1607 was three. This jumped to 40 in 1650 and declined to 20 in 1680, jumping again to 90 in 1752 and to 103 in 1787. As we have noted, these figures are indicative rather than authoritative.

In 1752 the total number of sugar refineries in the Netherlands was 145, including the 90 located in and around Amsterdam (Zunder 2010).

Table 3.5 Sugar Refineries in and around Amsterdam

Period	Number
1607	3
1650	40
1661	36
1668	34
1680	20
1752	90
1787	103

Source: Zunder 2010.

According to Davids:

> [t]he reasons why sugar refining in the Netherlands became such a successful branch of the activity must mainly be sought elsewhere. Like distilling, sugar refining was excellently located with regard to both the supply of raw materials and the access to exports markets. The sugar refineries, almost all located in the major port cities Amsterdam, Rotterdam and Dordrecht, did not only receive supplies of raw sugar from Dutch colonies overseas (Java, Suriname, and for a short time, Brazil), but also drew on large amounts of raw sugar imported, directly or via France, from the French isles in the West-Indies. A substantial part of the refined sugar was shipped to the Rhineland, while smaller amounts were exported to the Southern Netherlands and other regions in Europe. (Davids 2008: 190)

The state took an active interest in the sugar industry:

> Like distilling, sugar refining enjoyed government protection from an early date, too. Weigh fees, cargo fees and other duties weighing upon refineries were reduced or abolished between the mid-1650s and 1680s, whereas import duties on syrup (a by-product of refining) were raised in 1668. After 1750, government support for the industry was even further extended by the reduction or

suspension of export duties on refined sugar, the increase of duties on the transit of raw sugar or foreign refined sugar and the payment of handsome export premiums. (Davids 2008: 190)

The trends in sugar refineries in and around Amsterdam in the seventeenth and eighteenth centuries indicate that like all economic systems, plantation-based slave economies evolve through a series of stages, beginning with the acquisition and clearing of land and proceeding through planting and tendering to harvesting and transportation of goods to the Netherlands. This makes them susceptible to competition among slaving nations and to technological change. According to Zunder, Reesee reports that due to wars, the price of sugar rose around 1650. These developments partly explain the rise and decline of plantations in Suriname, and of sugar refineries in and around Amsterdam. This in turn has influenced perspectives on the relationship between Atlantic slavery and the Dutch economy. However, Dutch historians, relying heavily on the activities and archives of the WIC for their narrative on the 'slave' trade, not only isolate the 'slave' trade (as a means) from slavery (the end), but they also focus on book-keeping records of the WIC to the neglect of a broader economic analysis and function of slavery as a system. But they draw conclusions that have implications for general economic development (Emmer 1998; Postma and Enthoven 2003).

Emmer has done some shadow-boxing on the issue of profit and loss in the 'slave' trade:

> The trade was not particularly profitable and there were even periods when the slaving companies made a loss. The slaving losses made by the first WIC in Brazil have already been discussed although, incidentally, it is not possible to discover how great those losses were. They were undoubtedly tiny in comparison with the enormous cost of administering and defending the colony. It was that which brought the first WIC to its knees rather than the failure to make a profit from the slave trade. (Emmer 2006: 104)

With regard to the WIC, my correspondence with a Dutch history teacher, Cees Luckhardt, generated the following information:

> The cost price for a 'slave' was calculated at 93 guilders; the sale price between 300 and 400 guilders. But this profit margin appeared to be a paper affair because the 'slaves' were sold on

credit to Portuguese planters in Brazil. At a given moment the Portuguese owed the WIC 4.5 million guilders. The Portuguese planters did not pay; instead they revolted against the WIC, which declared bankruptcy and left Brazil in 1654. Between 1670 and 1730 the Dutch transported around 100,000 African captives from Curaçao to Spanish America. Unlike the Portuguese, the Spanish paid cash. (Personal communication)

In an attempt to come to terms with Dutch involvement in Atlantic slavery in relation to the development of the Dutch economy, Emmer has stated that:

> The Dutch were not very important in that part of the World ... In the Atlantic, *the Dutch suffered bad luck* ... In spite of these negative developments, the importance of the colonies to the Dutch economy increased because, after 1750, Dutch shipping and trading firms were driven out of the competitive markets in Europe, which increased their dependence on the protected colonial markets (in the East and West). (Emmer 1998: 4; emphasis added)

(If slavery brought *bad luck* to the enslavers, one wonders what sort of luck it brought to the enslaved!)

It is true that the physical presence of the Dutch in the Atlantic was in Suriname and the Antilles, and was thus less significant than that of other European states such as Spain, Britain, Portugal and France. However, behind Emmer's statement is an attempt to challenge the well-known Williams thesis that slavery made an important contribution to capital accumulation and the development of the industrial revolution in Britain. Emmer however, unlike Williams, does not supply enough evidence to support his thesis (Blackburn 2011: 101–6). As we noted above, the number of African captives the Dutch processed and transported to the Americas was nine times higher than the number of Africans the Dutch physically enslaved.

Emmer's view is however of a different order from that of Enthoven, who states that 'the Dutch were deeply involved in various aspects of the Atlantic World during the ancient regime, and that trade with the Atlantic Region enriched the Dutch Republic even more than the Asian trade of the VOC' (Enthoven 2003: 4).

Information gathered from archival sources has led mainstream Dutch researchers to the conclusion that the WIC was not a profit-making company and therefore had to be liquidated –

and by implication, that Suriname was not a profitable colony (Goslinga 1990; Emmer 2006). Although it succeeded in inflicting heavy losses on the Spanish–Portuguese enemy, this did not always result in profits for the company. This can be established from disappointing financial results, the non-repayment of loans, slow and irregular distribution of dividends, and recurrent state subsidies (van Stipriaan 1993).

The idea of viewing Dutch slavery in Suriname through the prism of profit and loss has given rise to two book-keeping models and perspectives on the subject. The first of these, which is the dominant one, uses the liquidation of the WIC and the direction of state finance as the frame of reference. Here it is argued that there were various reasons for the WIC's failure: the starting capital was insufficient – certainly not enough to pay the enormous expenses of war, insurance, management and staff; the company's management would have included a greater number of speculators than genuine entrepreneurs, precluding intelligent planning for the future; the internal conflicts between Holland and Zeeland were disadvantageous; and, last but not least, there was strong competition from similar English and French companies.

According to Willemsen, the plantation system in the West Indies yielded enormous profits, more in the eighteenth than in the seventeenth century. The most important commercial development in the seventeenth century (and more specifically at the end of that century) was the growing market for European products, caused by migration. Willemsen had earlier noted that Wallerstein does not get lost in ineffective assessments regarding the precise contribution of transatlantic trade to the Dutch economy. Instead, he wonders why these profits were more beneficial for the French and especially the English, than for the Dutch. The answer is that establishing such a system was a difficult and time-consuming undertaking, which was financed by the Dutch. However as they were on the verge of reaping the harvest, the period of Dutch hegemony was coming to an end. It was England, more powerful at that moment, which succeeded in amassing the profits.

Working in the same book-keeping model, but using his own accounting method, Zunder (2010) has set out to prove the contrary, and argues that slavery in Suriname was profitable to the Dutch.

It should be noted however that so far as the enslaved are concerned, the issue of profit and loss is beside the point; after all, the enslaved did not sign an agreement with anyone to work for them. But the impact of the book-keeping model on Dutch social thought should not be underestimated. For not only were the enslaved considered subhuman, but also, in declaring the slavery colony of Suriname to be unprofitable, the logical conclusion from the narrative is that the enslaved themselves were considered worthless. In other words the enslaved were more of a liability than an asset. In addition, the enslavers unilaterally assigned value to the enslaved; how much to pay for them, how much to sell them for, and how to use them. But assigning a value to captives and 'slaves' does not make economic sense, because the enslaved did not sign any agreement with anyone and therefore had no obligation to produce.

The underlying assumption of those who claim that slavery was not profitable to the Dutch is that Dutch economic development (and for that matter, why not the economic development of every country on earth?) was and is independent of every external circumstances.

On the development side, it can be argued that goods are not produced for the sake of production; they are produced for consumption. For the enslaving nations, using other people's land for planting potatoes and maize presumably relieves pressure on land more suitable for other crops. Also, sugar from slave colonies supplied calories to Europe that it did not have to provide for itself. 'Later of course, imports of wheat and meat from the New World fed millions of Europeans and permitted them to put their scarce land to other uses, as did the import of cotton, replacing wool from sheep that had grazed enclosed land' (Frank 1998: 63).

It does not make sense to attribute economic development of the world, a region, or a country to one factor; slavery is no exception. However, throughout history societies have continually attempted to eliminate factors that hinder development and add factors that foster development; slavery was one of the factors that was added and maintained for more than two centuries.

Enslaved populations had to be managed in order to produce. This brings us to our next subject, namely, pacification and resistance.

PACIFICATION AND RESISTANCE

Slavery is essentially an issue of freedom. The claim of one person to own another person through the institution of slavery can be maintained only by violence, or the threat of it. Violence is therefore crucial in the perpetuation of slavery. This finds its expression in pacification and resistance. Slavery-based domination requires pacification; even extreme violence is an aspect of pacification, because the ultimate aim of slavery-based domination is to enforce or extract submission through deterrence. Thus deterrence serves as psychological warfare; in turn, resistance has a psychological component. Those who resist need to have an understanding of the strategies of domination of those who dominate and adjust their resistance strategies accordingly. Slavery-based domination and anti-slavery resistance go hand in hand; this is human nature. However, the idea that resistance is a constituent part of domination may not hold true for those who consider Africans as having been subhuman at the time (if then, why not now?). The absence of resistance to slavery becomes an issue when it is assumed that the enslaved are subhuman.

As we noted above, under slavery, the enslaved worked in the plantations or performed menial domestic tasks so that the enslavers could pursue their non-menial activities. In the process, to paraphrase Lewis Gordon, under slavery, the enslavers led ordinary lives under ordinary conditions; but the enslavers expected the enslaved to lead ordinary lives under extraordinary conditions. The question therefore is not whether slavery required pacification and resistance, but what kind of pacification strategies were applied by the dominant Dutch group to enforce slavery, and what type of strategies were used by the enslaved to resist slavery? (Small and Walvin 1994).

To begin with, the major classification of a society built on slavery is the grouping of people into those who are 'free' and those who are 'unfree'. The enslavers and those whose freedom was deemed necessary in order to help perpetuate the institution of slavery belonged to the 'free' people; the enslaved belonged to the category of 'unfree' people. Different rules, norms, values and codes applied to 'free' and 'unfree' persons.

But the contradiction between slavery and freedom was not always clearly discerned. Eric Foner (1983) notes that slave-drivers in the south of the United States were long convinced that slavery formed the basis of freedom: in their view, an individual was only truly free when he was able to support himself independently of others. In this sense, the possession of slaves contributed to the extension of someone's economic autonomy and thus to his freedom. Foner cites a member of the American Congress who stated that thanks to slavery, white slaveholders in the southern states were as independent '*as the bird which cleaves the air*'. So freedom was not always viewed as the antithesis of slavery.

Writing on Barbados, Beckles has noted that:

[t]he first comprehensive slave code for Barbados was the 1661 'Act for the better ordering and governing of Negroes.' This slave law, according to Richard Dunn, 'legitimised a state of war between blacks and whites, sanctioned rigid segregation, and institutionalised an early-warning system against slave revolt'. It formed the legal basis of slave–planter relations and represented an attempt to legally structure the social order of the plantation world. (Beckles 1990: 33)

This observation can be extended to the control of enslaved populations in the Dutch orbit. Part of the 'slave codes' were in response to anti-slavery revolts that took place in the slave colonies. We return to this below.

Apart from physical violence, religion was a useful tool for pacification. The role of Christian missionaries thus became crucial, especially as the day of legal abolition approached. As we see below, in Dutch mainstream historiography, the emancipation of the Catholics is important. However there is no evidence that the emancipation of the Catholics in the Netherlands led to any sympathy for, or solidarity with, the enslaved on behalf of the Catholic church. On the contrary, for decades, slave society had seen a close collaboration between church and state. When the state postponed the legal abolition of slavery time and again, it found an ally in the church, which also defended the idea that the enslaved were not mature enough for liberty.

During this long delay, the missions went to work on what they referred to as 'preparing the slaves for their emancipation'. Long before 'the big day', missionaries tried to prepare the baptized enslaved in a spiritual sense for their forthcoming freedom. This spiritual control, also referred to in colonial reports as 'the conciliation of the slaves', was primarily the work of the Moravian Brethren (also known as the 'Hernhutters'), and – to a lesser degree – of the Catholic missionaries. These two were the true churches of the people. The Reformed and Lutheran churches were little interested in the fate of the enslaved and did not make any attempts to convert them. They were and remained the churches of the white enslavers, and later on of the more educated coloured people. According to Helman, Christianity was presented to the enslaved by the Hernhutters (and the Catholics) as a 'religious doctrine that emphasized mercy and salvation, suffering and compassion. It led to a "way of life" that showed humility, patience, resignation and submissiveness with regard to the ruling classes' (Willemsen 2006a).

The social situation on the Dutch Antilles islands was very different from conditions under other Europeans in the rest of the Caribbean. Current historiography suggests that the enslaved were treated with a relative liberalness that contrasted sharply with the harsh and cruel regime prevailing in Suriname (Hoetink 1973). Thus, manumission occurred rather frequently: in 1848, the number of free blacks was larger than the number of slaves.

It should be noted that the 'free' white population were not usually referred to as 'free'. This is because being free was normal. But freedom was not normal for blacks. But what was the status of the 'free' blacks? Were they Africans, Dutch, Antilleans? Did they have passports? Could they travel freely? What would happen if they travelled to another slave colony? Were they free from being bought and sold?

In identifying 'free' and 'unfree' people, race was the most significant criterion. Available data indicate that in 1738, 2,731 people were classified as free persons in Suriname; of these 2,133 were identified as white, 598 as coloured or black. The number of 'free' persons jumped to 6,006 in 1787: 5,356 white, 650 coloured or black. The figures in the same year (1787) in Curaçao were 3,964 white and 2,776 coloured or black. In 1817 the number of 'free' coloured persons (4,549) in Curaçao exceeded the number of 'free' white persons (2,780).

In Suriname the ratio of enslaved Africans to European enslavers and their organs (such as police, colonial administrators and missionaries) was about nine to one. Specifically, in 1790 the total population of Suriname was around 58,000; of these, 53,000 were classified as 'slaves', 5,000 were classified as 'free'. The number of 'free' persons in Suriname declined (from 6,006 in 1787) to 5,000 in 1790, of whom 3,240 were white and 1,760 were coloured or black.

In 1815 the total population of Suriname was around 57,041; of these, 51,937 were classified as 'slaves', 5,104 were classified as 'free'. There are no details on the composition of the free people, but the available data indicate that in 1816 there were 658 European soldiers in Suriname. This means that more than 10 per cent of the free people in Suriname at that point in time were European soldiers (Zunder 2010). The number of 'free' persons in Suriname rose to 7,850 in 1831, of whom 2,696 were white and 5,150 were coloured and black (Buddingh 1995: 108; do Rego and Janga 2009).

These demographic changes should not be taken at face value. After all, the Africans who arrived in Suriname and the Antilles, just as with the other slave colonies in the Americas, were all captives and they were all black. So how and why did some of them become free blacks? How and why did some of them become 'coloured'?

Underlying the notion of 'coloured' persons was the cruelty against enslaved women, namely, rape. Most of the coloured persons owed their 'coloured' status to rape. It was the children who were born to enslaved African women through the rape of the enslavers who became known as the coloured. They were assumed to be between Africans and Europeans. Since the European enslavers had declared the enslaved Africans subhuman, but did not refrain from raping the very people they had classified as subhuman, and since the 'slave codes' the enslavers had enacted prevented the enslavers and the enslaved living as equals, the enslavers resorted to manumission to prevent their 'children' from becoming slaves. This also explains why more women and 'coloured' people gained some freedom through manumission than blacks (ten Hove and Dragtenstein 1997). Thus manumission emerged out of the contradictions in the slavery system; the difficulties in enforcing slavery gave rise to the notion of manumission.

What about the 'free' blacks? The blacks became 'free' through the institution of manumission. We appreciate the work some career historians have done in salvaging the data on manumissions from official archives (ten Hove and Dragtenstein 1997). For our present purposes, however, we are more interested in how the enslavers used manumission to manage slavery.

Manumission had three functions relevant to pacification, namely, economic, social, and psychological. With regard to the economics of manumission, recall that slavery was built on the assumption that it should be profitable. But profit is not generated on production and exploitation alone. Other activities, including gambling and speculation can also generate profit – profit and loss go hand in hand. Even under super-exploitation enslavers can lose money. Thus, in Curaçao, it became common for the enslavers to give the enslaved permission 'to go and work for a living' in times of economic hardships for the enslavers. From here it was just a small step to manumission.

Before the abolition of the 'slave' trade it was standard practice to prevent marriage among the enslaved. However, after the abolition of the Atlantic slave trade by Britain in 1808 and its subsequent suppression, the flow of African captives to Suriname was interrupted. After 1826 the Dutch state, under the administration of General J. van den Bosch, reduced restrictions on marriage among the enslaved population (Buddingh 1995).

Socially, in addition to gender differentiation, manumission gave rise to 'class' differentiation among the black population.

As we noted above and will become clear below, slavery in the Dutch Antilles was complementary to the plantation-based slavery in Suriname. Thus the Baud Committee had already urged the colonial authority to prepare the slaves in Curaçao for a short emigration to Suriname. But on second thought, the committee realized that this was not going to work, because 'Suriname stands with them in bad repute because of its damp atmosphere, watery soil, distasteful food, unusual labor, strange language and the prevailing custom that forbids slaves to wear shoes' (Willemsen 2006a).

Psychologically, manumission served as a palliative, helping the enslaved to accept their position in the hope that if they behaved well and submitted themselves to slavery, they would become free one day. This brings us to resistance.

We noted that resistance took several forms. There were nearly 60 major recorded slave rebellions in the Caribbean; but rebellion does not constitute liberation; many of the rebellions were crushed; in fact there was rebellion from the day of captivity till the day of abolition.

From the perspective of active resistance, the eighteenth century was the era of organized revolt and rebellion in the Caribbean. There were at least 17 major rebellions between 1725 and 1795. There were revolts in Nevis (1725), St John (1733), Antigua (1735), and Grenada (1765). There was also a prolonged revolt known as the Black Carib War in St Vincent (1769–73) and further revolts in Tobago (1770–71, and 1774), Dominica (1785–90) and Martinique (1789–92). Guadeloupe and Grenada also experienced revolts in 1789 and 1795 respectively. There were major revolts in Jamaica in 1760 and 1795 and in Suriname in 1763 and 1772. Belize and Saint Domingue experienced revolts in 1765 and 1771 respectively (do Rego and Janga 2009).

While elsewhere in the Dutch colonies the enslavers were carefully avoiding the subject of emancipation, those on Sint Maarten were crying out for a swift proclamation of its enactment. This occurred, among other things, in a petition to the Dutch king dated 21 August 1844, a few years before the abolition of slavery was proclaimed in the French colony. The petition failed, but the enslavers appear to have evaluated the situation correctly: France abolished slavery in the French colonies in 1848; the enslaved put down their tools and many defected to the French part of the island. The enslavers held a meeting on 1 June 1848 and unanimously decided henceforth to consider and treat the enslaved as free people, and to conclude labour contracts with them as if they were free workers.

In response to the enslavers' request for compensation, the government said that it 'was impossible to order emancipation in one colony and maintain slavery in another. Neither can one give compensation to some and withhold it from others.' This situation was seen by the enslavers, as well as by the minister of colonies, as a partial abolition and not as a complete emancipation. This is evident in the seriousness with which the enslavers kept insisting upon complete emancipation over the following years. In other words, freedmen were now working for wages, but the enslavers had not (yet) received any compensation for their loss of capital. Compensation, so the minister of colonies said, would only be given when the national budget would allow it.

Another form of resistance was 'escapes', which gave rise to Maroon communities. There were many escapes during the last years preceding the abolition of slavery, especially from Curaçao. The many legal provisions passed specifically in this period limiting the enslaved's freedom of movement mirrored their growing desire to shake off the yoke of slavery. These legal provisions were mostly intended to discourage gatherings of the enslaved: the enslavers assumed that any assembly of even a few enslaved indicated secret plans of escape or rebellion. Therefore, any enslaved who walked the streets in the evening without permission were arrested and mercilessly punished. On every island, stealing canoes and boats was harshly punished. All sorts of regulations were issued regarding the security of ferries, canoes, boats and ships. These measures limited the number of successful escapes, but they could not prevent them completely.

The enslaved primarily escaped to the province of Coro in Venezuela. In 1821, Venezuela had been liberated by Simon Bolivar. Slavery was gradually abolished and ultimately completely eradicated in 1854. Thus the enslaved kept running away to Venezuela until the abolition of slavery in 1863: between 1857 and 1860 more than 500 every year. They were not sent back because the extradition treaty concluded between the Netherlands and Venezuela in 1841 was never upheld.

Henriquez points out that women were every bit as good as men when it came to escaping; every year, the number of escaped women was about as high as that of men. Some women took the extra risk of running away with their small children. An alternative to leaving the island was to hide in the caves outside Willemstad or in Otrabanda on the other side of the bay from the city. Henriquez quotes an official letter from the governor, Van Lansberge, in which he describes the impotence of the government in preventing the escapes:

> The slave population is becoming impatient ... it seizes every opportunity of escaping ... The money my predecessor spent on guarding the bay against cholera, but in reality against the escape of slaves, is becoming a heavy burden on the colonial funds. Aside from using the military police, the expenses of the national guards are costing the considerable sum of 10,000 guilders per year. (Willemsen 2006a)

Therefore, as a precautionary measure, police and military forces were enlarged. The number of soldiers in Curaçao in 1831 was 190. This jumped to 344 in 1833 and to 395 in 1835 (Zunder 2010).

The police force was reorganized and enlarged by 50 men. In 1863, a corps of military policemen was established, consisting of 122 non-commissioned officers and men ready for action. On the evenings of 1 and 2 July, police patrols marched through the city as a precautionary measure. They were able to pass through the streets without any trouble. The Surinamese armed forces of more than 800 men were enlarged by a company of 200 marines and 144 riflemen.

These changes came about because a committee in the Netherlands had submitted a petition to the minister of colonies on behalf of the enslavers and interested parties in Suriname, urging the necessity of reinforcements. By 10 February, 200 marines had arrived with the frigate *Landbouw*, carrying a large amount of ammunition. The other troops arrived from the Netherlands over the following months aboard the military vessels *Cornelis Dirks*, *Stavoren*, *Delfzijl* and *Dommel*. The navy was further reinforced with a steam-powered corvette, four steam-powered flotillas and a schooner. All of these military reinforcements were at the expense of the depleted Surinamese budget for the fiscal year 1863.

Furthermore, the Court of Justice was expanded by three lawyers from the Netherlands. This expansion was deemed necessary because of the resolution of 26 June 1863 against idleness, vagrancy, vagabondage and begging – a measure intended to solve the enslavers' labour problem by discouraging freedmen to roam about without a contract. Offenders against this resolution would be punished.

News of the military reinforcements was later published in the *Arnhemse Courant* in the following terms:

We received a letter from Suriname, dated June 20: six ships are now lying here: *Zoutman*, a steamer with a screw propeller first class; *Dommel*, *Stavoren*, *Delfzijl* and *Amstel*, ships with screw propellers fourth class. And finally the *Schorpioen*. Arenden de Wolff, commander of the *Dommel*, arrived here on June 12. Due to a fear of disturbance in the various districts, the ships are going to disperse. On June 21, the *Amstel* is leaving for Demerary to bring the official news of the emancipation and will strive to be in the district of Nickerie on July 1; the *Stavoren* is sailing up the Upper-Suriname to the 'Guineesche vriendschap' plantation, the *Delfzijl* up the Cottica River to the Sardam plantation, while the *Schorpioen* is going to Saramacca at the government's plantation Catharina Sophia. If nothing special occurs, the ships will return mid-July. Everything looks all right, although one can never know for sure. Starting from July 1, two government steamboats will navigate twice a week up and down the river to bring passengers to the various plantations if problems arise. Furthermore, on the morning of July 1, a salute of 21 shots will resound from Fort Zeelandia and the military post at Nickerie to announce the joyful news to the population (Willemsen 2006a)

Cultural resistance was also common. One of the first acts of the enslavers had been to obliterate the ethnicity of the African captives in order to destroy their identity, humanity and memory. This took several forms, involving physical violence to ensure submission, and including the separation of people from their ethnic groups so that they would be unable to use their own languages to plan revolt. But the enslaved created new bonds, new languages and new cultures that became instruments of resistance.

During slavery, every gathering of the enslaved made the enslavers fear rebellion. Even the announcement of a tambu meeting would arouse this feeling. Tambu is amusement, but at the same time social criticism. Though the word has different meanings, it conveys the interrelation of dance, songs, music, religion and social organization, which form a strong unity. Matters of public interest were brought up by the presenter. In the songs, infringements of norms and values were denounced. Since emancipation was such a long time coming and because, according to the enslaved, King William III did nothing to further it, these topics found their way into tambu songs.

The colonial authorities were strongly against this 'slave dancing', which they described as shameless and pagan, and during slavery the organization of tambu meetings was strictly prohibited.

It should be mentioned that as emancipation drew nearer, the enslaved became more rebellious. Repeated promises of freedom and repeated postponements caused the enslaved to lose their patience, and they became mutinous and unmanageable. Men and women who had seemed the most 'devoted' to their enslavers were the first to cease working and abandon the plantations. The Surinamese plantation owner Bartelink, who had managed several plantations, said:

> Quick abolition of slavery has been repeatedly promised and every time this promise had been broken. [The slaves] were grumbling about the disappointments they had to endure, but they did it in silence. In their immediate surroundings they had loyal friends who comforted them and urged them to be patient, who were also supporters of their freedom. If the Moravian Brethren, to whom I am now referring, had not been in the colony, the population certainly would have rebelled against the Government. But the gentleness and love of these missionaries managed to prevent many things. (Willemsen 2006a)

Regarding the continuous postponement of emancipation, another Surinamese eyewitness noted:

> This made the slaves more and more rebellious. If the order was restored over here, new disturbances occurred over there. The government had its hands full with the awakened spirit of the slave population that had previously been plunged into a deep sleep. (Willemsen 2006a)

These developments, coupled with the decline of the slavery economy, remind us of the rationale behind legal abolition. We now turn to this subject.

4
Abolition without Emancipation

This chapter is devoted to the legal abolition of slavery in the Dutch Atlantic orbit. After more than three centuries, the contrast between the social institutions and values prevailing in Europe and those in the overseas territories controlled by European countries led to the overthrow of the chattel slavery system. Of all the social processes transforming the world in the nineteenth century, none had such far-reaching social implications as the legal abolition of slavery. The abolition came about in various ways: through revolution (Haiti, 1804), through legislation (British colonies, 1838; Dutch colonies, 1863) or through civil war (United States of America, 1865). Not only did it eliminate the foundations of an institution that was more and more in direct conflict with the moral values of the times, it also raised fundamental questions about the system of economic and social relations that were to shape the post-slavery period.

EUROPEAN AND SYSTEMIC CONTEXT

Unlike Great Britain, the Netherlands never had a mass movement against slavery. Only a very small number of people were active in the public debate or politically engaged in this issue. The absence of a public anti-slavery debate characterized most of the nineteenth century in the Netherlands, with the exception of some initiatives taken in 1848 after the emancipation of the enslaved in the French colonies.

In the Netherlands, the legal abolition of slavery never became a social movement and was never a subject that captured the heart of the entire nation, even though the Netherlands, at that time, had a higher degree of literacy than England and, like England, it had a compact geography, which facilitated the spreading of new ideas (Willemsen 2006a).

From the European perspective, chattel slavery was both a legal and an economic system. Like any legal and economic system, it had its own cycle and dynamics. The Atlantic slavery system survived for more than 300 years partly because of continuous flows of captives from Africa and their forcible transportation to, and subsequent use in, the Caribbean and the Americas. From a systemic point of view, it is logical that, as a labour system, slavery would end when the supply of slave labour was interrupted. That occasion came with the British Abolition of the Slave Trade Act of 1807 and the subsequent suppression of the transatlantic slave trade.

This in turn had an impact on the slavery system in the Caribbean and the Americas. Thus, the 1807 abolition act, and the subsequent suppression of the transatlantic slave trade, formed the European and international context of the legal abolition of Dutch slavery.

The enslaved population in Suriname was at its peak in 1774, when around 60,000 people were classified by the Dutch state as slaves (see Table 4.1). The number grew from 37,835 in 1752 to 59,923 in 1774 and dropped to 48,155 in 1795.

Table 4.1 Enslaved Population in Suriname and the Dutch Antilles

Year	Suriname	Antilles	Total
1699	n/a	3,313	
1735	n/a	6,286	
1752	37,835	n/a	
1774	59,923	n/a	
1795	48,155	21,879	70,034
1800	n/a	n/a	
1813	44,155	n/a	
1816	n/a	12,202	
1836	46,879	n/a	
1849	40,311	n/a	
1850	39,679	n/a	
1851	39,676	n/a	
1852	39,309	n/a	
1853	39,130	n/a	
1854	38,689	n/a	
1855	38,006	n/a	
1856	37,759	n/a	
1857	37,175	11,803	48,979
1858	36,963	n/a	
1859	36,501	n/a	
1862	36,484	n/a	
1863	33,621	11,654	45,275

Sources: van Stipriaan 1993: 311; Willemsen 2006a: 87.

The general trend was that the enslaved population started to decline after the British abolition act of 1807, and the subsequent suppression of the transatlantic slave trade. In 1813, Suriname recorded 44,155 people classified as enslaved; the figure for 1836 was 46,879, and it dropped to 39,679 in 1850. Between 1849 and 1859 the number of the Surinamese enslaved population declined by 10 per cent; it was 40,311 in 1849, it had fallen to 38,689 in 1854 and declined further to 36,501 in 1859; on the day of emancipation in July 1863, the enslaved population stood at 33,621.

It should be noted that the Dutch legally abolished their part of the Atlantic 'slave' trade in 1814. However, as the above table shows, the number of the enslaved population increased from 44,155 in 1813 to 51,937 in 1815, then to 53,033 in 1831 before systematic decline set in. The initial increase in the enslaved population may have been a consequence of illicit trading in African captives after the legal abolition of the 'slave' trade, or of natural reproduction within the colony (Klooster 1997; Sherwood 2007).

The enslaved population under Dutch control in the six Antilles territories (Aruba, Bonaire, Curaçao, Saba, Sint Eustatius and Sint Maarten) nearly doubled, from 3,313 in 1699 to 6,286 in 1735 and then trebled again to 21,879 in 1795. It declined however to 12,202 in 1816. By the time of legal abolition in 1863, the figure was slightly down to 11,654. Specifically, the enslaved population in Aruba grew from 30 in 1795 to 502 in 1857 and dropped slightly to 480 at the time of legal abolition; that of Bonaire grew from 97 in 1699 to 819 in 1857 and dropped to 758 at the time of legal abolition; that of Curaçao grew from 2,400 in 1699 to 12,864 in 1795 and dropped to 6,751 at the date of legal abolition; that of Sint Eustatius grew from 385 in 1699 to 4,950 in 1795 and dropped to 1,138 at the time of legal abolition; whereas that of Sint Maarten grew from 300 in 1699 to 3,148 in 1795 and declined to 1,878 at the time of legal abolition. Only Saba saw a constant growth in the enslaved population from 131 in 1699 to 666 in 1857 and 710 at the time of legal abolition. In short, the enslaved population in Suriname declined nearly 40 per cent between 1800 and 1863; that of the Dutch Antilles declined nearly 35 per cent during the same period.

These figures should be treated with caution because, as we noted in Chapter 2, the Dutch transported more African captives than they actually enslaved (Klooster 1997). They transported nearly 200,000 African captives across the Atlantic Ocean between 1601 and 1725. The breakdown of the figures is: 39,900 between 1601 and 1650; 59,500 between 1651 and 1675; 97,400 between 1676 and 1700; and 74,500 between 1701 and 1725 (Eltis et al. 1999).

These figures however are not included in the data for the enslaved population in Suriname.

As we noted in Chapter 3, this in turn affected the production of the goods the enslaved produced, especially sugar.

To fully understand the debate that was held on the issue of freedom – while the bill regarding the legal abolition of slavery was being deliberated – one must become acquainted with the views of the State Committee presided over by J.C. Baud, the former minister of colonies.

FROM REGULATION TO INTERVENTION

Installed on 29 November 1853 by Royal Decree No.66, the Baud Committee was responsible for examining the measures the government should take regarding the enslaved population in the colonies. This set in process the transformation of the state from being a regulator of slavery into being a manager of slavery on behalf of Dutch citizens; it constituted a move from regulation to intervention.

As early as 1844, Baud had informed King William II that Suriname could only be kept as a colony if the enslaved were emancipated:

> Therefore, emancipation is ... a measure of material necessity; otherwise Suriname will inevitably perish because of the extinction of its agricultural workers. When emancipation is operational, *Suriname will produce less than today*, but will be preserved from complete devastation. In short, it seems that emancipation is the only way to save Suriname. (Quoted from Willemsen 2006a: 86; emphasis added)

The implication of the above statement is that the state viewed enslaved labour as more productive than free or alternative forms of labour. In other words emancipation was not an end in itself; it was a means to an end, namely, the preservation of Suriname as a Dutch colony. We noted above that one of the major reasons for the decline of the enslaved population was the legal abolition and suppression of the 'slave' trade. Another reason for the decline was, as everywhere in the Caribbean, the discrepancy between the mortality rate and the reproduction rate. The hard and heavy work of the enslaved took its toll on life expectancy. In total, 13,081 'slaves' died between 1850 and 1859 (1,224 died in 1850, 1,482 in 1855 and 1,391 in 1859) (see Table 4.2). During the same period (1850 to 1859) there were 12,234 recorded births, 2,722 manumissions, and 822 people classified as escapees or as unfit to be used as slaves in the labour process. The enslaved population was not reproducing itself.

Baud had arrived at this conclusion on the basis of statistics from the Ministry of Colonies: he found a sharp decline in the slave population, from 42,272 in 1833 to 34,773 in 1841 – a drop of 18 per cent, amounting to an annual average of 2.25 per cent.

Table 4.2 Enslaved Population in Suriname

Year	Total	Numbers of Enslaved			Escaped/Written off
		Born	Deceased	Manumitted	
1849	40,311				
1850	39,679	1,342	1,224	258	138
1851	39,676	1,250	1,544	331	80
1852	39,309	1,227	1,250	281	118
1853	39,130	1,205	1,053	302	137
1854	38,689	1,153	1,191	328	92
1855	38,006	1,079	1,482	237	96
1856	37,759	1,250	1,194	281	22
1857	37,175	1,220	1,572	215	17
1858	36,963	1,289	1,180	236	85
1859	36,501	1,219	1,391	253	37
Total		12,234	13,081	2,722	822

Note: Table reproduced from 'Explanatory Memorandum, Annex 3, Deliberations of the Provincial Council 1861–1862': 462.

Nevertheless, production remained unaltered, due to an increase in productivity on the sugar plantations. This was partly caused by the merger of several plantations and by the transport of enslaved populations from coffee and cotton plantations. But the main reason, as we indicated in the previous chapter, was the development of modern technology.

Before 1855, there were no less than 29 draft abolition proposals. To these, the State Committee added three of its own making.

The committee accomplished its task and reported on a series of questions related to the problem of slavery. The question arose of whether to proceed to immediate and direct emancipation, or to start with the proclamation of a transitional period that would remove slavery without immediately giving absolute freedom. The committee also wondered whether a more substantial improvement in the fate of the enslaved – while preserving slavery itself – would be a better option.

In its assessment of emancipation, the committee argued strongly in favour of governmental authoritative measures over freedmen and several kinds of forced labour. Within this context, it was expressing clear opinions and beliefs about civilization and barbarism, such as the laziness of 'the Negro', his backwardness, and his inevitable failure as a free citizen. These opinions, points of view and beliefs would completely dominate the debate in the Dutch Parliament regarding the legal abolition of slavery.

While discussing the abolition bill, the Dutch government and certain members of parliament repeatedly referred to these ideas and beliefs. The State Committee referred to notions of progress and civilization derived from the perspective on European history that prevailed during that period (Césaire 1972). This perspective assumed that mankind experiences a long series of historical stages. Each step is characterized by a certain degree of development entailing socio-economic progress when compared with the previous phase: the first people were hunters and gatherers, later they applied themselves to cattle breeding and agriculture, and so on. According to this line of reasoning, only Europeans had attained the highest level of development and civilization by the nineteenth century, because their society was driven by commerce and industrial production. This degree of progress was defined as civilization. In the committee's view, a society with slaves was clearly situated on a lower scale of development: in order to attain civilization, the removal of slavery was required, because slavery is an inferior form of employment. The enslaved as a group were considered 'savages', in need of a transitional period to master the essential work ethic, behaviour, standards and values of a civilized and well-ordered society. A cultural campaign led by the state was necessary to end the remnants of African 'backwardness' and 'barbarism' (Willemsen 2006a).

The State Committee formulated a number of general principles and basic assumptions which would influence the debate for years to come. First of all, the committee stated that slavery in the West Indian colonies had:

> [b]een expanded and protected by the Sovereign of that time ... and that a series of legal clauses, from later times as well, has stipulated that the slaves in the West Indian colonies are the legal

property of their masters; they are negotiable matter, the object of legal business and the subject of deals. (Willemsen 2006a)

Thus the legislature had created legal rights that could not be removed or abolished without giving something in exchange: hence the committee's position that the state could not bestow emancipation without first compensating the enslavers.

The committee was far less benevolent towards the enslaved population. First of all, it was the emancipated enslaved who would have to foot the bill for their liberation: they would have to reimburse the state as much as possible.

The committee argued that the enslaved were at the low end of civilization and morality; even those who could be called Christians were guilty of 'polygamy' and 'polyandry'. Therefore, if the state decided to legally abolish slavery it had to do so for the benefit of religion, civilization and the public interest. Furthermore, every emancipated enslaved person should be constrained to labour. This could be realized if the domination of the enslavers was substituted by the authority of the state. Finally, the experience of the British and French colonies should serve as an example to the Dutch state that the ownership of land by the emancipated should never result in 'a training school for laziness' (Willemsen 2006a).

It is remarkable that the State Committee refused to use the word 'emancipation', 'because the nigger would understand it as a permission to idle his days away without any regular job, to indulge in lustful passions and to prefer living in the woods, beyond the pillars of civilized society' (Willemsen 2006a).

The committee preferred talking about 'the removal of masterhood', because emancipation presupposed a far-reaching reorganization of society, and that was the last thing the committee wanted. It considered the enslaved as children who had to be placed under wardship, thus legitimizing governmental authority:

> It is not enough to liberate slaves and give them the jurisdiction to enjoy freedom in a barbaric way; they have to be guided, to be taught the meaning of freedom in a social sense – a sense that does not exist in slavery – with all ensuing commitments. The untying of the bonds (the true characteristic of slavery) must not go hand-in-hand with the sudden release of every commitment that was enforced during servitude; most of all, the means must be preserved to enforce one of the commitments of every social club: the commitment of labour. (Willemsen 2006a: 80)

The assumption here is that the enslaved had not been working.

As we see below, this point of view, adhered to during the debate by subsequent governments, members of parliament and factions, could be traced back to the committee's report. Its publication also gave the public discussion about the legal abolition of slavery a serious boost, causing the crystallization of various opinions and social currents. At the beginning of the 1860s, at a time when England and France had long since abolished slavery in their colonies, public opinion in the Netherlands had also evolved. Thirty years earlier, people talked about emancipation as 'an interference with the law of God ... a liberal vision'. Now it was no longer possible to avoid the issue: the Netherlands simply *had* to emancipate its enslaved.

It is worth noting that neither the State Committee, the government, nor members of parliament had any first-hand knowledge of the colonies in the West Indies. Hardly any of the authorities had visited these countries or spoke the language of the enslaved population. Aside from the committee, so-called 'experts' (who had close ties with some of the enslavers) were consulted about the social condition of the enslaved. Other sources of information were the many pamphlets and addresses of interested parties, articles in journals, official letters by governors and, based on these, documents written by public servants of the Ministry of the Colonies. The enslaved population's opinion was never sought. The 'silence' that we encounter in the archives on this subject is an indication of the structural exclusion and inequality with which the black population have had to struggle.

Subsequent governments proposed no less than five bills based on the reports issued by the State Committee in 1855–56. Every single one of them was rejected by the Second Chamber. Twenty-nine emancipation motions submitted by various individuals met with the same fate. The rejection of so many proposals was caused on the one hand by high hopes and on the other by the conflicting interests that came into play. In order of priority, we should first mention the interest of preserving Suriname as a colony producing sugar for the benefit of its master country. The second interest is that of the Dutch state. The third is the interests of the enslavers. At the bottom was the 'interests' of the enslaved population.

It was obvious that one or more of these interests would suffer and would even be sacrificed for the sake of the others. But still the Second Chamber was unable to choose from among these proposals. Only on 16 November 1855 did the Second Chamber decide 'that slavery would be abolished at a time to be determined later in a way that would be determined by law'.

It should be mentioned that until 1856/7, the government maintained the principle that the enslaved themselves would have to pay the expenses caused by their emancipation. But when parliament unequivocally disapproved, it dropped this principle (Willemsen 2006a). In 1861, the government was on the eve of voting for the final bill regarding the legal abolition of slavery in the Dutch West Indian colonies. What were the main points of the proposed bill?

First, with regard to the preservation of Suriname as a colony, emancipation had to go hand-in-hand with the immigration of free labourers to work on the plantations.

Secondly, the expenses of emancipation should not be paid by the enslaved population but by the state. Here, Asia was called in to the rescue. After all the discussions over the heads of the enslaved, the Dutch state decided that the abolition of slavery in Suriname and the Dutch Antilles was to be financed by surplus from the exploitation of Java (Indonesia) (the so-called 'Indian benefits'). To keep these costs as low as possible, a committee was appointed (in government circles known as 'the committee for verification of the slaves') to monitor and accurately record the number of enslaved reported by the enslavers.

Thirdly, the planters were entitled to a form of compensation. The amount of financial remittance the planters would receive as compensation would be calculated on the basis of the recorded numbers.

Finally, emancipation should not be entrusted to private organizations, but would be managed by the state.

This does not mean, however, that all members of parliament were completely convinced of the necessity for the legal abolition of slavery. Not everyone wanted to remove 'the stain on the Dutch escutcheon because slavery still exists in some of our colonies'. Not everyone wished to 'wipe out the stain that rests upon our fatherland as a slave holding state', and 'put an end to a situation, where one subject of the Netherlands could arbitrarily trade another subject – his fellow man – as merchandise' (Willemsen 2006a).

There were enough people – and not just in the Second Chamber – who still considered the idea of emancipation a folly. As in earlier days, some of them continued to equate the enslaved more or less with stupid animals. But there were also people who were outraged by the mere thought that the Netherlands was the only country in Europe that was still protecting and preserving slavery. Yet even among those who were absolutely convinced of the inevitable legal abolition of an institution thoroughly incompatible with the principles of religion, enlightenment and civilization, a difference of opinion existed regarding the extent of freedom to be granted to the liberated parties – indicated by the divergent views about emancipation.

As a follow-up to the State Committee report, on 20 November 1861, Mr Loudon, minister of colonies, introduced a bill to abolish slavery in the Dutch West Indian colonies. He had been assisted by a small committee consisting of C.P. Schimpf, I.J. Rammelman Elsevier Jr, Esq. and A.D. Van der Gon Netscher. Rammelman Elsevier and Schimpf had previously been governors, the former of the Antilles, the latter of Suriname. Van der Gon Netscher was considered an expert on Suriname because of his close ties with the enslavers and his many publications about the colony; this led to the remark of one member of parliament, Pieter Philip van Bosse, that the Surinamese enslavers had had a considerable impact on the bill through their connection with Van der Gon Netscher. The enslaved population were not consulted; their voices were not heard.

The bill was based upon four principles. These principles, also known as 'the complete economy of the law', were summarized by Uhlenbeck, minister of colonies following Loudon:

> that the declaration of freedom must go hand-in-hand with a compensation or indemnification for the owners; that the declaration of freedom must not be established gradually but immediately; that the slave upon his liberation must also realize that he is a free man, accepted in the society from which he was excluded by birth or any other circumstance; that the declaration of freedom must go hand-in-hand with the import of new labourers. (Willemsen 2006a: 89)

The four principles upon which 'the complete economy of the law' was based and which the minister deemed immutable were:

1. Emancipation had to take place right away and not gradually.
2. The master enslavers were entitled to some sort of compensation or indemnification.
3. The government would supervise freedmen/women for a period of ten years.
4. Immigration was to be under the control and supervision of the government.

Let us now take a closer look at the deliberations and the debate surrounding the most important articles of the bill, to ascertain which views and notions about liberty prevailed and whose interests were given priority. We do this by going beyond narrow historic narratives, within a broader world political, economic and historical context. This is necessary because legal abolition had implications for social formation and social thought.

MODALITIES OF ABOLITION: PROGRESSIVE CONTROL VERSUS TRANSFORMATIVE CHANGE

Given the fact that the legal abolition of the trade in humans had been imposed on the Dutch by Britain and the enslaved population was on the decline, the question was not why Dutch chattel slavery had to be abolished, but when and how much freedom the liberated enslaved should be given. The government set the parameters for the policy direction and opened the floodgates of parliamentary debate. Not only did the question of how much freedom the would-be emancipated people would get generate parliamentary debate, but also the policy and practice that emanated from that debate determined the quality of emancipation. Let us take these issues in turn, starting with the debate.

Abolition and Progressive Control

Part of the essence of chattel slavery is to force people to work without their consent or contract and without pay (Fogel 1989). The purpose of legal abolition was to ensure that those who had once worked without consent or contract would after legal abolition work with consent or contract, and with pay. In other words the Atlantic slavery was a legal institution sanctioned by the state. The state provided the policy framework and the police and soldiers needed to ensure security for the enslavers to help suppress the enslaved. The state also taxed the enslavers to bolster the state. State officials, including monarchs, also had shares in companies that dealt with the 'slave' trade and slavery. The State Committee recommended that the process of consent or contract had to be done in such a way that it did not get out of control or threaten the enslavers or the Dutch governing authorities. This process constitutes what Mullard has referred to as *progressive control*. Progressive control is defined as a dynamic process:

[w]hich, observed in and endorsed by policies, practices, official statements and the like, is oriented and continuously moves towards *newer forms of control* which, in turn, are called for as a result of changes in the material and structural conditions, consciousnesses and resistances that distinguish the character of a Europeanized society at any specific time. (Mullard 1988: 362; emphasis added)

According to the adherents of progressive control, a law that 'suddenly' liberated the enslaved population would be interpreted by that population as 'the license to lead an idle and drifting existence' (Willemsen 2006a). They did not go so far as to openly approve of slavery, but they thought that the black population had to be prepared for freedom; they considered that complete freedom was premature.

So progressive control does not mean *no change*; but rather a change that maintains and regulates existing dominant–dominated relations. Those who supported this view belonged to the advocates of state control and, though the enslaved were not consulted, claimed that this control was in the best interests of the enslaved. In an earlier explanatory memorandum, the government had supported this point of view, stating that the enslaved population was unfamiliar with family life (Willemsen 2006a).

We have seen that the enslaved population was already in decline under the supervision of the enslavers. And according to the line of thinking of those who advocated progressive control, liberated enslaved persons would not take the slightest interest in the fate of the handicapped, the elderly and the sick, or women and children; this lack of care and help would bring about the untimely deaths of many people, further reducing the population.

Therefore, the black man needed to be prepared for social freedom, educated into becoming a religious and morally more mature person, and moulded into an industrious and worthy member of society. This might succeed by forcefully restraining 'idleness and vagrancy' among the freedmen. One delegate wondered whether emancipation would improve or worsen the condition of the enslaved. In his opinion, the biggest problem was not so much the cost of emancipation as 'the slave's nature'. Given his 'nature', freedom could only civilize a black person 'when he is put in a situation where labour is inevitable for the gratification of his needs and where he finds the opportunity to communicate with more civilized people'.

In justification of why the freedom of the emancipated population should be restricted, one of the parliamentarians, Dirks, reminded the chamber that:

> [a] negro remains a negro, and attempting to make anything other of the blackmoor is futile. Labour in the field is particularly problematic. The white man, it is said in Suriname, does not work in the field, which means that it is shameful. A free man, says the slave, wears shoes and a blue or yellow hat. But a free man does not work. Free is equal. I can do anything and do not have to work. (Willemsen 2006a: 91)

Apparently the honourable parliamentarian had taken upon himself to think for the enslaved without the latter's consent.

Another line of reasoning of the enslavers was that the work of the enslaved population could not be counted as work. Thus most members of parliament felt that black people would simply translate freedom into the right to wear shoes and an exemption from labour. The common view was that black people have few needs and that a piece of land with a cabin and some poultry would suffice to succumb to a life of *dolce far niente*. The black population would want to lead a life secluded from civilization – and the abundance of fertile land in a country as sparsely populated as Suriname would offer them every opportunity to do so. Therefore, the black man had to be prepared for his freedom and gradually taught what life in a 'civilized' society meant. In other words the enslaved, who were to be 'emancipated', should not confuse freedom with equality. To ensure that the would-be emancipated did not confuse freedom with equality, a speaker, de Raadt, further noted that:

> [c]ivilisation does not tolerate jumps, and social freedom, in its most noble meaning, is not achievable for those who can enjoy it on the basis of a combination of disposition or training and self-control ... But it is then doubly necessary to guide them in the process of transition from slavery to freedom and to protect them from themselves and from giving in to temptations that would corrupt them. (Willemsen 2006a: 92–3)

These members of parliament forcefully and repeatedly argued that the black population had a low level of civilization and thus would not be interested in regular jobs. Abandoned to his fate, the black man would return to his natural state, 'which seems so alluring to these barbarian people'. Once liberated, the black population would view freedom as idleness and vagrancy, as a deliverance from work and/or a flight to the woods to seek their own interpretation of liberty: mere pleasure. This tendency towards idleness, emptiness and vagrancy – which the advocates of this way of thinking called 'the harmful consequences of freedom' – must be vigorously suppressed. For this very reason these people supported a period of transition controlled by the state, or 'state control'.

From their patronizing point of view they pleaded for the institution of apprenticeship, analogous with the system that was introduced by the British government. They viewed the enslaved population as stupid and lazy people who had to get used to freedom and therefore had to be protected against themselves. They gave the impression that they did not want to abandon the liberated slaves to their fate, but were instead aiming to help and protect them. In their rhetoric, the enslaved were depicted as passive and submissive creatures. Slavery was represented as a form of humanitarianism, combining a paternalistic relationship with camaraderie between enslaver and enslaved.

Again, the important implication of these views is that we should not confuse legal abolition with emancipation. Legal abolition is an act of legislation, whereas emancipation is a cultural, social, political and economic process. This process, it was articulated, should be guided by the state. Moreover,

> state supervision is not so much needed for the improvement and education of the adults, who have already developed their characters and acquired certain habits, but it is useful and necessary for the next generation, to give this generation a different perspective to their parents by means of Christian and academic education and good examples. (Willemsen 2006a: 96)

The black population had to be socially engineered.

Supporters of this position alluded to 'foreign colonies' where, according to the authorities, 'a significant part of the Negro population is living in the woods; instead of bettering themselves, their laziness, immorality and vulgar wrongdoings have sharply increased, causing a severe deterioration of their situation'. The Netherlands should not follow this example, for otherwise the millions spent on emancipation would be put to bad use. Therefore, the freedmen had to be guided during a period of transition and must learn to make more efficient use of their newly acquired freedom, not only for themselves but also for the benefit of society. Furthermore, they must be taught to lead an industrious and orderly life and to use their freedom well and sensibly by sustaining their livelihood without becoming a burden to others.

We noted earlier that not every African was fit to be captured in Africa to be transported for enslavement in the Americas (see Chapter 2). In a similar vein, according to Mr de Raadt, not all the enslaved were fit for emancipation. To drive this message home, the speaker noted that:

> [i]t may be necessary to declare that this is applicable to the entire generation that is currently undergoing emancipation. Giving complete freedom without any restriction to people who will now act as children in society and who view inactivity as the primary right of freedom, who can obtain everything that they need in an exceptionally mild climate, with few needs, without performing any work worthy of note – I wonder, where would that lead to? (Willemsen 2006a: 98)

This speaker seems to have had the ability to predict the inevitable social formation that would emerge after legal abolition!

The majority of the members of parliament were not willing to grant the enslaved population unconditional liberty. The enslaved were considered as being at the low end of the scale of civilization, people who would behave as children and for whom freedom meant the privilege of not having to work. To strengthen their argument, these members of parliament repeatedly referred to the French and British colonies, where disturbances had occurred after emancipation and where freedmen had supposedly been unwilling to accomplish regular (i.e. forced) labour on the plantations.

In support of this perspective, another parliamentarian, Duymaer van Twist, posed two questions, and answered them, as follows:

> What is the slave's great objection to slavery? What is, for him, the essence of slavery? Labour – labour that he is forced to perform from his youth by the lash of the whip. This is why he hates labour and slavery.

Mr van Twist went on to pose a third question, namely: 'Or do you believe that he is oppressed by slavery because the deprivation of *human rights* prevents him from developing freely and independently?' (Willemsen 2006a: 99; emphasis added).

Van Twist's reply to his own question is this:

> I do not believe so. It is the labour that oppresses him. For him, freedom is the freedom not to labour. It is the freedom that he desires, that he will seek and that prompts him to flee into the wilderness, where he is sure that he will not be found and where his urge not to work will prevail. (Willemsen 2006a)

Two observations may be made about this statement; first, clearly Duymaer van Twist knew what human rights were; but he thought they were not applicable to blacks or the enslaved. The second observation is that van Twist observed that the notion of freedom among the enslaved was bound to be different from that of the enslavers. These observations undermine the views of historians such as Eltis and Emmer, who argue that we cannot use our current knowledge to judge the actions of past generations.

To conclude his plea, van Twist posed and answered two final questions:

> What is there to prevent him from doing this? What would prompt him to work? Neither in his habits, nor his minimal needs nor his current level of development and civilization can such a stimulus be found. And as long as such a stimulus is lacking it must be imposed from the outside, he must be forced to work and not flee into the wilderness if necessary. The law, in accordance with nature, gives the father power over his child, the guardian power over the minor. A person who has not achieved a level of civilization and development that will enable him to be free and independent will abuse the freedom. (Willemsen 2006a)

The racist context of their plea aside, those of van Twist's persuasion had made their point, namely, that legal abolition is not the same as emancipation. They were in favour of legal abolition, but not of emancipation.

As we noted above, progressive control does not mean lack of change, or no change. Rather it refers to changes on a horizontal continuum designed to maintain the dominant–dominated relationship for which change was called for in the first place. One of the ways to maintain control over the emancipated enslaved was to tie them to the plantations and thus ensure the availability of their labour through a system of apprenticeship. However, as we see below, the official discourse revolved around the notion that apprenticeship was necessary to civilize the enslaved after legal abolition; they were not capable, it was argued, of taking care of themselves.

Let us consider alternative views on legal abolition and emancipation in the Dutch parliament at the time.

Abolition and Transformative Change

Emancipation entails the liberation of the enslaved from slavery or bondage. In a narrow sense, the act of legal abolition of slavery can be considered as emancipation. However as we noted above and argue below, this is not sufficient, because the Dutch governing authorities went a step further by compensating enslavers for losing formal control over the enslaved. The state took over the task of control. Emancipation is embedded in *transformative change*, which:

> [e]ntails a special kind of break from former policies and practices and the relations in which they arise. Such a break encompasses not only a qualitatively different perspective from that which dominates, but, in the challenge, there also lives an idea of an opposite conception of approach, policy and practice; one which reflects a transcension rather than a progression from one state to another state of things. In other words, the kind of break which characterizes this kind of change cannot be seen merely as a shift from one position to another within a preconceived or determined framework. It is a break which necessitates the occurrence of a *transformation* of the existing, dominant framework, or, in policy terms, the social transference and exchange of one set of policies based upon one set of beliefs to another oppositional set based upon an oppositional set of beliefs. (Mullard 1988: 363; emphasis added)

Clearly transformative change aims at vertical change in which the dominant–dominated relationship is transformed into one of equal relations. This brings us to the perspectives on legal abolition and emancipation of those parliamentarians whose views were in opposition to those on the progressive-control continuum.

To begin with, in response to the view that the unrestricted freedom of the enslaved would neither be good for them nor safe for the enslavers, one speaker, Mr Van Zuylen van Nyevelt, posed the following question: 'Has the terrible yoke that oppressed slaves for so many years not taught them enough about this, so that it is necessary to devote another ten years to teaching them how to work?' (Willemsen 2006a: 94).

The speaker posed another question and answered it as follows:

> After all, what motivates the slaves to flee into the jungle? Nothing other than slavery, but, when they are freed, why would they not enjoy their freedom in the colony as much as in the jungle, which would not then be so exceptionally attractive? (Willemsen 2006a: 100)

Elout van Soeterwoude, a former member of the Executive Committee to Abolish Slavery (Maatschappij tot Afschaffing van de Slavernij), was among the members of parliament who favoured legal abolition and emancipation. These members cited examples that proved that the liberated black population, in Suriname as well as in the English colonies, was anything but lazy. For instance, in 1861, enslaved Surinamese who had been liberated thanks to collections taken up by sympathizing citizens of Amsterdam succeeded in saving, out of their own wages, the sum of 4,958 guilders in order to purchase the freedom of others.

> I believe that this is proof that they are not actually so inferior, or that they have some realisation of the value of freedom, some understanding of decency, some feeling of gratitude towards those who helped them, that they desire to preserve the worthiness of what they have received and to share it with others. (Willemsen 2006a: 94)

As in England, where almost every abolitionist was against the system of 'apprenticeship', active anti-slavery forces in the Dutch parliament opposed this bill. One of their most important arguments was that a government in favour of state control and coercion does not have much trust in the principle of freedom. The adherents of this point of view – who constituted an absolute minority – wanted to liberate the enslaved population without further delay. They strongly objected to the fact that the enslaved would not get full possession of their freedom, and characterized the proposed freedom as some sort of 'intermediate situation' between slavery and freedom, which could hardly be called total freedom. Slavery, some members claimed, would continue to exist for another ten years in the colony of Suriname, though under a different name.

The advocates of this view wished to grant the enslaved their freedom *'purement et simplement'* as one of them said, without reservation, without restriction, without delay. Therefore, they pleaded for a simple and immediate declaration of freedom with no limitations, modifications, clauses or conditions. Otherwise, they reasoned, the enslaved would be mystified. They insisted upon immediate and full emancipation with no period of transition or apprenticeship, which they called 'half-hearted', 'double-faced' and 'camouflaged slavery'.

Some critics of the bill stated that it was impossible to know the joy of freedom without *being* free. They called the idea of trying to make people familiar with freedom through forced labour an illusion. They also referred to the example of the English colonies, where in 1833 the enslaved were declared free but actually were not – because of their apprenticeship. At first, the duration of the supervision was set at twelve years, a little later at six years, and soon afterwards, when its pointlessness was recognized, it was reduced to four years.

The supporters of this idea did not think that the state should place adults under guardianship. The wonderful principle of freedom, soon to be granted to the enslaved, could only be restricted through attempts to keep law and order in the colony. They did not object to some preventative and, if necessary, repressive measure in the period before, during and after emancipation. They stressed that the subjugated black population had been promised liberty for 30 years, and they blamed the government for not keeping its promise. They mocked a bill that began with the words, 'You are free', and then continued, 'but for such and such a number of years you will not fully enjoy freedom'.

The most forceful advocate of emancipation and opponent of progressive control of abolition at that time was the parliamentary liberal van Bosse. He invited those who were in favour of progressive control and apprenticeship to imagine their own reasoning as follows:

> You are free, but you are obliged to continue labouring, to stay in the district where you live. You will be punished by the police if you rest for too long or if you show the least resistance to the precautionary measures that we approve. Is that the situation that is least similar to the image that an average slave's mind can and must have of freedom? Is that a situation that the slaves will meekly accept when they compare it with what they

know about their brothers in neighbouring colonies? Will they not sooner regard it as a deception that means that being free may have worse consequences than if, *purement et simplement*, freedom is granted? I fear that such a situation will produce much worse consequences than unconditional freedom. (Willemsen 2006a: 102)

Van Bosse argued that the enslaved population would be greatly disappointed. The impact of emancipation upon the enslaved would be intensified by feelings of disappointment and mystification when it became clear that freedom amounted to little more than false freedom. The fear that a return to slavery remained possible – even after liberation – would never leave the minds of the enslaved population.

Van Bosse considered the bill incompatible with the way he felt the enslaved thought about liberty. They would view the proffered freedom as a mystification. He proved to be the strongest advocate of immediate freedom '*purement et simplement*'. According to Willemsen, the way van Bosse has been depicted in Surinamese historiography – as someone who did not always make the best decisions for Suriname – must be put into proper perspective and revised (Willemsen 2006a). Few members in the chamber pleaded so openly for the introduction of a system of free labour in Suriname. Apart from van Bosse, Van Zuylen van Nyevelt also belonged to this group. It was the desire of these members that, after their liberation, the enslaved would have the freedom to choose the labour they preferred. Van Bosse attacked the so-called free labour that the bill wanted to introduce in Suriname. He put forward an amendment to give freedmen the best opportunities to work for themselves; to conclude labour contracts voluntarily and to discuss their salaries freely with the plantation owners. He was the only one who wondered whether it would be acceptable, from the principles of modern economics, for the state to act as a deliverer of labourers and spend the taxpayers' money on making the plantation enterprises more comfortable and less expensive. He called the far-reaching state intervention with the supply of new labourers for the plantations a 'big economic heresy'.

To prevent any misunderstandings, it must be noted, however, that the members of parliament who favoured legal abolition also imposed some limits on the freedom they wanted to bestow upon freedmen. No one was clearer on this subject than the member Heemskerk Azn. Those who defend liberty, he said, do not want lawlessness; they are merely aiming at personal, not political freedom. Personal freedom has its limits and is compatible with rigid enforcement of the law by the police and with measures concerning public order. 'It is out of the question to give a Negro who was a slave yesterday political rights tomorrow.'

During the debate, adherents and opponents of the bill bombarded each other with all kinds of arguments. Thus, advocates of the law said that it was based on the advice of people who were living in Suriname or who knew the colony. The critics were reproached for never having visited the colony and never having seen a slave. The retort was that it was unnecessary to be acquainted with slaves in order to judge the principles of the law. In this context, an imaginary conversation with a black slave was mentioned, which we do not want to withhold from our readers. Member Tutein Nolthenius, a supporter of the law, reproached his critical colleague van Bosse for having had an imaginary conversation with a black man in which he said: 'You are free.' Tutein Nolthenius went to the 'heart of the matter' along the following lines:

> 'You are free.' When the negro jumped for joy he added: 'but you must continue to work here, and if you do not work hard enough we will punish you'. The negro replied: 'That is a deception', and left angrily. He had now become dangerous. If I had been there I would have told the shouting negro: 'A propos, friend, come here for a moment. This gentleman has told you several things, but has actually not yet told you about the heart of the matter. He has forgotten a few minor issues, which I shall add. He has forgotten to tell you – you can henceforth no longer be sold, and you may also be pleased to learn – you will henceforth have to *work like me and others* in order to earn your daily bread, but you will be paid for all your work, and what you receive for it will be your property. You will therefore be able to own property and have a family, and your children will no longer belong to the slave master as slave children, but to you. And if you behave properly and meet your obligations, you will be completely free in ten years.' This is what the esteemed delegate forgot to say to the negro; but if that imaginary negro received the idea of naively asking me: 'Why has the other master only told me half of what he knew?' then, Mr Chairman, I would find it somewhat difficult to answer him. (Willemsen 2006a: 104; emphasis added)

Though Tutein Nolthenius was holding an imaginary conversation, it can be discerned that it contained elements of truth, for example, about deliberate social engineering to prevent the formation of families under the enslaved.

In response to this, van Bosse questioned why we should equate legal abolition with emancipation and continued in the following words:

> If that reasoning and thinking negro of the speaker from Hoorn (Mr Tutein Nolthenius) was present at this meeting, what would he say? You give me a great deal, but what have I discovered? People tell me: you will own property. I was told that 25 or 30 years ago. You will have a family. I had been told this long ago. You will not be moved from one plantation to another. That was already part of the government regulations when I was a slave. What has become of all these privileges? Nothing! Now people say: there will be one law. But the speaker from Hoorn is starting to go further than the law. 'If you behave properly', he says, 'you will be free in ten years.' But this is not part of the law – it simply states that I will be under the supervision of the state for ten years. You now start to talk of a period that may still be extended ...
>
> You see, gentlemen, that if a negro were to reason along these lines he would quickly draw the conclusion, 'You are just telling stories.' If I wish I can obtain my freedom by crossing the border into the British colony. But there I can get everything that you give me, and something more, and to which I attach much greater value – the freedom to travel and work as I please.' (Willemsen 2006a: 104–5)

We noted above that the legal abolition of the Atlantic slave trade was imposed on the Dutch by Britain; van Bosse's observations also indicate that the earlier legal abolition of slavery in the British and French territories had an impact on the Dutch parliamentary debate.

Following the example in the English colonies, the advocates of granting immediate and complete legal freedom tried to shorten the period of state control from ten to four years. Though admitting that reducing this period did not remove their objections to forced labour, they considered this option the lesser evil. This attempt failed because the government did not want to give up the ten-year state control, and the minister of colonies threatened time and again to withdraw the law if 'the economy of the law' was endangered. What the government did accept was the proposal to introduce the words 'not exceeding', so that the ten-year period could not be extended; if circumstances permitted, it could even be reduced.

The anti-slavery forces in the Second Chamber wanted to give the enslaved – following their liberation – the freedom to choose the job they preferred. A liberated enslaved person should not be coerced into forced labour; it should be up to him to decide which work he wanted to do. He should be provided with opportunities to work for himself, to conclude labour contracts voluntarily and to negotiate his salary freely. In short, this was a plea for a direct transition to the system of wage work. Compulsory labour should only be inflicted upon those who did not want to work and who abandoned themselves to vagrancy and idleness.

But is emancipation involving forced labour any different from camouflaged slavery? In such a case, is individual masterhood not simply substituted by the authority of the state? In the preceding pages we have produced many arguments that endorse such a point of view. In the chamber, Member Boreel van Hogelanden developed a strong counter-argument:

> Is a slave paid for all the labour he performs? Can he choose where and when he wishes to labour, change masters every year, be the father of his own family, master in his own home, become the owner of his field, live under the same criminal and civil law as other inhabitants, to whom only the law will say – you will not be idle in the interests of society, just as the law here says, for the benefit of society – you will not beg on the street in order to live off charity. (Willemsen 2006a: 106)

Obviously, Boreel van Hogelanden defined freedom in a negative sense: as slavery without floggings and without detention of person or property.

Unlike in Suriname, the enslaved population in the Dutch Antilles was immediately 'brought into the full enjoyment of man's most valuable possession' on 1 July 1863. The enslaved got their freedom right away, without being subjected to any kind of forced labour. The government's proposition to establish state control (except for Curaçao and Sint Maarten) for a maximum of five years was rejected by a vote of 28 to 24. One might then ask why the enslaved on the islands got their freedom immediately, while those in Suriname did not.

In the English system, the enslaved remained enslaved as long as the apprenticeship lasted. In practice, apprenticeship differed very little from slavery. In the Dutch system, the enslaved were liberated but state control was forced upon them. The English apprentices were obliged to remain with their enslavers; in the Dutch system, freedmen had, at least in some cases, the limited possibility of choosing their own 'masters'. That was the only important difference. As Member Van Luynden stated: 'In the Dutch system they say: "You are free", followed by: "during so many years you will not fully taste the joy of freedom."' (In the French colonies, emancipation had occurred in 1848 without state control or apprenticeship.)

The State Committee remarked that there were no forests on the islands (in contrast with Suriname) where one could withdraw and be self-supporting. The islands were not plantation economies: to a large extent they were barren and had to obtain provisions from elsewhere. For freedmen this implied that they inevitably had to work to buy provisions. Hence the remark by Mijer, a conservative member of parliament, that 'hunger [will] take care of what in Suriname only the fruit of wise state intervention can achieve'. This strong incentive to work was absent in Suriname. Nearly all the land on the islands, however, was private property and there was a surplus rather than a shortage of work. For freedmen, the only real alternative to starvation was wage work, if necessary combined with some sort of self-sufficiency. The influence of this incentive caused the group of free people, which on Curaçao was twice as large as the slave population, to set the latter a good example. 'The continual contact between these two parts of the population made the slaves more adaptable to the joy of freedom than elsewhere' (Willemsen 2006a: 109).

Thus the colonial authorities considered the gap between free coloured people and the enslaved on Curaçao less important than in Suriname. For example, it was not deemed necessary to deny the enslaved the right to wear shoes. On holidays, the enslaved were just as well dressed as their enslavers. Still, the government thought that the islands, apart from Curaçao, could not do without state control. They proposed this measure to combat so-called excesses and lawlessness. Van Bosse criticized this position, pointing out that countering lawlessness was always the government's obligation.

Whereas in the case of Suriname state control was deemed necessary for the preservation of sugar production, no such argument existed for the islands. A considerable part of the chamber was eager to emphasize that the enslaved on the islands were predominately craftsmen, with a higher level of development than the ordinary enslaved man who worked in the field. Therefore, they were more 'open' to freedom than the mass of labourers on the sugar plantations. Not only did craftsmen usually have a higher level of development; at auctions they also fetched higher prices than other enslaved men. State control would give freedmen less freedom of movement than they now had; this would be similar to the case of many shipyard workers who, in spite of their situation, seldom attempted to escape. The enslaved on the islands were also 'more open' to liberty because almost all of them were Christians. The general propagation of Christianity would guarantee that the transition to freedom would be less problematic. Finally, the enslaved on Sint Eustatius and Saba had the advantage of speaking English, the language of their masters. Consequently, they were familiar with the white man's mentality, particularly concerning emancipation.

The argument that the enslaved on the islands would be more open to freedom is somewhat curious since many carpenters and other craftsmen were active on every sugar plantation in Suriname. Moreover, as we see in the next chapter, the influence of the Moravian Brethren and the Roman Catholic Church among the enslaved population in Suriname was underestimated. On the other hand, it is true that the enslavers in Curaçao had invested in the enslaved population and had schooled a great number of them in some type of craft; the rental income from these craftsmen's labour was the livelihood of many enslavers. But whether all these arguments were valid or not, state control was never established on the islands; immediately after legal abolition, freedmen were granted complete freedom and all civil rights.

As will become clear in a moment, at the end of the debate, those in favour of transformative change were in the minority. This gave those in favour of progressive control the power to translate their perspectives into policy and practice.

It is worth mentioning that in England, the discussion regarding the emancipation law lasted more than three months, and in the Netherlands it lasted eight days – from 2 to 10 July 1862. This was unparalleled in Dutch parliamentary history; even later, 'the West' never preoccupied the chamber for such a long period. This was mostly because of the deliberations surrounding Article 2: 'Because of the abolition of slavery, slave owners will receive compensation.'

Indemnification or compensation for *slaves* was not on the agenda. Willemsen has noted that Elout van Soeterwoude was the only member of parliament who casually wondered if the enslaved were entitled to some sort of compensation. In the Dutch Parliament he was the first who, with remarkable foresight, raised the matter of *reparation* or *compensation* for the enslaved population – an issue that 140 years later would again arouse emotions. So far as we can discern, nobody in the chamber took this up and the matter of compensation for the enslaved died a premature death.

So here we are again. Three centuries after Las Casas and Sepúlveda debated the humanity of Native Americans and Africans, the Dutch parliament was debating the humanity of an enslaved population; but this time not in the name of God, but on behalf of Dutch citizens. Let us return to the issue of citizenship in order to understand why the government decided to compensate the enslavers and not the enslaved.

ABOLITION AND CITIZENSHIP

We mentioned in Chapter 2 that after the French Revolution, European citizens became stakeholders in their states. At the background of the issue of slavery and abolition is the fact that European citizens, who became colonists of large territories such as the United States and Brazil, had revolted against their mother countries and formed independent states to manage their own enslaved populations (see Chapter 6). Thus, viewed in the context of 'citizens as stakeholders in the state', the legal abolition debate was a discussion between the government as the custodian of the state, and representatives of the enslavers as citizens. The enslaved were considered as subhuman and non-citizens. Abolition and emancipation thus constituted a conflict resolution between the Dutch state and sections of its citizens.

To enforce their point of view, as we have seen, supporters of the bill repeatedly referred to the disturbances that had taken place in the English and French colonies. They viewed these events as a classic example of the way things should not be handled: the plantation owners were ruined, freedmen had turned away from the plantations and refused to work when there was enough land where they could settle, the English treasury had lost a great deal of money, and the British economy was suffering from reduced imports from the Caribbean territory.

To members who supported legal abolition, the West Indian form of emancipation was, on the contrary, a source of inspiration from which lessons could be learned. And so they wondered why the government, in spite of the negative experience of the British with apprenticeship, still proposed establishing state control.

What lessons could be learned from the emancipation in the Caribbean territory? This was the subject of an intense debate throughout the nineteenth century. Alexis de Tocqueville concluded in 1839 that a period of transition after emancipation was necessary to keep the plantation system from falling apart; at the same time, he remarked that the system of apprenticeship had failed, because in the eyes of the black population it was too close to slavery. He suggested another solution: the state should intervene between the two parties – planters and liberated slaves. The state had to see to it that the blacks would still offer their services to the plantation owners – that is, on the government's conditions – and that they would not fall back into barbarism and idleness.

It is clear that white people defined freedom for blacks in a very narrow and limited way, as though they could not understand what freedom meant to the blacks. They realized that the government had liberated the blacks, but on the other hand they still wanted to exercise supervision over them. That is why conflicts arose from the very first working day. To the plantation owners, freedom still meant hierarchy and masterhood – not a right for the black population, but a privilege. In their concept, legal freedom did not signify economic independence or equal civil and political rights for the blacks; hence the pressure on freedmen to negotiate labour contracts, while they were denied equal rights. In addition, severe punishments were meted out whenever a contract was not honoured – a desire to preserve the plantation system remained (Willemsen 2006a).

The equation of labour with civilization can be found in the Dutch answer to emancipation. What was the difference between the English system of apprenticeship and the Dutch system of state control? According to Uhlenbeck, the minister of colonies, the Dutch system was completely different: while the English apprenticeship was actually a substitution for slavery, the Dutch declaration of liberty *preceded* state control. In the words of the minister of colonies:

> That kind of control is completely different from what this Government is proposing. The Negroes remained slaves and that is the reason why that supervision had an adverse effect. England had to give in to the pressure of the Negroes: on the one hand, they were somewhat released from the most crushing bonds, but on the other hand, they did not have the feeling of being free since they remained bound to the masters, obliged to work for them without getting paid and bound to the penal

code that was enforced upon them under the pressure of slavery. What the Netherlands intends to do is of a completely different nature. We merely want to restrain lawlessness when the bonds of slavery are untied; we want supervision to avoid a large number of labourers being unemployed and therefore unable to provide their own livelihood. (Willemsen 2006a: 108)

Not only was the Dutch government using Britain as a mirror to its policy but also, following Uhlenbeck's lead, the government took the point of view that the enslaved population was uncivilized, stupid, childish, lazy and incapable of handling liberty. Uhlenbeck felt that the enslaved would not understand the true meaning of freedom and should learn to become industrious and useful. They should acquire notions and feelings that would bring them closer to those who were born free. In the explanatory memorandum for the bill regarding the legal abolition of slavery in the colony of Suriname, prejudice and racist views are abundant. There is, for instance, mention of the fact that daily contact between a white and a black person is the motor of civilization for blacks.

This line of thinking implied that there was no room for the independent economic development of the black population – for example, as farmers. Using the future alienation between blacks and whites – which would be 'detrimental to the black civilization' – as a pretext, the enslavers' interests were served. According to Willemsen, this explains why the government and the colonial authority were for a long time disinclined to stimulate small agricultural projects among freedmen. Even access to the land was denied, forcing them to work on the plantations.

Furthermore, the government clearly stated that reason and experience had taught them that, in the transition from slavery to civil liberty, the joys of freedom should at first be somewhat restricted, in the interest of the persons involved as well as in the common interest. During the general discussion, the minister of colonies stated that from his knowledge of 'the nature of the negro and the character of tropical tribes in general, state control would be necessary and useful' for those who were going to be released from their crushing bonds. In line with the dominant social thought, the minister argued, with great bravura, that the nature of black people made it necessary 'to treat them as infants who need council, guidance and support from their guardian'. He defended state control with the argument that 'it was necessary to teach the liberated slaves to live within a family, to make them accustomed to labour for their own profit, to restrain them from excesses, and most of all, to lead adolescents to a higher social level through schooling and religious education'. He received much support, especially for what he called the reform of character – in particular of black youths.

> This state control is not absolutely necessary for the amelioration and education of those who are already adults, whose character and behaviour have embraced a specific way of life, but it is useful and necessary for the coming generation, in order to give that generation, through Christian education, proper schooling and good examples, an attitude unlike that of their parents. (Willemsen 2006a: 96)

This is the world turned upside down; the very people who abducted Africans and prevented them from forming families under slavery now turn to accuse them of being incapable of family life.

The Dutch government believed that a period of ten years would be necessary to accustom the freedmen to wage work. The idea, as we saw above, was that without firm guidance from the state, the liberated slaves would discard any kind of personal labour contract and flee to the woods in pursuit of the pleasure they thought freedom entailed: the privilege of not having to work. Therefore, this proclivity to idleness and vagrancy should be forcefully suppressed.

Some members of parliament defended state control out of a sincere concern for the freedmen they were trying to protect. They thought it impossible to liberate 33,000 Surinamese natives one day and then abandon them to their fate 'without any courtyard or roof'. If the enslaved did not possess any shelter or land the day after their liberation, they would have every reason to move into the woods and revert to a primitive state. To prevent such disorder and chaos, the Netherlands needed to be willing to undergo some sacrifices for these freedmen, because immediately after legal abolition, the black population would possess nothing at all, except freedom. Many were reluctant to leave the freedmen to themselves during that first period. An act referring to the government's special involvement with freedmen should be written into the law to help and protect them. The advocates of this point of view actually pleaded for some sort of guardianship for adults, not so that their former owners might continue to boss them around, but to help, instruct, and raise them from the situation to which slavery had brought them. In theory this line of thought points to some form of compensation or reparations. In practice it harboured elements of the racism that was then (and is still now) common. In their paternalistic rhetoric, they proposed that state control should serve the interests of freedmen and protect them. Precisely this element of protection, however, was lacking in the bill, which dealt only with surveillance in the interests of agriculture and the plantation owners.

Another argument for legitimizing state control considered the already existing legal process of manumission, which also entailed state control for ten years. A decree from 1844 that prevented 'idleness and vagrancy' saw to it that a manumitted person did not immediately obtain the liberty to do whatever he or she wanted, but was obliged to choose a profession or business and practise it for ten years under the supervision of an employer. This profession or business had to be recorded in the manumission papers, and practising the job regularly was obligatory, on penalty of indictment for idleness or vagrancy. If condemned, a manumitted person could be put to work on 'some task of public usefulness'.

It was argued that, since they were familiar with manumission, the enslaved already knew that the transition from slavery to freedom involved restrictive conditions. Therefore, the state reasoned, they would not mind if the massive manumission that was now to take place had similar conditions. Thus there would be no legal difference between a manumitted and a liberated slave; the only distinction was that his employment would now be managed by the state.

During state control there would exist some sort of police supervision over freedmen. They would be given the same rights as any other citizen, but only after a period of ten years. It was quite difficult and complicated to be released from state control prior to that. Freedmen remained 'minors', so to speak. They were forced to be contractually employed and if they did not fulfil this obligation, they could be punished with penal servitude. Furthermore, once liberated, they were not allowed to leave Suriname, in case the opportunity to enjoy more freedom elsewhere presented itself. Such restrictions of civil liberties were deemed necessary to get the freedmen accustomed to an occidental form of family life. For as long as they were enslaved, marriage had been strictly forbidden and the government thus anticipated 'that many mothers were going to require guidance, reprimanding and special protection for the needs of their families'.

Finally, the law also encouraged 'civilization and Christianity': freedmen had to be given schooling and religious education. The unanticipated consequence of this progressive control was that in

Suriname compulsory education was instituted in 1877 – much earlier than in the Netherlands (Willemsen 2006a). All these measures were intended to establish a proper civilization that would turn freedmen into decent people and lay the foundation for a well-ordered and industrious population.

A few members of parliament wanted to go beyond the government's proposal. They wanted to extend the ten-year period of state control and:

> [i]f necessary, apply it to the entire generation that is going to be emancipated. Absolute freedom without any restriction for people who in our current society culturally behave as children and who view the principal notion of freedom as the privilege of doing nothing, who in an exceptionally mild climate can get everything they want within their small needs without considerable effort – what would be the outcome of all this? (Willemsen 2006a: 98)

What influence did those members of parliament who were inclined to accept abolitionism exert upon the law? Did these 'freedom fighters', as member Voorhuysen called his own group, succeed in obtaining a larger form of freedom for freedmen than the government had proposed? The debate in the Second Chamber resulted in a law that was certainly more liberal in its enforcement. Or, as member Van Zuylen van Nyevelt said: 'Our handling of the law has improved it.' On some matters, the government started from completely different principles during the debate than those it had envisaged when it first introduced the bill. This is without a doubt due to the liberal persuasion of Uhlenbeck.

First of all, the duration of state control was established at ten years and was *not to exceed that period*. Furthermore, it became theoretically possible to be exempted from state control. A few things were also changed editorially: several sections of the law concerning agreements between freedmen and plantation owners were initially formulated as being unconditional; for those sections of the law about supply and demand (for instance Article 33), the draft was changed or the words 'not exceeding' were added, resulting in some flexibility between the parties. At first, it was not planned that freedmen would come into possession of their own parcels of land. But after having been questioned by members van Bosse and Mijer, the minister promised that this would become possible.

We have mentioned above that Elout van Soeterwoude brought up the matter of compensation for the enslaved and that the entire

Second Chamber ignored his request. More successful, however, was his intervention to apply the common civil code to freedmen for the acquisition of property. Thus it became possible for them to obtain private property, insofar as this did not conflict with state control. Article 22 was altered in this respect and became: 'The common civil and penal code is applicable to freedmen, barring the exceptions necessitated by state control as long as they are subject to it.' This meant that freedmen still had to do forced labour and could be brought into action by the government for jobs in the public interest, but that they also had the opportunity to perform free labour if they were in possession of a parcel of land or were capable of practising a trade (Article 24). In reality, acquiring a parcel of land proved to be extremely difficult.

The bill for Suriname was passed on the eve of 9 July 1862, with a vote of 47 to 11, and the bill for the Dutch Antilles passed the following day, with a vote of 45 to 7. It is remarkable that a few members of parliament who supported legal abolition, as well as some fierce critics of the bill (such as van Bosse) voted against the bill in the case of Suriname, but for it in the case of the West Indian islands. Apparently, the different extent of freedom in the two bills was enough to make them vote in the one case for, and in the other against, the legal abolition of slavery.

Thus, after many struggles for control, a bill that had been doctored for the fifth time was accepted, and the stain that marked the Netherlands as a slave-holding state could be wiped out. In August 1862, King William III, at his vacation residence in Wiesbaden (Germany), signed the law regulating the abolition of slavery. The enslaved were informed of this event, but they had to wait until 1863 to witness the day of jubilation they had been looking forward to for such a long time.

In the tradition of progressive control, as a means of appeasing the enslaved population somewhat, those enslaved who belonged to the government (the so-called government's slaves) were permitted to wear shoes. This news travelled fast and reached the enslaved on private plantations. It resulted in feelings of discrimination and anger, which caused even more unrest. To counter these side effects, regulations about using the whip were relaxed and lighter punishments were inflicted. This reduction of punishments actually restricted the power of the plantation owners. 'Behold the beginning of redemption.'

Even before the bill was approved there was commotion on the plantations and revolts broke out. The number of escapes also increased – even on the coffee plantations, where escapes were a hitherto unknown phenomenon. 'Het Koloniaal Verslag over Suriname' ('The Colonial Report Concerning Suriname') mentions excessive disturbances on various plantations, with order being restored only after military intervention. These disturbances reached a culmination at the end of 1862, when the entire enslaved population of the Rac a Rac plantation escaped following a festival. Troops called on for help were met with gunfire and forced to retreat. Further military actions were discontinued as a general amnesty for the Maroons was promulgated on 20 October 1862. This early date was fixed in the hope that the refugees would return before the deadline – the moment when all enslaved had to appear before a verification committee. As we have seen, these data would form the basis for the enslavers' compensation (Lamur 2004).

It does lend the colonial authority some credit that it ordered the translation of the various Dutch documents and laws regarding the abolition of slavery and the new situation of state control into the native language of the liberated enslaved (Sranan). In this way, a group of freedmen who could read Sranan but who had never mastered the Dutch language could become acquainted with their newly acquired rights and duties and with the policy intentions of the colonial authority. This news was passed on by word of mouth (*mofo koranti* = mouth paper).

But the authority was rather selective in translating these texts. The laws and regulations relating to the enslavers were often not translated, leaving freedmen uninformed of these regulations. Thus, one of the most important clauses of the law regarding the abolition of slavery was not communicated to the liberated population. It concerns Article 2 of the law, dated 8 August 1862, regarding the legal abolition of slavery in the West Indian colonies. This article stipulated that the Surinamese enslavers were to receive the sum of 300 guilders as compensation for every living enslaved person. This important article was omitted from the translation of the law into Sranan (Willemsen 2006a).

Why was this article omitted? As mentioned before, the enslavers and the colonial authority were afraid that the enslaved population would want to seek revenge after liberation. The ruling class truly believed that freedom would incite the enslaved to insurrection and insurgence. If liberated 'slaves' learned that planters were to be compensated while they themselves would get nothing, their bottled-up anger would rise to fever pitch. All this must be viewed against the backdrop of the general preparations to keep the situation regarding legal abolition under control: troops were sent to Suriname and military vessels were posted at the river estuaries. So perhaps the fear of insurrection was the reason why it was decided not to translate this very important article of the law, keeping it from the liberated population. That it was painstakingly concealed is an undeniable fact; there is no mention of it in colonial literature and we do not know whether the liberated population was in some other way informed of it. This concealment has remained unnoticed for well over 130 years (Willemsen 2006a).

This selective information given to the enslaved population must not be viewed as an isolated event. Missionaries, for instance, long concealed from them scriptural passages that advocate equality among men (Rodney 1974). Now we notice that policy makers were also hiding specific ordinances from the enslaved. Thus we encounter an important characteristic of the slavery system, for the essence of this system was twofold: on the one hand the extreme exploitation of the enslaved, on the other the intense distrust between the enslavers and the enslaved. The enslavers distrusted the enslaved and vice versa, but their mutual distrust had different origins: the distrust of the enslavers was a consequence of the constant fear of 'slave' rebellions and revenge for the injuries that had been brought upon the enslaved; the distrust of the enslaved manifested itself in their behaviour, since they could never take at face value anything the enslavers told them.

We have seen that the enslavers had previously depended on the constant import of new captives from Africa, but since the 'slave' trade had been abolished, the supply had simply ended. In the government's own words:

> The cause of decline of this colony – despite the fertility of its vast soil, its many rich forests and navigable rivers and creeks that run through it – is to be found in the unremitting decrease of the slave population, caused by the yearly manumissions [i.e. of slaves who purchased their own freedom], the unfavourable proportion between birth and death rate, escapes and social expulsion on account of contagious diseases. As the merchandise for the European market is exclusively produced through the labour of slaves, and as said population can no longer be replenished by new supplies, the production must eventually come to an end.
>
> The hands that gradually will be lost to agriculture can only be renewed by an ample supply of apt free labourers, but to achieve that goal, complete abolition of slavery is an absolute priority;

to be sure, it has been proven (here and there in Suriname on a small scale and in Cuba on a large one) that free labourers can be employed in a slave colony, but only the abolition of slavery will remove the moral grounds responsible for the fear in our fatherland and particularly elsewhere, that this supply would represent nothing less than camouflaged slave trade.

As an inevitable necessity and a means to preserve and regenerate the colony, while discharging many fertile plantations of the burden of prevalent mortgage debts, the government proposes the abolition of slavery, while preventing the present manpower from becoming extinct through the provision of a constant renewal of labourers, and also while granting a reasonable compensation for slave owners. Thus the uncertain situation that was paralysing the colony as long as it remained unresolved, has now come to an end, while the use of fresh capital and all kinds of improvements are being stimulated, and the enterprising industrialist finally has a good prospect to make a profit. (Willemsen 2006a: 84–5)

Thus the government's policy with regard to Suriname was entirely in accordance with the advice of J.C. Baud, the chairman of the State Committee, 'that Suriname could only be kept as a colony if the enslaved were emancipated' (see above).

It should be mentioned however that the reason the government gave for abolishing slavery on Curaçao and other dependencies was of a completely different nature. The Malthusian hypothesis for sugar and slaves did not apply here. There was no significant decrease in the enslaved population on the Antilles. (In 1816 the enslaved population in the Antilles had stood at 12,202; this had declined slightly to 11,803 in 1857, and to 11,654 in 1863.) The real reason was that the government could not abolish slavery in one of its West Indian colonies while maintaining it in another, particularly since it had claimed that the enslaved on the islands had reached a higher level of civilization than those in Suriname and therefore were more familiar with the notion of freedom. Again, in the government's words:

> The manifest importance of the colony of Curaçao and its subordinates demands the abolition of slavery though not entirely for the same reasons as in Suriname. Here is no decrease of the slave population, no need for agricultural workers to replace the ones we lost; moreover, the advanced intellectual, religious and social development of the slaves on these islands devoid of

heathens, brings about another urgent reason: the impatience of the slaves that has manifested itself here more than in Suriname when the long awaited emancipation did not come about, notably through clear indications of unwillingness and in repeated and manifold escapes, often undertaken with great peril of life and which the local police cannot always adequately prevent, but which cause much damage to the owners. (Willemsen 2006a: 88)

The contradictions in the above statement should not be overlooked. If the enslaved population in Curaçao were freer than Suriname, why would they escape?

The island of Sint Maarten was a rather special case. Here, the enslaved had freed themselves in June 1848 when France had abolished slavery in the French part of the island. But until 1863 the Netherlands had always refused to abolish slavery officially.

On 1 July 1863, slavery was legally abolished in the Kingdom of the Netherlands. That day, more than 45,000 enslaved people in Suriname and the Dutch Antilles obtained their freedom. As we see below, several Dutch newspapers referred to this event as an historic and joyful day, always to be commemorated because the stain that had been defiling the Netherlands could now finally be erased.

The way in which the abolition debate was organized and structured, and the outcome it led to, not only impacted the trajectories of emancipation but they were also to shape the Dutch debate on race relations in subsequent years. This is the topic to which we now turn.

5
Trajectories of Emancipation: Religion, Class, Gender and Race

In Chapter 4 we delineated the discrepancy between legal abolition as progressive control and emancipation as transformative change. This can be formulated as follows. From a legal and legislative perspective the abolition of chattel slavery constitutes a transformative change in theory; in policy and practice however the Dutch legal abolition of slavery rested on progressive control. We also noted that abolition and emancipation are not two sides of the same coin. With regard to slavery there should be abolition or revolution before emancipation; but abolition does not automatically lead to emancipation. In the previous chapter we focused on abolition; here we focus on emancipation.

As will be noted below, abolition – a legal act – broadens the emancipation space, but does not necessarily end the dominant-dominated relation on which slavery rested.

For historical, cultural and emotional reasons, the term 'emancipation' has different connotations for different groups. However it is assumed that emancipation has to include a process whereby a *social grouping* who find themselves in a dominated position in society, or considered second rate by a dominant group, struggle to improve their conditions and attain a fully fledged place in society integrated into existing the social order (Winkler Prins Encyclopedie 1968, quoted from Mullard, Nimako and Willemsen 1990: 25). On this score emancipation is a sociological phenomenon; it relates to an identifiable social group rather than to individual social mobility.

At the broader historical level these processes give rise to different trajectories and narratives of emancipation. On the progressive control continuum, emancipation can lead either to assimilation or segregation. Under assimilation, some members of the emancipated group may be culturally, socially, politically, and economically absorbed into the dominant group; others may be marginalized or segregated and controlled, which in turn will lead to resistance and new demands for emancipation.

On the transformative change continuum, emancipation can lead to integration or separation. Theoretically, integration gives rise to upward mobility without the group having to give up its cultural and social traditions; this upward mobility of some of the emancipated group can even give rise to separation or a conscious break from former oppressors.

We return to some of the historical and empirical aspects of these developments below. In particular we argue that issues related to segregation and separation in emancipation go some way towards explaining why Dutch social scientists have neglected or failed to integrate race into the analysis of emancipation.

We have seen that one of the main organizing principles of chattel slavery was race. It follows that emancipation would also be racialized, which is one of the themes of this chapter. We deal here with the discrepancy between emancipation as understood by mainstream Dutch historiography (for example, Verwey-Jonker 1983) and what universal emancipation should entail.

In the post-Westphalia history of the Netherlands, three events are primarily associated with this term: the political emancipation of the Catholics in the early nineteenth century, the emancipation of the working class in the late nineteenth century, and the political emancipation of women in the early twentieth century. The first two, Catholic and working-class emancipation, gave rise to what became known as 'pillarization' in Dutch political history (Lijphart 1968). In Suriname and the Dutch Antilles, however, 'emancipation' is primarily linked with the legal abolition of slavery on 1 July 1863 (Oostindie 1996; Willemsen 2006a).

Why do Dutch citizens have different trajectories of emancipation? These trajectories epitomize parallel histories and intertwined belonging, concepts which we introduced at the beginning of the book and return to in the concluding chapter. For the moment suffice it to say that emancipation evolved in different directions.

But this does not mean that emancipation struggles should be analysed in isolation. They should be analysed in relation to broader struggles that were taking place within the Dutch state, social formation and social thought. These were struggles of religion, class, gender and race. What is the relationship between the legal abolition of slavery and the emancipation of the Catholics, the working class and women? We argue that the integration of the legal abolition of Dutch Atlantic slavery into the emancipation discourse enhances our understanding of Dutch historiography, state formation, social formation and social thought, then and now.

RELIGION AND EMANCIPATION

We noted in Chapter 2 that modern Dutch sovereignty emerged out of the Peace of Westphalia, which in turn was a consequence of what is known as the Thirty Years' War. The Thirty Years' War has been classified in textbooks as religious. These religious wars gave rise to 'Protestant-dominated states' and 'Catholic-dominated states'. The Netherlands became a Protestant-dominated state. We also noted that not only did the Peace of Westphalia delineate the boundaries of modern Dutch sovereignty, but also it contributed to the clarification of the 'wealth of nations'. With regard to the wealth of nations, Spufford has given us the following insight:

> In the last quarter of the eighteenth century, Dutch banking had however become extremely vulnerable. Amsterdam's bankers, despite the city's pre-eminence as a financial centre, had suffered a severe blow as a result of the crises of the 1760s and 1770s. Even some of the largest firms like Hogguer, Horneca & Co, or Goll & Co. were not immune. It is not surprising that many of them, foreseeing Amsterdam's possible collapse, transferred some of their assets to other places, particularly London, like Gerard van Neck and the Barings, and, in 1760 Abraham Ricardo, the father of David Ricardo the economic theorist ... Hope & Co., the most considerable banker remaining in Amsterdam, arranged ten loans to Sweden (1767–1787) and then eighteen to Russia (1788–1793). From Amsterdam Henry Hope handled the Spanish loan of 1792 when Spain was fighting against France. When Henry Hope moved to London in October 1794 it was a sign that the end had come. Alexander Baring was left to follow in January 1795. Weeks later the Dutch Republic collapsed in the face of the French invasion. (Spufford 2006: 167)

In other words the French invasion was precipitated by economic crisis. But what has this got to do with emancipation?

One of the major contradictions in the evolution of Dutch sovereignty was the French occupation of the Netherlands between 1795 and 1813. On the one hand, the French occupation eroded the sovereignty of the Dutch state. On the other, the Napoleonic occupation of the Netherlands resulted in a Unitarian state and a modernized state apparatus; this was legalized by the 1815 constitution. In this arrangement, all citizens were to be subjected to the same system of justice and to receive equal rights, although the large Nederlands Hervormd Kerk (Dutch Reformed Church) took up a privileged position, while the Roman Catholic Church took second place (Buiting 1990: 58). These developments culminated in the 1848 constitution. According to Buiting, the 1848 constitution was a product of 'revolutionary storms' which raged throughout Europe in 1848. Although the Dutch urban proletariat agitated for only a short while, King Willem II was so afraid of more unrest that he made an important concession to the liberals. A representative of theirs, Thorbecke, was allowed to write a new constitution (Buiting 1990: 59).

The 1848 constitution had three elements relevant to our discussion. The first of these was the introduction of a limited franchise for elections to the Lower House, whose members were to be directly elected by the adult male inhabitants. The second element was the separation of church and state. The third was the legalization of denominational-based education. It was under these initial constitutional arrangements that individuals and groups within the Dutch sovereignty made their claims for emancipation within the Dutch state.

More than two centuries after the emergence of the Netherlands as a Protestant-dominated state, partly thanks to the French, Catholics started to reposition themselves within the state. This took place in the context of religious and political equality (gelijkberechtigd staatsburgerschap) in relation to the dominant Protestant group.

In the wake of the French Revolution, the concepts freedom/liberty, equality and fraternity had become more than mere words. They were part of the lexicon around which political (freedom), economic (equality) and social (fraternity/solidarity) issues were articulated and public programmes emanated (Wallerstein 2004).

However, as we argue below, unlike in the case of slavery, in which legal abolition and freedom are the starting points for emancipation, the focus for the Catholics was equality. This involved the demand for employment within the state and government apparatus and for equal participation in social and socio-economic life. At the same time the Catholics demanded less government or state interference in the religious and cultural activities of the Catholic community. In other words the Catholic community demanded relative autonomy. Catholics did not seek to be assimilated into the dominant Protestant religious culture, but rather to be integrated into state institutions, without losing their religious identity. This constituted the making of a plural society and a unitary state.

The period between 1850 and 1960 has been characterized as the period of the emancipation process of the Catholics (Stuurman

1983). This reached its climax after 1945; since then no government could be formed without Catholics.

By the turn of the twentieth century the Dutch population (excluding its colonial subjects) was said to be divided into three major pillars (*zuilen*); the Catholic pillar, the Protestant Christian pillar, and a general pillar consisting of people without church affiliation (*vrijzinnigen of andersdenkenden*). These three traditions found their expression in the intellectual traditions of Catholicism, the Reformation and Humanism. Each pillar lived in its own world, independent of the others. This isolation was more social than geographic, though there were regions in which one or other pillar was more represented than the others, such as the Catholics in the south.

It has been observed by some scholars that through these three vertical pillars ran a horizontal 'line': the socio-economic dividing line (*scheidslijn*). The economic and class contrasts were sharp; the elite and the working class were very clearly defined. In the nineteenth century, after the rise of the nation and the emergence of nationalism, the pillars became organized and institutionalized. Religion and ideology were used and mobilized in the service of organizational and political practice. These ideological and principles-based organizational forms found their expression in the media, the party system and the system of interest groups.

The elites were in a position to overcome this segmentation through permanent political compromises. One of the important 'rules of the game' of this pacification politics after 1917 was the principle of 'proportionality'. State subsidies, for instance for education and health care, were divided among the pillars on the basis of proportionality, with the assistance of several permanent umbrella organizations. The institution of the Social–Economic Council in 1950 formed the apex of these developments.

The impact of proportionality went further than just financial matters. It was also applied to matters related to available time for radio and television broadcasting associations (Willemsen and Nimako 1993).

Thus, like the legal abolition of slavery, the emancipation of the Catholics was precipitated through a legal act, namely, a constitutional arrangement made under Napoleonic occupation. This created the space for a cumulative emancipation process resulting in more equality with the dominant Protestant group. However, for the enslaved population it was freedom that was the first priority; equality as an emancipation project was to follow, of which more below.

CLASS AND EMANCIPATION

As we saw in the previous section, the socio-economic dividing line (*scheidslijn*) that cut across the pillars of Protestantism, Catholicism and Humanism constituted a class line separating sharply contrasted elite and working classes. There are those who argue that pillarization emerged or was called into being by the elite in each religious pillar to regulate or pacify class struggle or prevent working-class emancipation (Stuurman 1983). Nevertheless working-class movements and socialist parties emerged around the end of the nineteenth and the beginning of the twentieth centuries.

In his study of labour movements in the Netherlands, Henny Buiting (1990) informs us that until the middle of the nineteenth century the Netherlands remained a predominantly agrarian country. Due partly to this, labour movements did not take off until the late 1870s. We can discern from his study that the Dutch working-class movement began in 1867 and was consolidated as an institutional emancipatory project in 1906. The narrative is as follows.

The first organized labour union, the General Dutch Union of Typographers (Algemeene Nederlandsche Typografenbond, ANTB) was founded on 1 June 1866. Its main focus was the improvement of the wages and conditions of its members. Three years later, in 1869, the Dutch Working Men's Association (Nederlandsch Werklieden Verbond, NWV) was formed. The NWV had a socialist agenda and was affiliated to the First International.

The NWV succeeded in setting up the first trade union of factory workers, namely, that of the confectioners in Amsterdam. However, according to Buiting, the NWV's radicalism put off most artisans and workers and this led to its demise around 1874. The founders and leaders of the NWV found a temporary home in the General Dutch Working Men's Association (Algemeen Nederlandsch Werklieden Verbond, ANWV, 1871) (Buiting 1990: 61)

There were major strikes between 1889 and 1890; these resulted in a rapid increase in the number of trade unions. According to Buiting, the Social Democratic League (SDB), founded in 1881, helped set some of the trade unions up and:

[i]nitiated a number of large strikes by agricultural workers against the farmers and landowners, as well as a fight for universal (male) suffrage, thereby assuring itself of massive support ...

Of importance for the further development of the SDB and trade-union movement was the successful strike by the Rotterdam dockers in 1889, which precipitated a strike wave which allowed the trade-union movement to organize new groups of workers ... [The SDB] also started a movement for an inquiry, in which data on wages, working times and workers' household budgets were collected as a propaganda weapon against the horrors of capitalism. In this period, too, the Dutch parliament, worried by alarming reports on women's and child labour, ordered a parliamentary inquiry into the situation in factories and places of work. Agitation by the SDB, massive strikes and progressive–liberal lobbies all played their part, and the inquiry finally resulted in the labour legislation of 1889, which restricted to some extent the most blatant forms of exploitation of women's and child labour. (Buiting 1990: 66)

The unions under the SDB did not all describe themselves as socialist. According to Buiting:

The SDB accepted this situation and no longer considered the trade unions as extensions of its own organization. Ultimately the League set up an independent trade union federation. In 1893 the National Labour Secretariat (*Nationaal Arbeids Secretariaat*, NAS) was founded – also at the instigation of the Second International – and presented itself as 'neutral' ... [To this effect,] 'a motion was accepted at the League's (SDB) Christmas congress in 1893 proclaiming that the League would 'under no circumstances, not even for campaigning purposes, take part in the [parliamentary] elections'. (Buiting 1990: 67)

The SDB started with 30 members in 1878; it grew to 4,000 in 1886, and then reached 5,000 in 1893; after that it declined to 2,126 members in 1897 and to 600 in 1898.

Buiting also notes that the decline in membership was partly due to radicalism: this 'anti-parliamentary', actually anarchist, position then led to the growth of a 'parliamentary' opposition in the SDB, which formed an independent organization on 26 August 1894: the Social Democratic Labour Party (Sociaal-Democratische Arbeiders Partij, SDAP).

Unlike the SDB, the SDAP wanted to attain socialism through both parliamentary and economic action:

> One favourable factor was the period of economic growth which began in the middle of the 1890s and which stimulated the growth and expansion of the 'modern' labour movement. The SDAP was strongly oriented towards its German sister organization, from which it derived its party programme as well as its organizational structure. (Buiting 1990: 67)

Another important event in 1894 ('an extremely important year for the Dutch labour movement') was the foundation of the General League of Dutch Diamond Workers (Algemeene Nederlandsch Diamantbewerkers Bond, ANDB) which, 'in the footsteps of the new English trade unionism, would be a model for the modern trade-union movement [in the Netherlands]'. (Buiting 1990: 68)

The ANDB had a tight organizational structure and a centrally directed policy, unconditional discipline, paid professional executives, an extremely efficient administration, high membership dues and therefore a large strike fund. It also supported only those actions which were under its own control. This was the organizational model on which the structure of the Dutch Trade Union Federation (*Nederlandsch Verbond van Vakvereenigingen*, NVV) was founded in 1906. (Buiting 1990: 68)

The labour movement activities went hand in hand with political activities. On the one hand, a long weavers' strike in Almelo in 1888 influenced the founding of Catholic trade-union organizations, 'with the particular aim of turning back the "red" tide'. The Patrimonium, founded in 1876, also opposed the SDB. 'In 1888 the *Patrimonium* declared its support for the "houseman's vote", that is to say the vote for heads of families, and, after a "Christian Social Congress" in 1891, ended its opposition to social security and strikes' (Buiting 1990: 64).

As we see below, the women's emancipation movements were tied to working-class movements.

From its foundation the SDAP demanded the abolition of all laws which put women in disadvantageous positions; furthermore, the party strove for the introduction of universal suffrage for men and women. In practice, however, especially in the parliamentary party, priority was given to realizing the right of men to vote, even after 1908, when the party explicitly stated that it wanted the vote for men and women. (Buiting 1990: 77)

To this effect:

[o]n 12 November 1899 [the SDAP] took the initiative in founding the Dutch Committee for Universal Suffrage (*Nederlandsch Comité voor Algemeen Kiesrecht*, NCVAK), which later organized countless demonstrations. The party also fought for social security legislation and attempted to set up a trade-union federation prepared to fight for economic as well as political aims ...

Massive demonstrations for electoral reform were also organized from 1910 to 1913; two of them – the so-called 'Red Tuesdays' in 1911 and 1912 – were especially impressive and undoubtedly helped precipitate the introduction of universal suffrage for men in 1917. (Buiting 1990: 69, 74)

On the basis of the above analysis, it can be concluded that the working-class movement evolved in response to, or as a consequence of, industrial development in the Netherlands in the late nineteenth century.

It should be mentioned that in his analysis Buiting does not make explicit reference to colonial labour as part of Dutch labour, thus discounting slavery as labour outside Dutch soil proper.

By the early twentieth century, Dutch society and politics had given rise to 'the politics of accommodation'. The emancipation of women cuts across the pillars that form the basis of this politics.

This brings us to the status of women in relation to emancipation.

GENDER AND EMANCIPATION

One of the most authoritative figures on Dutch emancipation movements is Verwey-Jonker (1983). According to her, the most successful emancipation movement in the Netherlands is the working-class movement. Verwey-Jonker further notes that the position of women in the Dutch agrarian setting was not very different from that of men. Industrial development, which she refers to as capitalist development, affected women in two directions: on the one hand, working-class women lost their job security due to temporary contracts; on the other, middle-class women also lost their independence in the labour process.

According to Verwey-Jonker, the mid nineteenth century should be considered as the low point of power for women. It is therefore not surprising that this period gave the first push to the women's emancipation movement (Verwey-Jonker 1983: 42). To this we should add that, like the working-class movement, the women's movement was also tied to industrial development in the late nineteenth century. What we can derive from this is that the women's movement was initially a variant or part of the working-class labour movement. However, the women's movement had two other aspects, namely, a private or household aspect, and a public aspect. In this section our focus is on the public aspect.

Like the male-dominated working-class unions, the initial demands of the women's movement were for good working conditions. According to Buiting:

> [t]he patriarchal and traditional–religious view of the world, which was connected with the 'moral nature of the nation', in many ways also determined the place of women in the labour movement. Neither in the trade-union organization, nor in political parties and other workers' organizations did women play a role comparable with that of men. This limited influence was largely the result of the very low percentage of [formally] working women in the Netherlands, who from 1860 to 1914 constituted an almost constant 18–19% of the total working population ... The ANWV and the *Patrimonium* opposed professional work for women, but opposition also existed in socialist organizations. This was particularly true for the right wing of the SDAP and broad sections of the NVV ... [I]n 1904 only 1,452 of the 160,000 female wage workers were organized in any way; the first women's trade union was only founded in 1897; the seamstresses' union All Are One (*Allen Een*).

The number of organized women increased sharply once the NVV was founded. By 1 January 1907, 4,499 of the 26,227 members were women and the NVV succeeded in increasing this number later. By 1911 40% of all organized women were members of the NVV. Nevertheless the NVV showed a certain ambivalence with regard to women's labour – the federation accepted wage differences between men and women for instance, and also wanted women to be prohibited from working in certain professions – while women had almost no influence at the top of the NVV and in the separate unions. (Buiting 1990: 76–7)

To increase their influence:

[i]n 1905 the first 'Social Democratic Women's Propaganda Club' was founded in Amsterdam, soon to be followed by others elsewhere in the country. Around the middle of 1907 there were nine clubs with 515 members and by 1914 all of them together numbered 1,500 members. The women's clubs published a newspaper, *De Proletarische Vrouw* [Proletarian Woman], and in 1908 the national 'League of Social-Democratic Women's Clubs' was founded. The aim of the clubs, as well as the co-ordinating League, was in the first place to propagate socialism amongst women. Afterwards, from about 1907, they also started working for women's universal suffrage, which in turn helped determine the position of the SDAP congress in Arnhem in 1908, that women should also have the right to vote. (Buiting 1990: 77)

Like the emancipation demands of the Catholics, equality was the driving force behind the women's movement; this culminated in the 1920s, when women were given the right to vote.

Viewed in the context of public demands, the women's struggle for emancipation was initially less complicated than the struggles for religious and class emancipation, because the focus for the women was clear: the right to vote. This required only legal intervention to lift the barriers; it did not require major changes in the social and economic sphere. Nevertheless, having the right to vote gave women more influence in politics, partly because of gender demographics. It institutionalized the emancipation claims of women in the public sphere and culminated in the formation of organizations such as the Vereniging voor Vrouwenbelangen (Association for Women's Interests) and Vrouwenarbeid en Gelijk Staatsburgerschap (Women's Labour and Equal State Citizenship) in the 1920s.

Today, within the state, women's emancipation claims find their expression in the institution of the Emancipation Council.

In sum, like class, gender also cut across the three pillars. Women did not, and still do not, have their own pillar. Their influence was articulated through existing pillars.

The chronology of the emancipation of workers and women should not be overlooked. Why did the Dutch working-class movement and the women's movement take institutional shape after the legal abolition of slavery? Let us take a closer look at this phenomenon.

RACE AND EMANCIPATION

Race is central to the issue of the Atlantic 'slave' trade and slavery, its legal abolition and the struggle for emancipation. This is because race was one of the major, if not the foremost, organizing principle of the 'slave' trade and slavery. Africa was the location for enslavement; race and skin colour were the objective criteria for identifying the enslaved (James 1980; Patterson 1973). This leads to the following question: if emancipation is a process, where does it start and end? Let it be said one more time: the abolition of Atlantic and Dutch slavery was a strict legal declaration and should be distinguished from the ensuing emancipation process. This should be emphasized, as emancipation can lead to assimilation, integration, segregation or separation. We argue that the legal abolition of slavery did not lead to assimilation or integration; rather it led to segregation. After legal abolition the former enslaved became racialized colonial subjects in the context of colonial rule: hence segregation.

The evidence suggests that the enslaved were able to distinguish between legal abolition and emancipation, because even when the exact date of legal abolition was known, there was still open resistance on seven plantations. The last rebellion before legal abolition took place in Suriname on the Schoonoord plantation at the beginning of December 1862. The plantation manager wanted to punish an enslaved African for his 'brutality'. The slave resisted and was supported by other enslaved Africans. The manager then enlisted the help of the troops quartered in Sommelsdijk. A corporal and six men were sent to Schoonoord to arrest the 'insubordinates' and transport them to Sommelsdijk. One enslaved person was arrested, but before he could be carried away he was rescued from the hands of the soldiers by other enslaved. To avert this dangerous situation, the commanding officer, accompanied by 15 men, came to Schoonoord. At first he tried to come to a mutual agreement, but the soldiers were booed and pelted with various objects. The commanding officer fired a few warning shots in the air. But this boomeranged because the fury of the enslaved turned into rage. Then the commander aimed at the unarmed group and killed several of them. Thereupon, most of the others fled into the woods and order seemed to have been restored; but this was only a sham.

When the soldiers left, the enslaved went to the manager's house and demolished it.

How can this resistance, so shortly before the date of legal abolition, be explained? Before the law abolishing slavery was passed in 1862, the enslaved population in Suriname already knew that many proposals contained a transition or 'apprenticeship'. Since they were also aware of the negative experiences in the British colonies and of the absence of any transition in the French colonies, many preferred an immediate and direct liberty. We can deduce this from the fact that the number of escapes significantly increased the moment it became known that there was a *proposal* to abolish slavery on 1 July 1863. Escape, an old strategy to obtain freedom, was resorted to more and more. On 20 May 1862, the governor wrote in his diary:

> Desertions will increase steadily ... because the slaves will be disappointed in their longing for freedom that will not be an independent one ...
>
> Nobody likes forced labor; when this stems from climatic needs or from inferior fertility, such as in Europe, one will submit to it because this pressure is not exerted by one man upon another; but when it is – in the Negro's mind – always enforced without any purpose, in a country where his needs are infinitely less than what a salary of six days per week will satisfy, then it becomes unbearable for a man who considers himself free. Perhaps a regular job is just as unpleasant for a Negro: during two, three days, he will work very hard chopping a few trees, but then, during another eight or ten days, he will refrain from any labor unless it is also relaxing, such as hunting or fishing. The knowledge that he is a slave, makes him submit to his fate, but tell him that he is free, and that submissive mentality will soon disappear. (Willemsen 2006a: 67–8)

What was also new was the enslaved resorting to manumission ('buying' their liberty), not to be delivered from the yoke of slavery, but to escape future state control. As soon as the law regarding the abolition of slavery was promulgated, the number of requests for manumission increased drastically. In 1862, 392 appeals were submitted.

According to a colonial report, there were 99 more manumissions in 1862 than in the previous year. In his journal, the governor wrote: 'This considerably larger number is to a great extent caused by the prejudices of the slave population regarding this liberation by the Government that is linked with state control – which at that time was absolutely new to them' (Willemsen 2006a: 68).

It was also noted that many requests for freedom were made by enslavers or others out of affection for, or because they had a 'special relationship' with, some of the enslaved. Enslaved persons also submitted petitions for manumission. For this, they had to pay large sums – on average, more than 300 guilders, in some cases even 500; and all this to be free on 1 July 1863 and to escape state control (Willemsen 2006a).

To put this in context let us take a moment to reflect on the notion of manumission. Like the concepts of 'slave' and 'trade' in the transatlantic 'slave trade' narrative, the concept of manumission is a historical and conceptual fraud. Manumission was a concept and practice imposed on the enslaved. Formally, manumission implies that the enslaved have bought themselves out of slavery. In the world of the enslavers, Africans were subhuman and thus might be bought and sold. Thus if the enslaved wanted their freedom they either had to escape or buy their freedom. This might happen when the enslaver needed money or had no need for the enslaved. Manumission expanded the options of the enslavers and limited the choices of the enslaved; it therefore became the other side of the coin of Maroonage. This same logic led the state to compensate the enslavers at the time of legal abolition.

The many escapes in 1862, so shortly before the date of liberation, were attempts by the enslaved to avoid state control, to which the enslaved population was strongly opposed. As the governor correctly noted, they considered it a form of camouflaged slavery. To put an end to all these escapes, on 20 December 1862 the governor was forced to proclaim a general amnesty for the Maroons.

Here was human agency and reason at work: the enslaved were not docile or passive. Though the white population was far outnumbered by the enslaved (in a ratio of one to nine), and the enslaved had therefore become a force to be dealt with, the enslaved population also realized that an armed revolt would amount to downright suicide. After all, slavery depends on physical power, and the enslavers, though in the minority, could at any time deploy an armed force that would not hesitate to inflict a massive bloodbath upon the enslaved.

It is well known to historians of Dutch slavery that, having decided to abolish chattel slavery, it took the Dutch governing authorities some ten years of preparation and parliamentary discussion to design and plan the freedom of the enslaved. The parliamentary discussions boiled down to three things. The first was how much the enslavers should be compensated. The second was what to do with the freed 'slaves'. The third was how much freedom the 'ex-slaves' would be given.

First, the issue of compensation also showed the two views on freedom. For enslavers, freedom also meant the right to compensation. Elout van Soeterwoude, as we saw in the previous chapter, was the one member of parliament who brought up the matter of compensation for the enslaved population. He denounced the fact that the enslavers were not only being indemnified by the state, but were also receiving a large profit from state control – which he characterized as a sort of camouflaged slavery. As he pointed out, through the system of forced labour the government was in a roundabout way increasing the enslavers' compensation. As someone who sympathized with the enslaved, he pleaded for free labour and wondered out loud what the difference was between freedom and slavery if freedom was ruled out. The enslavers, he argued, had a right to compensation from the state, but, he wondered, 'Would not [also] the slave be entitled to some compensation from his master – and from us in the Netherlands who permitted this injustice – for the bitter suffering that was passed on from father to son during two centuries?'

The question of indemnification for the enslavers was a different matter. The more conservative members of parliament took the view that through a series of legal terms the enslaved were the lawful property of the enslaver. Therefore, many members of parliament cried in unison, this is a matter of dispossession; the state, having itself benefited from slavery, cannot abolish it without compensating the enslavers.

The small group of abolition supporters hastened to help the minister. Compensation, they argued, means a complete restitution of damage. If the chamber accepted this principle, the amount of the reimbursement would be many times larger than what a 'subsidy' would cost. Even conservative members recoiled at this news. One member, Dirks, remarked that it was impossible to evaluate the price of an enslaved person, because not only did his age, energy and aptitude for work need to be taken into consideration, but also his spirit and morality. He said that compensation was out of the question, because in such a case one had to calculate the impossible, i.e. the precise amount of damage that was suffered. On the strength of these arguments, the term 'compensation' was dropped in favour of 'subsidy' – quite a change, indeed.

Another member, Van Nispen van Sevenaer, argued that dispossession was not an issue:

> Dispossession can only take place when a property is taken away to be transferred into the hands of the state or those of others. In this case the slave is not taken away, nor is he transferred. Bare, he returns to that natural state to which any human being, black or white, has an inalienable right. Actually, emancipation is nothing else than the government withdrawing the iron hand that until now has protected the right to possess a slave – a right that is not permissible within every concept of religion and humanity. And now you want to call such an abolition 'dispossession'? In that case, every slave code limiting a slave's working hours amounts to a partial dispossession, and yet nobody ever thought of paying compensation to the slave owners for such a limitation. (Willemsen 2006a: 113)

Van Bosse, who fiercely opposed the idea of compensation, stressed the fact that this property, by its very nature, was extremely precarious as it would ultimately be lost for the enslavers through the extinction of the enslaved. Those who sympathized with the enslaved argued that it was about the legal abolition of a system, the removal of an unnatural situation. Thus, a reasonable subsidy for damage suffered could be granted – but no compensation. Therefore, the legislator had every right to give 'our partners in nature' their freedom back without any indemnification. In the words of Mr Goltstein, the sharpest critic of compensation:

> There was talk about compensation, as if this was a case of dispossession. Their argument ran as follows: a slave is someone's property; when he is taken away, the owner is dispossessed and therefore entitled to compensation. I cannot acknowledge such reasoning: I am bound to react to it. No, a human being cannot be another's property. In this context, there exists no property. This is merely an unlawful situation. Here, compensation or indemnification due to dispossession is out of the question because there is no legal ground for it. In my mind, this is a truth that cannot be contradicted: one man cannot be another man's property. A subsidy, however, can be granted because this unlawful situation has been instituted by and on behalf of the state itself, because the

state has encouraged and recommended this situation. For this reason, it is fair and proper that in this case a subsidy is granted by the state that generated such a situation and put it under the protection of its laws. (Willemsen 2006a: 114)

One proposal granted the enslavers the amount of 300 guilders for every enslaved person in Suriname and 200 for each enslaved person on the islands. The government decided on this sum after having verified how much money was paid in the English and French colonies at the time of emancipation. According to the explanatory memorandum, the enslavers in the British colonies were paid on average slightly more than 300 guilders for every enslaved person, but the British government had actually reserved 20 million pounds as compensation for the loss of the 800,000 people who were liberated – which amounted to an indemnification of some 275 guilders per slave. On Martinique and Guadeloupe, an average of 450 francs per slave was paid, amounting to a sum of about 214 guilders. The compensation for the Surinamese enslavers, when compared with the amount paid to the English and French enslavers, was thus, if anything, rather high. But naturally there were complaints that this sum was too small.

Furthermore, the government had to budget money for the supply of immigrants, because in accordance with 'the economy of the law', it had linked the abolition of slavery to immigration: 'both will together regulate the way to preserve and expand agriculture and industry as much as possible'. For this reason, the government split the subsidy into direct restitution of money on the one hand, and the supply of labourers on the other. This way it intended to kill two birds with one stone: the enslavers were compensated, while contributing to the preservation of Suriname as a colony that could be exploited by the motherland.

At first the government reserved the sum of 3 million guilders for immigration. But after an amendment by van Bosse (who called this the worst form of protectionism ever conceived), it was reduced to 1 million guilders; private individuals could claim part of this money as a premium for the supply of workers.

Some members of parliament disputed the fact that the proposed compensation per enslaved person was lower on the islands than in Suriname; they wanted to reverse the situation. They argued that the enslaved on the islands were mostly craftsmen, particularly sailors, 'whose value was many times greater than what the slaves were worth in Suriname'.

The minister of colonies would not hear of it, because many enslaved persons were also active as craftsmen on the Surinamese plantations. Some members, on the other hand, took the position that the amount of compensation on the islands was too high, since they were not agricultural colonies. The conclusion was that the proposed amounts should remain unaltered: 200 guilders for every liberated slave on the Antilles, 300 in Suriname. The compensation for the enslavers in Sint Maarten, however, was only 30 guilders, because there the enslaved had more or less liberated themselves after 1848, when France had abolished slavery on the French part of the island.

The contradiction here should not be overlooked. In the previous chapter we noted that the state claimed that the enslaved on the islands were more 'civilized' than those of Suriname. One might therefore have expected the 'civilized' to have been worth more than the 'uncivilized'; but apparently the logic of slavery operates differently.

The compensation for the 'slave owners' amounted to 11,876,260 guilders, of which 9,874,360 went to Suriname. Only about a quarter of the sum that was paid to the enslavers in Suriname was actually paid there. The rest went to 'slave owners' living in the Netherlands. Many of them closed their businesses upon receiving their cheques. Nevertheless, the Surinamese economy received a small financial injection, causing brief illusory prosperity.

According to some historians, in the week before 1 July 1863, each enslaved person would receive from the colonial authority the sum of 60 guilders. This money was to be used to buy clothes and to provide for the enslaved person's livelihood. Indeed, the colonial authority had decreed that all adults would have the opportunity to conclude a labour contract by 1 October 1863, and these 60 guilders were meant to tide them over the first three months. But this never happened; the liberated slaves never got a cent. In one of the many bills introduced over the years, this idea had actually been brought up – as evidenced by a remark in the explanatory memorandum of the bill of 1860/61. This is to the effect that that the idea of giving freedmen a small sum out of *de uitgaanskas* (supplemental funds) might prevent unrest, but that the government 'has already spent so much on freedmen that it would be impossible to give money beyond this. A liberated slave who wants money in his pockets can get it, provided that he gets busy.' Not surprisingly, this resolution disappeared from the final bill.

Some enslavers took a pessimistic view of a future without slavery, sold their plantations and set sail for the Netherlands. According to Helman:

> [f]rom the national buildings, in particular from the 'Waaggebouw' on the 'Waterkant' in Paramaribo, cash was transported during the emancipation weeks in barrels and sacks on donkey carts to the office or home of the plantation owners. But soon the opposite started to happen. The large amount of cash sent from the Netherlands for compensation made it more attractive to pay the transfers or the available capital in cash instead of using expensive bills of exchange. Packed in barrels and boxes, huge amounts of money were transported to the harbor on the 'Waterkant' and sent by ship to every continent.

The consequences of the decline of the productivity of the slavery-based plantations in the Dutch West Indies colony were twofold. First it delayed the legal abolition of Dutch slavery, because the plantation owners, who considered the enslaved as their property, demanded compensation from the state before it granted the enslaved their legal freedom. To satisfy this condition, the Dutch state had to acquire resources from their East Indies colony to compensate the enslavers in the West Indies. The demand for compensation was citizenship at work; citizens have the potential and capacity to revolt – some more than others. Recall that the colonists of other major slave colonies had revolted against their mother countries and set up independent nations. The possibility that the Dutch colonists too might break away has been left out of the discussion of Dutch slavery and the colonial narrative. We suggest that the Dutch state *had* to compensate sections of its citizens if it was to survive.

Secondly, the decline of the slavery economy in the period of legal abolition has led to the incorrect conclusion among some Dutch scholars that slavery was not profitable to the Dutch people in general, and the Dutch state in particular. But we know that the planters instructed their government to set the date for the legal abolition of slavery after the enslaved had harvested the produce from the plantations. Clearly if profits had not mattered, the enslavers would not have insisted on compensation; nor would they have bothered about when their produce should be harvested

This brings us to the second issue, namely, what to do with the freed 'slaves'.

After it had been established in August 1862 by the Dutch ruling authorities that slavery would be legally abolished on 1 July 1863 and this message had reached Suriname, the mood of the enslaved awaiting their emancipation was communicated by a Dutch missionary named Jansa to an American newspaper as follows:

> The intelligence of the speedy emancipation of the negroes naturally awakens in me, who have so long laboured in this Colony, the most heartfelt joy. Having been requested by several planters to make known to their slaves the Proclamation of the Governor and the Emancipation law, I [Jansa] did so. They assembled, neatly dressed, in the church and I tried to explain everything to them, getting them to repeat aloud all that I said, so that there might be no misunderstanding. The joy and the praise of the poor Negroes were touching. They had previously heard, but refused to believe the news, saying: 'The whites have deceived us so often!' But now that I made known truth and told them, it is really so, our Saviour has influenced the King and his counsellors to set you free on the first of July, 1863, – they doubted no longer. Big tears of joy rolled down their black cheeks, and with jubilation they exclaimed: 'Our dear teacher tells us; we believe it; we will be free! What our mothers heard of before we were born, that is now to come pass, that we will see! Thanks, thanks unto God.' (Willemsen 2006a: 160)

It should be mentioned again that the article on compensation for the enslavers contained in the official proclamation was omitted in the version in the Surinamese language (Sranan Tongo) that was communicated to the enslaved (Willemsen 2006a).

Two things stand out in Jansa's description of the scene and the mood of the enslaved. The first is the issue of trust and mistrust; the enslavers could not announce the proclamation of the abolition of slavery to the enslaved themselves. The second issue is the reference of the enslaved to their mothers. They did not refer to their mothers and fathers, but to their mothers alone, which in turn reflects the type of family structures that had emerged under slavery. (Under chattel slavery the enslaved were not permitted to marry, so families could not live together. Children remained with and were raised by their mothers; they thus tended to know their mothers, but not their fathers.)

On 1 July 1863, 45,275 enslaved persons gained their formal freedom, and compensation was paid for 43,946 of these (see Table 5.1).

Table 5.1 Numbers of Enslaved Who Became Free on 1 July 1863

	Chattel slaves	State slaves	Total
Suriname	32,972	649	33,621
Curaçao	6,684	97	6,751
Bonaire	151	607	758
Aruba	474	6	480
St Eustatius	1,087	0	1,087
Saba	700	0	700
St Martin	1,878	0	1,878
	43,946	1,329	45,275

But where did the state get the money to compensate the enslavers? According to the official and conventional narrative, the state financed the abolition from its East Indies colony of Indonesia. But this is essentially creative accounting; the enslaved themselves paid for the legal abolition, by contributing to the wealth of the enslavers and the state.

This brings us to the third issue, namely, how much freedom the 'ex-slaves' would be given. Not only were the enslavers financially compensated, they were also assured of the pacification of the ex-slaves by the Dutch state. This led to the provision of security through the deployment of military and police forces by the Dutch government to the slave colonies to prevent the 'ex-slaves' from turning against those who held them in bondage. Another pacification method was religious education or indoctrination.

At the cultural level, the enslaved, who had been robbed of their African names and ethnicity and denied surnames for centuries, were given names; however, they were not allowed to have names that could be traced to their enslavers. In other words not only were the enslaved denied their physical freedom but also they were denied the right to choose their own names. Here was a contradiction that remained unresolved till the twenty-first century: whereas during slavery the enslavers had operated openly, publicly and with pride, following legal abolition they set out to cover their tracks.

We noted above that information on the 'slave' trade and slavery in various archives was obtained and preserved for a variety of purposes, and can therefore be used for the study of other phenomena. Humphrey Lamur does this in his interesting and useful study *Family Names and Kinship of Emancipated Slaves in Suriname* (2004). In his foreword to Lamur's study, Glenn Willemsen writes:

> As compensation for the emancipation, the [Dutch] government gave slave owners 300 Guilders for each slave or 30 Guilders if the slave was entitled to manumission. To be eligible for this compensation, they were obliged to submit lists of the slaves they owned. This list, the Statement of Registration, contains valuable information such as the names of slaves, their ages and dates of birth, religion, job and some comments on their personal circumstances. The majority of slaves were given a family name when they were emancipated, after which they were registered on the Emancipation Register.
>
> [Humphrey Lamur's study] has linked both files – the Statement and the Emancipation Register – which made it possible to create a database with significant information on individual slaves. This database was then supplemented with data on the slave owners and other socio-economic reference material, thereby creating an important source of information for further scientific research (Lamur 2004: vii).

As we have seen, the names given to the emancipated slaves were constructed so as to give no clues as to the identity of the slave owners. However by linking the Statement and the Emancipation Register, Lamur has been able to unravel the link between the enslaved and the enslavers. Lamur's work thus provides us with some of the most accurate and verifiable information on Dutch slavery to date. These two examples, namely, compensation and the construction of names, undermine the argument by some formal historians that we cannot use current moral perspectives to judge the past. In fact the two examples indicate that state officials at that time had some idea about the long-term consequences of their policies and practices.

Now that we have explained the government's and parliament's ideas about the extent of the freedom they were willing to grant the enslaved, it is necessary to examine how the enslaved themselves were thinking about freedom. History shows that liberty is not something you bestow on somebody; its development is too complex. People develop their own notion of freedom, subject to their own histories. For this reason, freedom had an entirely different meaning for freedmen than it had for enslavers.

Let us first examine how the enslaved population expressed the concept of freedom. The generation that Ira Berlin called the 'freedom generation' did not leave any written sources revealing its opinions about freedom. Access to the written word was denied to the majority of the enslaved. But this by no means implies that they did not reflect on freedom or know what it was; the *desire* for freedom was too great. The enslaved were acquainted with the events in the Maroon communities, and it was on this basis (among other things) that they were able to develop their own ideas about freedom. When they came into contact with missionaries and the Christian religion, they became inspired by the biblical story of the Exodus. In that narrative, a chosen people endures a long martyrdom in slavery, but salvation and freedom await them through God's intervention. The enslaved considered themselves simultaneously as individuals who were deprived of their rights and as a people unable to attain self-determination. Therefore to them freedom primarily meant two things: no further exposure to the iniquities of slavery (such as floggings, separation or separated sale of families, no access to education, sexual exploitation of women by enslavers) and collective empowerment, being treated as ordinary citizens.

The oral expressions by the enslaved (odos, *anansi tori*, songs) can also give us an impression of their ideas about freedom. In particular, proverbs and sayings dating from the period of slavery – called odos in Suriname – can indirectly teach us something about the (bad) conditions and practices of those days. It is an old African custom to utter criticism, not in a direct but in a symbolic way, for instance through an odo or in a song. We quote some of them, taken from a book by Albert Helman.

In spite of the hard and exhausting labour on the sugar plantations, the enslaved received little thanks for their pains. For this, they thought up the proverb, *Tangi foe boen na kodja*, 'Gratitude for a good deed is the stick.' An enslaved person who has been treated well must not think that he is no longer enslaved since even the best life of a slave can never be compared with the life of a free man. No matter how well an enslaved person was treated, his life was extremely uncertain: anything could happen to him. The enslaved were at the mercy of the enslavers' absolute arbitrariness. Just because they were missing what we today consider as our greatest gift, liberty, the whip could at any moment, without any reason, suddenly appear. Hence the odo *Si boen anga fri a no wan*, 'A good life and freedom are not the same thing' – so you had better not believe that you have reached your goal when you have only partially succeeded. Nowadays, we would say: 'One swallow does not make a summer.'

Whoever had gained his freedom (by whatever means) had good reason to be proud of it. Occasionally, however, recently liberated enslaved persons were treated as inferior or considered as semi-slaves by those who had obtained their liberty a long time before. The newly liberated enslaved defended themselves with the odo *Mi fri froe bakadina de so boen leki fri foe mamanten*, 'My freedom dating from the afternoon is just as good as your freedom dating from the morning.' Everybody who is feeling happy is happy, and it does not matter how long he has been happy or what his happiness consists of – as long as he is feeling that way.

While the majority of their brothers and sisters were still living as enslaved, freedmen found that the benefits of liberty were relative. Therefore they used the odo *Negre wani fri foe weri soesoe, a no sab'tak'na lekdoroe a e go kisi*, literally, 'Slaves long for the freedom to wear shoes, but they do not know it will give them corns.' In other words, do not yearn too much for what you do not really know, because it causes unknown troubles. Helman appropriately notes that no non-free person will ever believe this.

Everywhere in the Caribbean we notice some striking similarities in the enslaved conception of freedom. After abolition, freedmen expressed their liberation by travelling from one plantation to another, as if wanting to test the authorities and find out whether they truly were free and could do as they pleased. This going to and from plantations occurred particularly in Guyana, Jamaica, Trinidad and Suriname. But it also served another purpose: Ira Berlin points out that immediately after their liberation, freedmen in the United States started to look for relatives they had lost. This behaviour undermines the view that the enslaved did not have any family life during slavery. Reuniting their torn families was one of the very first things freedmen wanted to accomplish after abolition.

Another crucial element in the way freedmen experienced their liberation was their economic independence. They longed for a parcel of land that would enable them to be self-supporting through their own labour. Slavery meant working for someone else. Freedom, on the other hand, meant going to a place where you could lay hands on a piece of land. For many liberated enslaved persons, freedom also meant putting a great distance between themselves and the place where they had been bonded. Many turned their backs to the plantations in search of agricultural land or trying to acquire a craft.

The end of slavery meant the beginning of colonial experience and a new phase of another emancipation struggle, namely, decolonization.

THE IMMEDIATE AFTERMATH OF ABOLITION

The legal abolition of slavery and the institution of apprenticeship obliged former enslavers to confront the following key question: how do you suddenly, due to a legislative act, consider as human people whom you have always considered subhuman? On this score the legal abolition was a bittersweet affair. At one level the legal abolition was bitter, in the sense that those who had been in control of the lives of the enslaved lost that control (though they did gain materially and thus enjoyed the sweet fruits of financial compensation). At another level the legal abolition was sweet, in the sense that those who gained freedom rejoiced and became vocal (though the joy was tinged with bitterness since those who rejoiced did not become better off materially). This partly explains why one of the first demands of the 'ex-slaves' in Suriname was the opportunity to be able to send their children to school. On this score, whereas chattel slavery revolved around economic interests, emancipation revolved around human relations.

In certain districts of Suriname, freedmen soon came into conflict with plantation owners with regard to the amount of their wages. The law had stipulated that during state control, wages would be determined by the colonial authority. While discussing the bill in the Second Chamber, van Bosse had insisted upon an assessment of wages, but the government would not hear of it. For freedmen, though, salary was of the greatest importance. Freedom was seen as the opportunity for a man to support his family, which depended on his wages, whether he was married or not. The low wages of these days hardly allowed freedmen to do this. When freedmen spoke of liberty, they did so with reference to acquiring an income not as isolated individuals, but always in order to support their families, thus enabling the families (and not the individuals) to obtain some independence. The extent to which the man of the house was capable of protecting and supporting his family became central to the general definition of freedom and contrasted sharply with their situation during slavery.

During slavery, women constituted the backbone of the workers on the sugar plantations. Yet not only during slavery but also during state control they were extremely vulnerable to all kinds of abuse.

After state control, many women withdrew from work on the plantations. They were kept at home with their children to work within the family and on their own parcels of land. That is how freedmen wished to protect and secure their women and children. From now on, women exclusively had to take care of their children's education. This principle bears a remarkable resemblance to gender ideology in the Western world. But it also meant that women no longer accepted being abused in the fields. This way, they expressed what they meant by liberty: their bodies belonged to themselves and they had the right to be exempt from abuse and violence.

What can be concluded from the analysis of this chapter is the following.

In the Dutch context, the major difference between the emancipation of Catholics and that of the working class and women was that the emancipation of workers and women was brought about in relation to industrialization, whereas that of Catholics was brought about in relation to Napoleonic occupation. However the emancipation of Catholics, workers and women was different from that of the enslaved. For Catholics, workers and women, the object of emancipation was *equality*. For the enslaved, *freedom* was the entry point of emancipation; equality within the colonial setting; decolonization within the international setting; where decolonization is not possible, racism and sexism became the major obstacle to equality, and for that matter, the major object of protest.

The emancipation of the Catholics, workers and women was institutionalized within the Dutch state. The 'emancipation' of the enslaved was not institutionalized: hence it is an unfinished business. This is the subject to which we now turn.

6
The Legacy of Slavery: The Unfinished Business of Emancipation

The main legacy of slavery is *emancipation as unfinished business*.

In the preceding chapters we have reiterated that most countries in Africa, Europe and the Americas acknowledge slavery and racism as a part of their histories since the sixteenth century. It follows that each region has its own legacy of the Atlantic slavery.

We noted in Chapter 1 that until the end of the twentieth century, Dutch involvement in the Atlantic slavery system remained a non-issue in the public domain and in the collective memory of Dutch public institutions and Dutch society generally, except in the work of a handful of historians and anthropologists. This is in sharp contrast with the Surinamese and Antillean communities living in the Netherlands, amongst whom it was, and still is, an important and recurring topic of conversation. We also noted the different ways in which the historical day associated with emancipation is dealt with in the Netherlands and its former colonies. In this chapter we address some of the issues that inform the legacy of Dutch Atlantic slavery.

At the broader level, as the Atlantic slave colonies grew larger, the capacities of the 'mother countries' to maintain them waned. Colonists became alienated and revolted against the authority of their mother countries. Several colonies successfully revolted: the United States of America against England, Brazil against Portugal, Latin American countries against Spain, and Haiti against France. The larger colonies were more successful in setting up independent states and nations than the smaller ones. They did so in order to be free to continue to practise chattel slavery and make the indigenous peoples and people of African descent unfree. It is no accident that in many of these nations, the majority of those in control were European or of European descent. The dialectic of colonial revolt was that the colonists (predominantly white) sought their freedom from the mother countries in order to deny the conquered and enslaved (predominantly black) their freedom. This suggests that freedom had a different meaning for the white colonists than it had for the blacks, who became the subjects of the white colonists.

The colonists did not end domination in order to end slavery; on the contrary, they sought independence from the mother country so that they could continue to practise slavery, and to enjoy its fruits (economic profit, political control and social domination). Brazil, for example, having become independent of Portugal, was one of the last countries in the Americas to legally abolish slavery.

Thus, from the perspective of state formation, almost all the slave colonies in the Atlantic revolted against their mother countries in Europe – colonization breeds decolonization. But the revolts of the enslavers against their mother countries were much more successful than the revolts of the enslaved against the enslavers. In the Atlantic slave colonies, the emancipation of the colonists did not lead to the emancipation of the colonized and enslaved. Haiti is the only place where the enslaved successfully revolted against both the enslavers and their mother country to set up a state; but this did not lead to emancipation. For the smaller territories that were not strong enough to revolt against the mother country, the legal abolition of slavery transformed the former enslaved into colonial subjects. This set in motion another struggle for equality and made emancipation an unfinished business.

The move from unfreedom (slavery) to freedom (legal abolition), followed by the move from freedom to equality, constitute an ongoing process: the search for emancipation and the correction of historic injustice remain unfinished.

MEMORY AND DIGNITARIANISM

The fight to end the Atlantic 'slave' trade and slavery was superseded by a collective struggle to remember, and represent, the nature of slavery and the 'slave' trade, and the manner in which they were legally abolished. These activities involve groups, organizations and protests, as well as exhibitions, galleries and museums. They take place in private and in public spaces.

Through conquest, colonization and slavery, Europeans created an image of themselves and of the world (Hegel, quoted in Magubane 2006; Smith 1977; Darwin 1996); similarly, the peoples of the world outside Europe created an image of Europeans for themselves (Said 1978; Amin 1989; Dussel 1985; Quijano 2000; Asante 2007; Mignolo 2007). Underpinning the memory of the Atlantic slavery is the issue of dignitarianism. Ali Mazrui has broadly formulated dignitarianism as follows:

> The African people may not be the most brutalized people in modern history, but they are almost certainly the most humiliated. The most brutalized people in modern history include the indigenous people of the Americas and those of Australia, who were subjected to genocidal attacks by white invaders. Also among the most brutalized in modern times were the Jews and the Gypsies in the Nazi Holocaust.
> On the other hand, no other groups were subjected to such large-scale indignities of *enslavement* for several centuries in their millions as the Africans were. No other groups experienced to the same extent such indignities as *lynching,* systematic *segregation,* and well-planned *apartheid* as the Africans [did].
> It is against this background that Africa's dignitarian impulse was stimulated. A deep-seated African rebellion against humiliation was aroused. It has been a misnomer to call this rebellion 'nationalism'. This has not been an African quest for nationhood. At best nationhood has been just the means to an end. The deep-seated African struggle has been a quest for dignity – human and racial. (Mazrui 2001: 107)

In other words the quest for emancipation is tied to the quest for 'dignity – human and racial'. As a legacy of slavery, colonialism and racism, dignitarianism has given rise to a distinctive intellectual tradition and political agency known as Africana (i.e. relating to Africa and the African diaspora). Among those who have worked in the dignitarian tradition are W.E.B. Du Bois, Anton de Kom, Kwame Nkrumah, C.L.R. James, George Padmore, Aimé Césaire and Franz Fanon. Du Bois expressed this tradition at the turn of the twentieth century in the following words: 'The problem of the twentieth century is the problem of the colour line – the relations of the dark to the light faces of man in Asia and Africa, in America and the Islands of the sea' (1961: 23). It is also in the dignitarian tradition that Du Bois formulated his thesis of the 'Black problem', namely, when a people with some problems become 'the problem people'. These observations were made not long after the legal abolition of slavery. They clearly show that emancipation had not been achieved.

A better appreciation requires us to bring three things into relation with each other in order to complete the 'circle': the institution of slavery, chattel slavery, and race. C.L.R. James informed us about variations within slavery in the following words:

> In a slave society the mere possession of personal freedom is a valuable privilege, and the laws of Greece and Rome testify that severe legislation against slaves and freedmen have nothing to do with the race question. Behind all this elaborate tom-foolery of quarteron, sacatra and marabou, was the one dominating fact of San Domingo [Haiti] society – fear of the slaves. The mothers of the Mulattoes were in the slave-gangs, they had half-brothers there, and however much the Mulatto himself might despise this half of his origin, he was at home among the slaves and, in addition to his wealth and education, could have an influence among them which a white man could never have. Furthermore, apart from physical terror, the slaves were to be kept with the most obvious distinguishing mark of the slave – the black skin ... No Mulatto, therefore, whatever his number of white parts, was allowed to assume the name of his white father. (James 1980: 38–9)

Fifty years after Du Bois made his historic statement, on continental Africa Nkrumah reminded Ghanaians about the relevance of decolonization and emancipation:

> This country is ours. This land is ours. It belongs to our chiefs and people. It does not belong to foreigners, but we don't say that all foreigners should pack up and go. They can stay as traders, and work with us not as masters and rulers ... The age of politics of words is gone. This is the age of politics of action. We don't have guns. We don't have ammunition to fight anybody. We have a great spirit, a great national soul which is manifest in our unity. (Quoted here from Nimako 1991: 45)

Here, we are being reminded that, like slavery, colonialism could be maintained only through violence.

In the French Caribbean, Aimé Césaire and Franz Fanon are acknowledged figures who work in the dignitarian tradition. We have emphasised the role of race as an organizing principle of slavery. Like many Africans who work in the dignitarian tradition, Césaire noted that we cannot subsume class under race:

There are people, even today, [i.e. 1967] who thought and still think that it is all simply a matter of the left taking power in France, that with a change in economic conditions the black question will disappear. I have never agreed with that at all. I think that the economic question is important, but it is not the only thing ... I remember very well having said to the Martinican Communists in those days, that black people ... were doubly proletarianized and alienated: in the first place as workers, but also as blacks, because after all we are dealing with the only race which is denied even the notion of humanity. (Césaire 1972: 94)

This is also what Césaire means when he says 'there are no allies by divine right'. There you have it: the unfinished business of emancipation.

Reflecting on both slavery and colonialism in relation to race, Fanon made the following observation:

The disaster of the man of colour lies in the fact that he was enslaved. The disaster and inhumanity of the white man lie in the fact that somewhere he has killed man. And even today they subsist, to organize this dehumanization rationally. But I as a man of colour, to the extent that it becomes possible for me to exist absolutely, do not have the right to lock myself into a world of retroactive reparations.

I, the man of colour, want only this: That the tool never possesses the man. That the enslavement of man by man ceases forever; that is, of one by another. That it may become possible for me to discover and to love man, wherever he may be. The Negro is not. Any more than the white man. (Fanon 1970: 164–5; quoted here in Wallerstein 2009: 118–19)

In the Dutch Atlantic, Anton de Kom represented the dignitarian tradition. In his introduction to de Kom's book entitled *We the Slaves of Suriname*, John Jansen van Galen makes an interesting observation. He notes that in the process of editing the book the editors decided to exclude a chapter entitled 'Our Heroes'. Part of the chapter contained the following statement: 'our race ["ras" in Dutch] shall liberate itself when we are capable of producing great and conscious revolutionaries such as Baron, Bonni, and Joli Coeur again' (de Kom 1999: 8). (Baron, Bonni and Joli Coeur were people who led rebellions during slavery in Suriname.) Specifically Anton de Kom noted that '[n]o people can become fully matured when it is saddled with inherent inferiority complex. That is why this book attempts to arouse self-respect among Surinamese' (de Kom 1999: 17).

In the 1950s a cultural nationalist movement emerged in Suriname whose slogan was *wie egi sani* (our own thing). It was a cultural awakening for the black people not to be ashamed to speak the Sranan Tongo and be proud of their African heritage (Marshall 2003). A similar development took place in Curaçao with regard to the promotion of the Papiementoe language, under the leadership of Aaron Martinus (Martinus 1996).

Martin Luther King and Nelson Mandela might also be added to de Kom's list of heroes. During his trial in Pretoria in October 1963, Mandela made the following statement:

> During my lifetime I have dedicated myself to this struggle [against Apartheid] of the African people. I have fought against white domination, and I have fought against black domination. I have cherished the ideal of a democratic and free society in which all persons live together in harmony with equal opportunities. It is an ideal which I hope to live for and achieve. But if needs be, it is an ideal for which I am prepared to die. (Sampson 1999: 193)

During one of the numerous civil rights marches in the United States, when Martin Luther King was stopped and asked by a sheriff what he wanted, he said, 'dignity'. Today it is common for Antillean youth in the Netherlands to say they want 'respect'; perhaps they too mean 'dignity'. The memory of humiliation under slavery, and the awareness of racism now, are deep in the thoughts of many descendants of the enslaved.

In Chapter 3 we argued that ever since Columbus landed in the Americas in his search for an alternative route to Asia, the Atlantic world has had meaning only in relation to the Asian world. We also argued that not only did the goods the enslaved produced in the Atlantic world facilitate trade between Europe and Asia, but they also made it possible for Europe to colonize Asia. Colonization goes hand in hand with humiliation; in turn humiliation arouses dignitarian impulses. This is not peculiar to Black intellectual tradition in relation to the history of the Atlantic world. Though Wolfgang Sachs had a different project, his observations of the rise of China are relevant to our project:

Every time the Olympic flame is lit in front of the host country's president, the pulse of a nation quickens. But the Games have rarely been staged with more ambition to self-aggrandisement than in Beijing 2008, when China celebrated its arrival as a world power. Moreover, that which in the summer of 2008 was broadcast to the world through the language of the Olympics will in 2010 be reiterated in the language of a world exhibition in Shanghai, in which China presents itself to the global public as a platform for the scientific achievements of the twenty-first century.

According to Sachs:

> The Olympics and the World Expo are symbols of the secular shift that occurred around the turn of the millennium; the ascent of China – and other countries of the South – to the exclusive club of global powers. It is scarcely possible to overestimate the significance of this shift for world history, and in particular for the people of the South. After centuries of humiliation, they finally see a Southern country on a par with the powers of the world. Countries once treated as colonial underdogs now measure up to their masters, and people of colour take over from the white man. (Sachs 2009: vii)

Sachs further notes that:

> A quick glance at China may illustrate the point. The ascendancy of China to the ranks of a world power is balm on the wounds inflicted during her two centuries of colonial humiliation. And the success of the middle class is a source of pride and self-respect that puts the Chinese elite on a par with social elites elsewhere on the globe. The Chinese example brings to the fore what has been part and parcel of development all along: the desire for justice is intimately linked to the pursuit of development. (Sachs 2009: ix)

The common thread that runs through the above intellectual and political tradition is race, humiliation, slavery, colonialism and memory.

We have seen that the legal abolition of Dutch slavery was a consequence of pressures and intervention from Britain. Nevertheless when the day of emancipation came, the credit went to the Dutch king. Some Dutch newspapers, such as *De Heraut* and *De Rotterdamsche Courant* wrote positive comments about the legal abolition of slavery. However it was the editor of a provincial newspaper, *Utrechtsch Provinciaal en Stedelijk Dagblad*, who linked their commentary to memory, freedom, equality and legacy:

> Only where a civilization is founded upon natural principles of *freedom* and *equality* can prosperity and flourishing be expected in the *long run*. May this prosperity and flourishing become the destiny of our West Indian colonies so that in the future one will always – with even more joy – *remember* the first of July 1863 as a happy day in Dutch history, as a fortunate moment during the reign of Willem III. (*Utrechtsch Provinciaal en Stedelijk Dagblad*, no.155, 2 July 1863; emphasis added)

Let us pay special attention to the four words we have emphasized in the editorial above: freedom, equality, long run (i.e. legacy), and remember (i.e. memory).

In a sense, the Dutch king, Willem III, became the moral equivalent of William Wilberforce in Britain; the legal abolition of slavery was interpreted as resulting from the king's morality and magnanimity. But, as we have seen, the enslavers had to be compensated by the Dutch state before the enslaved could gain their legal freedom under the abolition act (Willemsen 2006a). Thus equality was out of the equation. So was memory: for more than 100 years very few people remembered what the newspaper editor expected them to remember; the happy day did not come; instead we got forgetfulness. This raises questions of knowledge production and representation. We return to this below.

In the last decade there has been an upsurge in the number of institutions that directly and explicitly focus on slavery. These reflect the successful efforts of Black communities in many nations to bring the discussion of slavery and its legacy into the broader public domain. These initiatives include successfully lobbying government and other agencies to persuade them to be more proactive in promoting discussion and dissemination of information about slavery, racism and discrimination (Small 1997; Willemsen 2006a; Young 2002).

It was against this background that, the Afro-Surinamese Cultural Centre (ASCC) organized a conference on 1 July 1998 in south-east Amsterdam to discuss the disregarded past of slavery. At this symposium, participants argued that the significant contribution the Atlantic 'slave' trade and slavery in the Caribbean made to the Dutch economy and society should be a required topic in the educational field. Those present also unanimously agreed that the erection of a monument would contribute to this endeavour.

State response to this demand gave rise to public (mostly on radio) and private discussions in the Afro-Dutch community, in which four perspectives might be discerned. First, there were those who then (and now) do not want to be reminded of the Dutch involvement in the transatlantic slavery system because it does not correspond to the self-image of the Dutch master narrative, namely, a culture of tolerance, freedom and democracy. In reality, those who held these views were afraid of the backlash from the white Dutch community. This, in and of itself, was a recognition of the culture of repressive tolerance.

Secondly, there were those who questioned why people should be bothered with an extensive discussion of slavery, and its commemoration and remembrance, since it pertained to a shameful period from the distant past. These people argued that the past, which was a nightmare, had better be buried so that we can focus on the future. This focus on the past, it was argued, constituted *victimology* by the descendants of the enslaved and reinforced the antagonism in society towards blacks, especially when initiated by the descendants of the enslaved (Mamadeus 2007).

Thirdly, there were those who opposed the discussion of slavery on purely psychological grounds. They argued that the issue of slavery has a traumatic effect on the descendants of the enslaved. It is better to spare them such trauma. What is peculiar about these three perspectives is that they are all racialized: the objections do not apply to white scholars; when whites write or talk about slavery, nobody says it is a long time ago; when whites talk about it, it is history education; when blacks talk about it, it is emotion. This stems from repressive tolerance. We encounter this problematic also in race and ethnic studies (Essed and Nimako 2006).

Finally there were those who argued that every aspect of history should be a subject for discussion, and slavery is no exception. This group demanded that slavery should become part of public history. They felt that the silence around the Dutch involvement in the transatlantic slavery system had to be broken. In the process, this fourth perspective attempted an epistemic intervention by introducing the concept of 'enslaved' into Dutch discourse. Such a concept could not be found in the Dutch lexicon, so they used the expression *tot slaaf gemaakt*, meaning, 'made into a slave'; this is more a phrase than a concept. Whether this is a consequence of the inadequacy of the Dutch language is another matter; but it constitutes conceptual disobedience (Mignolo 2009).

But the attempt to create a new concept as a challenge to dominant concepts is not a matter of semantics; it is a reflection of real life situations. The following statement by the Rev. Jesse Jackson (made on 28 March 2009 in Rotterdam) can serve as a starting point for the relevance of concepts as part of knowledge production: 'My great-great grandmother was my great-great grandmother; but for someone, she was a slave.' The point Jackson is making is that *he* cannot call his great-great grandmother a 'slave', even if those who held her in bondage called her a 'slave': the concept of 'slave' is used by the enslavers, not the enslaved. This has implications for accounting for slavery and its legacy. This also explains why, throughout this book, where possible, we have preferred the word 'enslaved' rather than 'slave'.

We have noted above that in response to the abolition of slavery in the Dutch orbit on 1 July 1863, a Dutch editorial newspaper implored that: 'We must always remember 1 July as the happiest day in the reign of King Willem III.' However, it took more than 130 years before the abolition of slavery was commemorated on Dutch soil – the official and formal monument to commemorate Dutch slavery was erected in 2002. Why did it take so long?

Here we should distinguish public history from private history, because before the official monument, there were unofficial or private commemorations and there were commemorators. Who were these commemorators?

COMMEMORATORS AND COMMEMORATION

Activities associated with the anniversaries of the abolition of slavery have occurred in Dutch colonies for many years, though not in the Netherlands itself until recently. The commemoration of slavery started immediately after the legal abolition of Dutch slavery on 1 July 1863. The first nationally organized commemoration by the descendants of the former enslaved took place in Suriname in 1913, 50 years after abolition. In 1963, on the 100th anniversary of abolition, 1 July was declared a public holiday.

As van Stipriaan has noted:

> Until the early twentieth century this day was used by church and secular organizations to celebrate the glorious granting of freedom to the enslaved by a generous (white) king and a benevolent

(white) church. It was a celebration of the colonial status quo, and particularly the status quo of a racial hierarchy. Year after year 1 July was a time when the need for moral emancipation was emphasized as a corollary of physical emancipation implying the need to adapt to Western civilization. (Van Stipriaan 2007)

A celebration of this type is an example of progressive control, defined in Chapter 4 as a dynamic process which 'continuously moves towards newer forms of control' as a result of changing conditions (Mullard 1988: 362).

Such a mode of commemoration was not satisfactory to some of the descendants of the enslaved and led to new initiatives. Van Stripriaan notes that:

[i]n the early twentieth century ... a new dimension was added to this abolition and moral emancipation discourse which eventually transformed Emancipation Day into a vehicle for anti-colonialist ideas. This reflected a cultural and socio-economic emancipation of the Afro-Surinamese population which was linked to nationalism as well as to the African diaspora discourse. In the 1920s, committees emerged publishing emancipation papers and organizing Afro-Surinamese rallies on Emancipation Day giving voice to mounting ethno-nationalist feelings which eventually formed the basis for national independence, supported mainly by Afro-Suriname politicians. (Van Stipriaan 2007: 214)

This change of emphasis constitutes a change from progressive control to transformative change. It should be restated that transformative change 'entails a special kind of break from former policies and practices and the relations in which they arise', and requires a change from 'one set of policies based upon one set of beliefs, to another oppositional set, based upon an oppositional set of beliefs' (Mullard 1988: 363).

The transformation from progressive control made the descendants of the enslaved the commemorators. For them it was the end of humiliation and the beginning of the struggle for equality. In the course of time, slavery and its legacy have been remembered in poetry, song and music, in carnivals and street festivals, in religious gatherings and memorial services, and in group discussions and celebrations of anniversaries. In other words, while remembering and commemorating slavery were non-issues, marginalized issues, or motivations to resentment and hostility in white mainstream communities, they were important and recurring topics of conversation, social interaction and community celebration in Black communities (Small 1994a 1994b; Brundage 2005; Clark 2005; Willemsen 2006a; Willemsen and Nimako 2008).

On the Dutch Antilles, the situation is more complicated. On Sint Eustatius 'Freedom Day' is always commemorated, and since 1981 the abolition of slavery is remembered with African drumming, recitations of poetry, and lectures about the island's history. On Curaçao, 1 July was initially commemorated, but this soon passed into oblivion; 1968 was the last year in which Emancipation Day was officially commemorated. The present generation experiences the abolition of slavery as a distant act by a Dutch colonial legislature, an act that no longer has any meaning in modern society. Far more important is the celebration of the great slave revolt that broke out on 17 August 1795, under the command of Tula. With the slogan 'Victory or death', the enslaved fought for their liberty. Therefore, on the island of Curaçao, 17 August is officially recognized as the 'Day of the Struggle for Independence'. On the Leeward Islands, 1 July has long since been forgotten.

Many Surinamese who travelled to the Netherlands to work or study after the Second World War had some memory of commemoration. In the 1960s, Surinamese students organized parties on 1 July at various locations, including Hotel Krasnapolski in Amsterdam, as part of the commemoration of the legal abolition of Dutch slavery. According to Willemsen, when Surinamese immigrants and settlers arrived in large numbers in the Netherlands in the mid 1970s, they were disappointed to find that no formal recognition of 1 July existed in the metropolis itself. Some Surinamese workers took the day off for commemorative purposes.

Nevertheless, the relatively small Black communities in the Netherlands have been central players in a wide range of activities (Willemsen 2006a; Horton and Kardux 2005; Nimako, Cain and Small 2010). Black communities organized community remembrance and commemorations, and issues of slavery and its legacy were addressed in churches, in community organizations and events, in festivals, and in music and poetry. As we have argued several times in this book, it was initiatives from within the Black community that led to the National Slavery Monument (formally unveiled in July 2002) and to the establishment of NiNsee (The National Institute for the Study of Dutch Slavery and its Legacy), which opened on July 2003 (van Stipriaan 2007). As Willemsen points out, 'before the official monument for commemoration, there were commemorators' (Willemsen 2006a). He then asks, 'Who were these commemorators?' His response is that they involved a series of black groups and organizations that laid roots in the Netherlands and expanded with the migration and settlement of Surinamese in the 1970s. These groups were 'the seed bed for the development of organisations in the major cities of Amsterdam, Rotterdam and The Hague' (Willemsen 2006a). And it should be highlighted that the transformation of Surinamese migrants from the status of colonial subjects to that of fully fledged Dutch citizens within Europe was instrumental in legitimizing their claims.

One of the association's organizing activities around 1 July is the National 30 June /1 July Committee, which created a tradition of commemorating slavery in the Dutch colonies with a vigil on the evening of 30 June in Surinameplein in Amsterdam. An important leader of this organization was Winston Kout. In 1993, on the occasion of the 130th anniversary of the abolition of slavery, the committee proclaimed 30 June as a recurring day of reflection. This is followed by Keti Koti, the celebration of the abolition of slavery, on 1 July.

On the same 1993 anniversary, Barryl Biekman, leader of the Afro-European Feminist Movement, Sophiedela, announced her plans for a national monument to commemorate Dutch slavery. Shortly thereafter, Sophiedela presented a petition calling for the erection of such a monument to Tara Oedayraj Singh Varma, then a congresswoman of Surinamese descent who represented Groen Links (the Green Left Party); this took place during a conference organized by Sophiedela on the occasion of a number of anniversaries – the 135th of the abolition of slavery in the Netherlands, the 50th of the Universal Declaration of the Rights of Man and the 150th of the Dutch Constitution. In September 1998, the petition, entitled 'Traces of Slavery', was also offered to several congressmen who were permanent members of the Commission of the Ministry of the Interior and Kingdom Relations, and was subsequently discussed in Congress in February 1999.

At the seventh memorial service (in 1999), a tablet was unveiled in Surinameplein. The name of the organization, the National 30 June /1 July Committee, was deliberately chosen as an analogy of the National Committee of 4 May/5 May, which annually commemorates the Dutch victims of the Second World War on 4 May and the liberation of the Netherlands from Nazi occupation on 5 May. The message is therefore clear: slavery is as much a part of Dutch history as the Second World War. The implicit message is even more provocative: namely that slavery was also a holocaust, with the Dutch as actors instead of victims.

Another high-profile organization is De Stichting Eer en Herstel, Betaling Slachtoffers van de Slavernij in Suriname (Foundation for the Honour, Restoration and Compensation of Victims of Slavery in Suriname), under the chairmanship of Roy Groenberg, also known as Kaikusi. This association planted a tree in Het Martelarenwoud (The Forest of Martyrs) in Jerusalem in 1996 to commemorate all natives and Afro-Surinamese who were killed during the slavery era. This gesture was also intended as a token of reconciliation with the Jewish community, which accounted for a large number of enslavers in Suriname. On 1 July 1998, the Honour and Restoration Foundation pleaded, in an open letter to the Second Chamber of the Dutch Parliament, for a series of activities, in particular the erection of a monument, to honour the victims of slavery, to commemorate their disregarded history and to 'repair' their sufferings. Every year, the foundation organizes a ceremony in which a wreath is placed in the Anton de Kom Square in south-east Amsterdam.

A 1 July Committee was also created in Rotterdam, where the annual Bigi Spikri (Great Mirror) Parade, in which the descendants of the enslaved parade in colourful traditional garments to celebrate the beauty of their culture, always attracts thousands of spectators. On 1 July 1999, the committee presented a petition to the municipality of Rotterdam, requesting that the municipal authorities use their influence with the national government to proclaim 1 July a national holiday.

All of these initiatives gained momentum when the government complied with the request from Sophiedela, and the new minister for urban policy and integration of ethnic minorities, Rogier van Boxtel, adopted the idea of a national slavery monument, making it the key point of his policy to promote the social integration of ethnic minorities. At the insistence of the Ministry of the Interior, several Afro-Surinamese, Antillean, Aruban, African, Maroon and Native organizations met in May 1999 to create a large umbrella organization, the Landelijk Platform Slavernijverleden (Nationwide Platform for the History of Slavery) (LPS), which became the official interlocutor with the government. Because of the political sensitivities surrounding this topic, the government required the LPS to have a large backing of public support. The ensuing collaboration between the LPS and the government, under the motto 'united by freedom', led to the generation and realization of a number of ideas, with the cooperation of the Ministry of the Interior and Kingdom

Relations and the Ministry of Education, Culture and Sciences. The installation of the management of NiNsee, on 24 June 2002, which became the new interlocutor with the government, was one of the highlights.

It should be mentioned that the 30 June/1 July Committee chose not to participate in the LPS. For this committee, the realization of its original idea of an *urban* monument in Surinameplein was more important than the broader perspective of the *national* monument that the LPS had in mind.

The efforts of the Honour and Restoration Foundation in particular, but also of the 30 June/1 July Committee and the LPS, have put Dutch slavery on the political agenda. This was the start of a public discussion about slavery and at the same time the cause of many emotional outbursts; it culminated in the unveiling of the Nationaal Monument Slavernijverleden (National Slavery Monument) on 1 July 2002 in Oosterpark in Amsterdam. The unveiling of this static monument in the presence of Queen Beatrix led to a dramatic situation. The crowd, consisting mostly of descendants of the enslaved population, was denied access to the monument's immediate vicinity. A crush barrier and high dividing walls covered with black plastic kept the multitude at a distance from the dignitaries and guests; police on horseback galloped into the crowd to disperse it. These safety measures elicited from the descendants not just an emotional explosion, but blind rage. They were completely left out, while the purpose of the national monument was to bring people together! The black population was deeply humiliated and cried out loudly that 'the days of slavery were not yet over' (Willemsen 2006a). Here is another illustration of the idea that the business of emancipation is unfinished.

The developments in the Netherlands relating to the slavery legacy ran parallel with international initiatives to combat repression and exclusion. During the World Anti-Racism Conference held in Durban, South Africa in 2001, van Boxtel spoke on behalf of the cabinet on the approach to the struggle against racism and racial discrimination. His speech included the following remarks:

> This World Conference in Durban is in our view a necessary moment to state to all people that racism and discrimination must be eradicated. But we can only be credible if we recognize the great injustice of the past. We express our deep remorse about the enslavement and slave trade that took place. But an expression of remorse as such is not enough and cannot be

used as an excuse for not taking any action in the present. It is important to take structural measures that have effects for the descendants of former slaves and the next generations ... Next year the Netherlands will unveil its national slavery monument, a symbol of national remembrance, in Amsterdam, our national capital. This monument is created in close cooperation with the descendants of former slaves. The monument as a whole will represent past, present and future. Madam, Excellencies, besides the unveiling of a monument we will also create a center of expertise on slave history, as a dynamic slavery monument. Together with better education, these centres will contribute to a better understanding and greater tolerance amongst young people. (Quoted from Willemsen 2004)

We continue this narrative with two observations. The first is that the minister made this statement without support from major mainstream Dutch public intellectuals. At that time, dominant public intellectuals were preoccupied with issues of multiculturalism and Islam. This is what we have characterized as *high intensity discourse*. High intensity discourse refers to the officially sanctioned discussions that gain more attention in the dominant media. The second observation is that within the Black community a *low intensity discourse* took place, of which four perspectives have been described in the previous section (Willemsen and Nimako 2008).

Let us take these perspectives and issues in turn.

INTEGRATION AND MULTICULTURALISM

We noted in Chapter 5 that the starting points of the emancipation struggles of the Catholics, workers, and women were different from that of the enslaved. The main differences revolved around the issues of citizenship and race. We return to this below. For the moment it is worth mentioning that there is an official state emancipation project which rests on the promotion of *social harmony*, and an unofficial emancipation project of the descendants of the former enslaved that continuously demand *equality*. The state emancipation project finds its expression in integration policy. This explains why it was the responsibility of the minister for urban policy and integration of ethnic minorities, van Boxtel, to respond to the demands of Surinamese and Antilleans for a slavery monument.

The genealogy of Dutch integration policy can be traced to three sources, namely, the East Indian colonial legacy, the Atlantic slavery legacy, and the legacy of labour recruitment ('guest workers') in the context of post-Second World War economic recovery. The East Indian colonial legacy found its expression in the presence of people of Indonesian ancestry and their agency; the legacy of Atlantic slavery found its expression in the agency of people of Antillean and Surinamese descent; and that of post-war labour recruitment found its expression in the agency of Moroccans and Turks. Each of these groups came with its own collective memories and manifested itself in different ways.

Recall that the Dutch tried to hold on to the 'slave' trade and slavery before pressure from Britain gave sway; when decline of the British and Dutch empires was imminent, the United States came to play the role of decolonizer similar to the role Britain had played in relation to the abolishing of slavery; thus, the Dutch tried to maintain its colonies until they had to give way under US pressure. This episode in Dutch colonial history has been described by Legêne and Waaldijk in the following words:

> The decolonization of Indonesia, which started with the nationalist movement in the 1920s and 1930s, culminated in 1945 in the Declaration of Independence by Soekarno. The occupation by Nazi Germany (1940–45) of the European part of the empire, and the Japanese conquest of the Indonesian archipelago (1941–45) accelerated the erosion of Dutch colonial rule. The Dutch political elite realized only slowly that an era was ending. Not until 1949, after several military interventions and heavy international pressure, did the Dutch government finally recognize Indonesian independence. Thereafter, the idea of the Dutch nation was narrowed down to the mother country in Europe. The mixed, public–private colonial canon became invisible in the national *historical* canon. The empire had passed into history, although, it did not disappear completely. (Legêne and Waaldijk 2007: 199; original emphasis)

With regard to memory, Legêne and Waaldijk inform us that

> [u]ntil the 1960s, the pupils of primary schools still had to know the geography of the Indonesian archipelago, drumming the names of the different islands into their heads. Moreover, elements of the empire also persisted in the more domestic discourse of literary fiction and popular culture. (Legêne and Waaldijk 2007: 199)

Not only did the end of the post-war economic recovery bring an end to labour recruitment, but also by the 1970s these three legacies had given rise to social configurations that required new social and physical accommodations. This was hastened by a revolt in the Netherlands of young people of Indonesian descent, referred to as Moluccans. Consequently, efforts were made in the Netherlands to develop a coherent ethnic-minorities policy to regulate race and ethnic relations along the lines of the policy adopted in the United Kingdom.

We have recorded this process elsewhere (Essed and Nimako 2006). A decade after a British home secretary, Roy Jenkins, had defined integration as 'not a flattering process of assimilation but equal opportunity accompanied by cultural diversity in an atmosphere of mutual tolerance', a Dutch Labour Party member of parliament, Henk Molleman, tabled a motion intended to introduce an ethnic-minorities policy in the Netherlands, on the model of the British Race Relations Act (1965) (Miles and Phizacklea 1984). In his speech to the parliament, among other things, Molleman noted that '[t]he Netherlands society has become a multi-racial society where (members of) minorities, as group and individuals, must be able to participate and *emancipate themselves* without giving up their own cultural identity and the reciprocal preparedness to dialogue' (quoted from Essed and Nimako 2006; emphasis added).

Ministerial approval of the motion led to the establishment of the Department of Ethnic Minority Affairs within the Ministry of Home Affairs, which set in motion the ethnic-minorities policy program. But as we note below, this experiment collapsed after five years. Following this, the East Indian legacy faded; the 'guest workers' legacy found its expression in discussions of multiculturalism; the slavery legacy found its expression in the demand for the slavery monument and institute.

The state emancipation project collapsed partly because it was dependant on the capacity of the state to finance it. This dependence on state funding is not peculiar to the minorities issue. A prominent scholar on pillarization, Anton Zijderveld, had observed that as the Dutch economy recovered from the destruction of the Second World War, groups that had initially depended on their pillars for support and funding turned instead to the government in The Hague. Not only did the state respond favourably to such requests, but also groups became dependent on the state. By the middle of the 1980s, the welfare state had become expensive and was in crisis; the foundations of pillarization began to shake, but were not destroyed.

This is the broader context in which we should view the revolt against the minorities policy and its replacement in 1989 with the *allochtonen* or aliens policy.

The new policy arose alongside a new official classification of groups in society into *autochtonen* (natives) and *allochtonen* (non-natives, or aliens). An alien is any person whose grandparents, one or both, can be traced to a Third World country. The aliens policy questioned the ethnic minority policy's focus on six groups and pleaded for the inclusion of all Third World migrants into a new immigration policy. Whereas the minorities policy had emphasized integration and emancipation, hence suggesting, at least in principle, a two-way social process of change between ethnic minorities and ethnic majorities, the aliens policy perceived only a one-way direction of change. It focused on an intensification of the general policies such as education, including adult (language) education, as a way of better qualifying ethnic minority groups to compete for employment opportunities.

For a while it was assumed by some scholars of pillarization that the 'guest workers' of Muslim backgrounds, such as Moroccans and Turks, were developing into another pillar. Zijderveld summarized the state of pillarization in the following terms. Ideological and political groups in the Netherlands were co-opted into a system of pillarization in the period following the Second World War. These non-secular pillars were organized and funded by the government. This included certain essential aspects of society (education, labour and health care).

The height of pillarization was in the 1980s. Pillarization was a part of the immigrant integration strategy of the Dutch government. It gave rise to a number of Islamic schools, television programming specifically created by and for ethnic minorities (Turkish, Surinamese, Moroccan, etc.), various community centres and ethnic associations, and so on. In short, the traditional Dutch strategy for negotiating differences between large religious groups (Catholics and Protestants) was extended to ethnic minorities in the Netherlands.

In response to this, we argued that whereas the Catholics, workers and women started their emancipation from within mainstream Dutch society, the emancipation of the minorities in question was from without (Willemsen and Nimako 1993) – the difference lay in the position in Dutch society of the members of the various pillars. No one questioned the right of Catholics or Protestants to live in the Netherlands or to be considered as citizens. The members of these groups already played a large role in the political and social realm; citizenship was a given for the stakeholders of the traditional pillars. The new pillarization, however, led to a form of segregation politics and marginalization under which ethnic groups were increasingly made dependent on the government. As a result, ethnic minorities remain outside the processes of defining the society in which they live and have limited access to resources and political power.

After the revolt against the minorities policy and its replacement with the aliens policy, the various groups went their own ways. The colonial subjects from East Asia (or Moluccans) were offered job projects and a museum; the Muslims became the object of multicultural discourse and ridicule; the welfare organizations of the colonial subjects from the West Indies were gradually dismantled. Against this background the commemorators of slavery emerged.

This discourse on Dutch multiculturalism reached its climax through the intervention of two public intellectuals, Pim Fortuyn and Paul Scheffer (Essed and Nimako 2006). Pim Fortuyn left academia to become a private consultant, columnist and politician. Paul Scheffer was a columnist who was invited into the academic world after the publication of an article entitled 'The Multicultural Drama' ('Het multiculturele drama', 2000). Published in the main (conservative) quality newspaper, the *NRC Handelsblad*, usually read by politicians and policy makers, the essay triggered heated debates. What Fortuyn and Scheffer had in common was that they set out to break the politics of consensus. A difference however was that Fortuyn directed his critique at the way Dutch society and politics as a whole were organized and operated, whereas Scheffer critiqued the discourse of multiculturalism and the minority research industry that supports such discourse.

The central Scheffer argument was that multicultural discourse has given rise to a 'culture of anything goes' and had clouded a proper understanding of Dutch history. Scheffer claimed that multiculturalism had failed Dutch society as well as its minorities. In the name of cultural relativism the autochthonous (native) majority (*autochtonen*), in particular the progressive elites, have become indifferent to the increasing segregation and isolation of *allochtonen* (non-natives), especially young people of Moroccan parentage, who are lagging behind socially, educationally and in the labour market. Scheffer's solution at the time: compulsory Dutch history lessons and assimilation into Dutch culture via familiarity with Dutch norms and values. Moreover, greater national pride amongst the Dutch would offer *allochtonen* additional reasons to want to belong. Scheffer also pleaded for a parliamentary inquiry into the ethnic minorities policy.

'The Multicultural Drama' caused widespread commotion, because many reduced the article to its most controversial statements, Scheffer's call for greater national pride ('a nationalist ...') and cultural assimilation ('... who wants to abolish cultural difference'). Few acknowledged his (self-stated) motivation: his outrage over the moral indifference of cultural relativists to the growing gap between *autochtonen* and *allochtonen*. It was argued that both the minority and aliens policies were anchored in the principles of progressive control and perpetuated segregation rather than fostering integration (Mullard, Nimako and Willemsen 1990; Essed 1996). But rather than writing about emancipation, anti-racism and transformative change in society, Scheffer's solution was in the tradition of progressive control: fix the ethnic minorities in order to enable them to live up to the culturally more advanced Dutch norms and values.

The political irony is that Scheffer's call for a uniform history had an unanticipated consequence. The demand for a 'uniform' national historical knowledge (high intensity discourse) to foster the integration of the *allochtonen* coincided with the demand for a uniform national historical knowledge of Dutch slavery (low intensity discourse) advocated by the descendants of the former enslaved, in which the Dutch Atlantic slavery is part and parcel of Dutch history and collective memory.

Since the erection of the National Slavery Monument (1 July 2002) and the establishment of NiNsee (1 July 2003), the Dutch state has commissioned and published a 'canon of Dutch history and culture' (2006). Grever and Stuurman report:

> In 2006 the Dutch Ministry of Education installed a committee to draft a national canon of history and culture, a government intervention in curriculum content that is unprecedented in the history of the Netherlands. The assumption underlying such policy statements is that the transmission of a coherent national past to younger generations will further the integration of [ethnic] minorities and contribute to responsible citizenship and social cohesion.

The authors comment that:

> [t]he flip-side of such a political role for history is that it can easily reduce history teaching to a branch of civics, guided by the political

priorities of the government of the day. Such a policy-guided approach to history would leave little room for dissenting perspectives and voices. Moreover, the cognitive functions of history as a scholarly discipline would easily be sacrificed to its ideological and moral functions. It might also prove to be counterproductive: a univocal history would be unlikely to nourish the competence to judge competing perspectives on historical trends and events. (Grever and Stuurman 2007: 2)

Furthermore:

[e]ducators and public moralists frequently recommend the canon as the only alternative to the postmodernist quandary of relativism and contingency. Yet, there are basic questions about the uses of history that all nations will have to address in the twenty-first century. Globalization, migration and post-coloniality will be on the world's agenda for the foreseeable future. So will the attendant cultural encounters and confrontations, in which gender, ethnicity and 'race' are often keenly contested and divisive issues. (Grever and Stuurman 2007: 8)

The canon identifies 50 'windows' on Dutch history and culture which education institutes should consider essential in understanding Dutch history. These 50 'windows' include Dutch slavery and multi-culturalism; slavery is considered in the context of 'history' whereas multiculturalism is considered in the context of the 'present'.

NINSEE AS A CONTESTED PROJECT

The Dutch canon of history and culture gives NiNsee some legitimation to exist. But it also makes it a contested project, for six reasons.

The first reason is the sources of funding. The Ministry of Education, Culture and Science is the main funder of NiNsee and determines the level and duration of funding. Like all national institutions dependent on state subvention, there are never enough resources. Thus NiNsee has to balance its ambitions with a level of resourcing that the ministry deems appropriate for such an institute.

Formally, NiNsee's task is to put the issues of Dutch Atlantic slavery and its legacy into the public domain. This makes NiNsee a 'public history' institute. NiNsee fulfils this task in a number of ways – remembrance and commemoration, education, exhibition, research, and documentation. These tasks cater to different publics, interest groups and stakeholders.

The second reason why NiNsee is a contested project relates to its position in relation to academia and scholarship. Public history institutes draw part of their knowledge resources from academia. With regard to education and research, NiNsee is positioned between academia and the public. On the one hand NiNsee brings knowledge and scholarship produced in academia to the public attention. It does this through the organization of seminars and public lectures and the publication of books. We noted above that different countries have different dominant narratives and research interests. In Britain the emphasis is on the legal abolition of the 'slave' trade. In the Netherlands there is more research interest in the 'slave' trade and less on how slavery affected the enslaved and its legacy. Dutch mainstream academia is relatively silent on issues related to race and racism, even though, as we have emphasized throughout this book, race was a major organizing principle of slavery. But these are issues that concern some of the stakeholders who campaigned for the erection of the slavery monument and the institute.

This raises the question of whether NiNsee should ignore the issues of race and racism, following the lead of mainstream academia, or take up these issues in their research agenda in response to the demands of stakeholders. A review of the historical record demonstrates that racisms articulated during slavery (e.g. racism as 'necessary evil', 'positive good', religious and scientific racisms) were then superseded by racisms in the post-slavery world ('new racism', cultural racism and sociobiology) (Banton 1977; Omi and Winant 1994; Essed 1991; van Dijk 1993; Ansell 1997). In the twenty-first century, these racisms continue to fuel the patterns of inequality and institutional discrimination entrenched during slavery, and thus continue to prevent full emancipation for the descendants of the enslaved. Their effects are experienced in the world of citizenship, work, politics and education. They continue to impede or prevent access (especially by black organizations) to political power and knowledge production processes in the struggle over collective forgetting and remembering. And they continue to shape attitudes towards public history and the collective memory of slavery, especially in its institutional forms in exhibitions, galleries and museums (Small 1997). Intellectuals play a role in shaping public histories; in turn institutional public histories are major players in distorting the historical record. These two sets of activities – post-slavery and rearticulated racisms – continue to frame our understandings of the relationship between the slavery of the past (including the relations between Africa and the West) and the post-slavery activities of the present (including understandings of emancipation and obstacles to the trajectory of full emancipation).

Dutch academia is interested in the legacy of slavery largely through the study of artefacts – a project called AWAD, the Atlantic World and the Dutch 1500–2000, has been called into being for this purpose. NiNsee works with AWAD through exhibitions and through its educational domain. Internationally this trend involves museums, galleries, exhibitions and monuments, as well as the heritage of stately homes and mansions, gardens, and ships and maritime structures, all of which were established during slavery and empire, and funded from their profits. The institutions involved have, until very recently, ignored, downplayed, or marginalized explicit discussion of slavery and its legacy, and have focused mainly on material culture, rather than on humans (Tibbles 1994), a subject we return to below.

On the positive side, NiNsee brings public concerns on the topic of slavery to the attention of academia and researchers. Here stakeholders play a role, of which more below. For the moment suffice it to say that a small group at NiNsee conducts research on slavery, resistance and its legacy. Like all research enterprise, the products emerging from NiNsee can either complement or challenge existing research and knowledge production. However, NiNsee is known more for its national remembrance commemoration activities on 1 July than for its research and other activities.

A third issue that makes NiNsee a contested project is the role of the media. The way the dominant media decide to report on slavery and its legacy also affects the image of NiNsee. In general the 1 July remembrance and commemoration get national and local media attention. The media also generate debates about the relevance of commemorating the abolition of slavery.

Competing narratives of these events also pervade education systems and popular culture. Though the Utrecht newspaper reported in July 1863 that 1 July would always be remembered, in reality it was not remembered in the national media for over 100 years. The media thus played a role in the institutionalized practice of the social forgetting of slavery in the Netherlands. This social forgetting was fuelled, collectively, in processes and practices prevalent across the public realm – in government, in the media and across educational institutions. It was also abundantly evident in museum exhibitions and galleries. It has analogues with similar effect in the historiographies of slavery in various nations, as reflected in the priorities assigned to research and teaching in the academy throughout the twentieth century. Social forgetting is achieved largely through the elimination of discussion of slavery from historical analysis; or through distortions, marginalization or trivialization of slavery and its importance for the growth of empire in the nation. It is also achieved by virtue of the dominant nationalist self-reference frame. In most nations that previously had colonies with enslaved populations, the media today highlights nationalist commitment to freedom, tolerance and democracy. In Great Britain this frame includes the prominent feature of the British as leaders of the abolitionist movement (see examples in Draper 2010). In the Netherlands it includes an emphasis on emancipations of various kinds (Wekker 2009). These self-images in both nations have involved systematic efforts of social forgetting (Draper 2010; Horton and Kardux 2005).

The fourth factor is the position and role of stakeholders. Who are the stakeholders and what do the stakeholders want NiNsee to do? This question is worth posing for the sake of public history. We have argued elsewhere that until about a decade ago the issue of slavery on the one hand, and the commemoration and remembrance of Dutch involvement in the Atlantic slavery in the Netherlands on the other, was history. It was *history* in the sense that it was taken for granted that 'only' formal historians, and perhaps only the marginal among them, should be preoccupied with the issue of slavery. However, as we have narrated above and as will become clear below, slavery became *a history* when a group of people, predominantly Dutch citizens of Surinamese and Antillean origin, asked the Dutch state for a place and a monument to facilitate their Atlantic slavery commemoration and remembrance 'rituals'. In other words, the issue of the request for a slavery monument, and the resistance and negative response to it from sections of the population, brought the parallel histories and intertwined belonging of Dutch social formation to the forefront (Willemsen and Nimako 2007 and 2008).

For a long time in the Netherlands, it was taken for granted that the Atlantic 'slave' trade and slavery had taken place long ago in distant countries; Africa, the Caribbean, and the Americas. The Afro-Dutch community was the seedbed for the development of organizations in the major cities of Amsterdam, Rotterdam and The

Hague that organized events on 1 July with the primary objective of commemorating the legacy of slavery and celebrating its abolition.

The fifth issue that NiNsee has to deal with is the role of the Black communities across the diaspora. Developments in the Netherlands do not take place in isolation. At the start of the twenty-first century in Great Britain and the Netherlands (as well as elsewhere in the West) multiple groups and movements continue to be active in separate, but overlapping spheres, with regard to their collective memories of slavery, its legacy, and the relationship of both to the widespread racial inequality and racism that are endemic in former slave-trading nations. This is also clearly the case in the United States and in the Caribbean.

Specifically, these activities articulate different understandings of the nature of slavery and its legacy; different understandings of why the 'slave' trade and slavery were legally abolished; and different understandings of the social conditions that followed legal abolition, particularly for the previously enslaved. They also embrace fundamentally different understandings of conditions that developed after the former British and Dutch colonies became independent (including migration to Europe); and of the relationship between slavery and contemporary racial inequality and racisms. The differences between these groups are fundamental, and highly consequential; access of these groups to political and social power, and to knowledge production, is extremely unequal; and the implications for social action are also markedly divergent.

Like the reparations movement, the remembrance and commemoration movement, is located in Black communities across the diaspora, from Great Britain and the Netherlands to the Caribbean and the United States. It is the movement that has most consistently recognized slavery and its legacies. These activities were most frequently confined to Black communities and their organizations, though increasingly, in the latter decades of the twentieth century, they forced themselves into the broader public realm, and into the political arena. Despite the harsh realities and consequences of racial inequality, and despite the daily necessity of confronting racial discrimination in immigration, employment, education and housing, Black communities of African descent across the diaspora remembered and commemorated slavery and its legal abolition from the day it happened (Sivanandan 1990; Willemsen 2006a; Brundage 2005; Clark 2005).

Across the many nations with Black populations that are the descendants of the enslaved, Black community organizations, including churches, educational groups, and community support groups, play a central role. Such activities have galvanized Black communities in various ways, including spiritual uplift, as they remembered their ancestors, confronted daily racism, and planned for the future. Across these nations, the exchange of diasporic resources – of ideas, ideologies, institutions (e.g. civil rights, Black nationalism, Black power, the Rastafari movement) and a range of cultural forms, such as music, literature, performance and dance – were and are central. These activities, with one or two exceptions, have remained marginalized in the academic literature on 'race and ethnic relations', and a full accounting of these groups, organizations and the wide range of their activities has yet to be undertaken.

These efforts to raise discussions about slavery – and to move discussions out of the realm of the Black community and into the larger public realm and to white populations – have increasingly gained strength, invigoration and support from diasporic exchange. There has been a much longer history in the United States, and activities are becoming evident in other nations across Europe, especially those with colonial legacies, such as France (Hine, Keaton and Small 2009). Such exchanges involve information, literature, insights and analysis, and take the form of symposia and conferences, some directly about slavery and its legacies, others about racial discrimination (for example, the United Nations Conference on Racism in Durban). They are not exclusively formal exchanges, but also involve significant consciousness-raising via music, art and performance.

Finally, international relations also affect the existence of NiNsee. For one thing, the UN conference on racism accelerated the erection of the National Slavery Monument. Additionally, as we noted above, when Glenn Willemsen became the first director of NiNsee he received invitations from various institutions across the country to give lectures on the Dutch involvement in the Atlantic 'slave' trade and slavery. He also received several invitations from institutions and universities across the globe either to take part in conferences or to give lectures on behalf of NiNsee. This trend has continued. NiNsee staff have become part of an international network that deals with slavery in various ways.

MUSEUMS AND GALLERIES

We have seen that museums, galleries and other institutions involved in the heritage of slavery have until recently presented and represented items associated with slavery, but without addressing slavery or its implications directly; or they have focused on slavery but without addressing the people enslaved. Heritage movements across nations that had large enslaved populations have created sites such as museums and tourist attractions that celebrate the spoils of slavery and/or empire (for Britain, see Coombes 1994; for the United States see Eichstedt and Small 2002). In recent decades, several commentators have criticised museums for their lack of attention to slavery and the 'slave' trade, and for their stereotypical representations of Africa and black people (Gifford et al. 1989; Small 1994c; Willemsen 2006a). Others have commented on the black people depicted in paintings and portraits in Britain in the eighteenth century, including some who occupied an ambiguous status between servant and enslaved person (Dabydeen 1992).

In the Netherlands, many museums possess objects, artefacts and art acquired during the period of slavery and the 'slave' trade (Legêne and Waaldijk 2007). These buildings, and others, also reveal an impressive range of architecture inspired by the Dutch colonies in the Caribbean, Suriname and in the Dutch East Indies. Many large houses were funded with the finances accrued during the 'slave' trade, slavery and empire. Many objects and artefacts in them came from similar sources. And many of the significant maritime buildings in the Netherlands (in Middleburg, for example) came into existence as a result of operations and trade directly and indirectly related to slavery. Some of the most important museums and exhibitions highlight acquisitions, art or architecture made during the so-called 'Golden Age' of the Dutch Empire – a period during which Dutch artistic expression reached a peak, both at home and abroad, while at the same time the Dutch were expanding their involvement in capturing and transporting hundreds of thousands of Africans into slavery.

In the majority of these institutions the issue of slavery and the 'slave' trade is currently avoided, or is addressed in an obtuse or highly circumscribed manner. There are some signs that one or two initiatives have broken through this previously impenetrable barrier. For example, a tiny number of museums, activities, galleries and exhibitions address slavery and the slave trade directly. For example, the Tropical Museum (KIT) in Amsterdam organized a small exhibition of photographs in 2003 called 'Sporen van Slavenhandel' ('Traces of the Slave Trade') which made reference to the 140th anniversary of the abolition of Dutch slavery. The Amsterdam Historical Museum organized an exhibition on sugar in 2005/6, in which marginal reference was made to slavery in Suriname. NiNsee, while not officially a museum, and lacking the artefacts typically held in mainstream museums, offers a permanent exhibition on slavery and a range of temporary exhibitions. There have also emerged recently several monuments to slavery in addition to the Nationaal Monument Slavernijverleden; for example, there is one in Middleburg, a town that played a significant role in the 'slave' trade (Horton and Kardux 2005). But taken collectively, these exhibitions and museums barely begin to scratch the surface. The Netherlands is a nation with several hundred museums, and it has the potential for a wide range of activities.

Due to dramatic social transformations – since the 1950s in the United States, the 1980s in Britain, and from the turn of the present century in the Netherlands – that have pushed discussion of slavery more and more into the public arena, we can now discern two trends operating side by side: the long-established trend in which mention of slavery is omitted or ignored; and the more recent trend in which slavery is directly and explicitly addressed. In the first of these trends, a small number of museums and collections display the physical remnants of slavery, such as chains, clothes and pottery, but, with few exceptions, they tend to highlight the magnificence, grandeur and originality of the historical architecture, the beauty of the gardens, the elegance and mores of historical white elites' lifestyles – with some attention to their gendered nature (Wallace 2006; Oostindie 2001) – and the originality, authenticity and beauty of cultural artefacts.

In Britain, foremost amongst those sites that follow the newer trend and are explicit on slavery was the Atlantic Slave Trade Gallery that opened at the Merseyside Maritime Museum in 1994 (Tibbles 1994; Small 1997). In 2007, its collections were expanded, it moved to a bigger location and it became the International Slavery Museum, which includes a Centre for the Study of International Slavery (in conjunction with the University of Liverpool). The museum now explores not only transatlantic slavery, but slavery in other times and places, including 'modern slavery'. There are plans in progress for further expansion. This is the first and only permanent museum in Britain dedicated to slavery and its legacies (though the Wilberforce House Museum in Hull also addresses these issues). The initial intent in Liverpool had been to focus exclusively on the 'slave' trade. But this changed fundamentally. The far broader nature and framing of the issues when the Atlantic Slave Trade Gallery opened in 1994 – covering life in Africa, a wide range of aspects of slavery, and especially the legacies of slavery, including reparations – occurred primarily because of active involvement in the project by Black organizations from Liverpool and elsewhere (Small 1997; Tibbles 1994).

Since that time, other (mainly temporary) exhibitions and galleries on slavery have been started: in London, for example, at the British Museum, the London Docklands Museum, and the Horniman Museum; and in Birmingham, Manchester and Lancaster. The activities at the Wilberforce House Museum have also been expanded. The British Empire and Commonwealth Museum, which opened in 2002, addresses these issues (Wallace 2006).

A far wider range of museums and galleries in Britain than ever before now mounts exhibitions on slavery. Some stately homes have also begun to address the ways in which slavery contributed to family wealth, social status and the acquisition of objects (e.g. Harewood House in the north of England). In Britain, museum activities were given added impetus during 2007, which was the 200th anniversary of the abolition of the slave trade in the British Empire (Littler and Naidoo 2005; Tulloch 2005; Monteiro 2009).

REPARATIONS

Though Elout van Soeterwoude, as we have seen in previous chapters, seems to have been the first person to raise the issue of reparations in relation to Dutch slavery, the subject has been largely absent from public debate in the Netherlands until very recently.

The demand for reparations has been stridently articulated in Britain for at least 20 years (Small 1994b; Brennan 2004, 2005 and 2008), and has increasingly been expressed in the Netherlands over the course of the last ten years, in both cases drawing heavily on movements in the United States (Munford 1996; Henry 2007). In both nations it has had a significant presence in Black communities, with only intermittent attention in the public domain: in Britain, for example, when the member of parliament Bernie Grant took up the issue in the 1990s; and in the Netherlands as part of the movement to memorialize slavery (which was itself closely intertwined with efforts to combat racial discrimination) in the 1980s and 1990s.

In 2000 an Afro-Dutch lawyer of Surinamese origin, André Haakmat, published an article entitled: 'Wiedergutmachung' ook voor slavernij' ('Compensation also for slavery') in the periodical *Contrast*. The article was written in response to the Van Kamenade

Commission report on the compensation for Jews by the Dutch state during the Second World War. Part of the article read as follows:

> if any group has the right to apology and financial reparations from the Dutch government, then it is descendants of slaves from Suriname, the Antilles and Aruba ... No reasonable person can deny the suffering of the Jews during the Second World War ... I do not see why the Dutch government should limit 'the past' to fifty years back from now. I find it justified that the descendants of slaves get compensation from the Dutch state for the injustice that has been done to their ancestors. (*Contrast*, 10 February 2000, Forum Utrecht)

The reparations issue was forced into the public realm on several occasions. For example, in the Black community a conference on reparations was organized by NiNsee in 2003 (Horton and Kardux 2005). Several events around reparations have taken place recently, the topic is being discussed in the public realm far more than ever before, and all indications are that it has gained a sufficient level of attraction to generate continued interest across a range of organizations and media. For example, two events on reparations for the descendants of the enslaved in the Dutch colonies took place in Amsterdam in June 2010. At the first of these, specially invited guests, representing organizations across the Netherlands, and from Suriname, the United States and France, met for an evening of discussion and fundraising.

The following day, a one-day international symposium was organized. Both events took place at Vereniging Ons Suriname (Union of Surinamese in the Netherlands), a long-established community organization. A series of papers were presented on a range of topics, and a new book on reparations was announced. The book, *Herstelbetalingen (Reparations)* by Armand Zunder, who also presented a paper at the event, had been publically launched the week before. In it Zunder provides an economic analysis of the profits acquired during slavery in Suriname, and calculates the cost of reparations at 50 billion euros. The book, and the symposium, received significant press attention in the Netherlands.

The reparations movement focuses on the issue of financial reparations and restitution for the descendants of the victims of slavery. It argues that the substantial profits garnered from slavery and the 'slave' trade, and invested in Britain and the Netherlands, led to benefits primarily for Europeans, and to costs primarily for

Africans; that these profits and losses can be calculated accurately; and that compensation in the form of financial reparations should be paid to Africans and their descendants across the diaspora. It points to similar payments of financial reparations to other groups who have been historically oppressed, including the Jews, and the Japanese in the United States. While most branches of this movement call for financial reparations, others call for other forms of restitution, including education and training.

Another element of reparations is the contention that museums across Britain and the Netherlands have plundered precious commodities, jewels and artefacts during slavery, that are now on exhibit, and that these items should be returned to their rightful owners (Small 1994b). Again, advocates of these actions point to the struggles for the return of artefacts in other national contexts, e.g. Egyptian demands upon British and German museums (for example, for Britain to return the Elgin Marbles). And while the topic of reparations was flagrantly absent from the academic literature on slavery and the 'slave' trade in both nations until very recently, the issue of profits has constantly been there, with most analysts coming down on the side of minimum profits (for Great Britain see the overview in Draper 2010, who argues against the main trend; for the Netherlands, see Emmer 2006).

Demands for reparations in Great Britain and the Netherlands draw on the long historical precedents that have existed across the diaspora, especially in the United States and the British Caribbean, dating as far back as the mid 1800s (Winbush 2003; Munford 1996). In these nations, black thinkers and leaders and those involved in movements for racial equality demanded reparations; but they did not have the necessary political power or knowledge to carry such demands into a broader public domain. But in the second half of the twentieth century, with the emergence of the Civil Rights Movement and Black Nationalism in the United States, and with large-scale migration of blacks from the Caribbean to Europe, demands for reparations have received renewed vigour (Henry 2007; Small 1994c). Bernie Grant was responsible for moving reparations into the public realm in Britain in the 1990s. As founder of the African Reparations Movement: UK branch, he was involved in international conferences on the topic (notably in Jamaica and Nigeria), made a series of public statements on the issue, which garnered substantial press attention, and raised the matter several times in the House of Commons. He coordinated the activities of several Black organizations, organized meetings and events, a series of press statements and information leaflets, and recruited black scholars to undertake lectures on reparations throughout Britain, in particular at British universities, in the early 1990s. Scholars such as Stephen Small were also recruited to undertake work on museum artefacts associated with slavery. Grant also worked alongside Lord Gifford, QC on these issues.

ANNIVERSARIES AND APOLOGIES

The trend towards celebrating anniversaries and issuing apologies is a recent development, having begun mainly in the last 15 years, with examples in Great Britain, the United States and, much more recently, with signs that it is taking roots and emerging in the Netherlands.

Apologies (or expressions of regret, or remorse) have occurred in the public realm, amongst politicians, public officials and the leaders of churches and large corporations. There have been formal apologies in the United States and in Britain. Anniversaries and apologies typically involve formal acknowledgement of slavery, or the 'slave' trade, and its abolition, and ceremonies attended by politicians and other dignitaries and the public. These activities are sometimes accompanied by religious commemorations and calls for redemption. It is a trend that involves ephemeral and uneven acknowledgments at the local, regional or national level of the facts of slavery and its abolition. While the official events are largely led by whites, the religious commemorations are largely led by blacks. The largest anniversary events to date occurred in Britain in 2007, the 200th anniversary of the abolition of the slave trade (Monteiro 2009).

In 1999, the Liverpool City Council formally apologized for its involvement in slavery and the 'slave' trade. It also promised to work with Black communities and others in Liverpool to tackle racial inequality (Christian 2007). In 2007, the then mayor of London, Ken Livingston, formally apologized for slavery and the 'slave' trade and called on the British government to do the same. A formal apology also came from the Church of England. The British prime minister, Tony Blair, expressed 'deep sorrow and regret' but did not go as far as a formal apology, though the Archbishop of York, Dr John Sentamu (himself an African) indicated that Britain should have gone further and set a higher standard.

There have not yet been any formal apologies for slavery or the 'slave' trade from officials or government in the Netherlands, though

Black organizations have called for them (as well as for reparations) (see Horton and Kardux 2005). To date, the involvement of city and national government representatives in the 1 July ceremonies in Amsterdam, celebrating Slavery Emancipation Day, which began in the early 2000s, come closest to expressions of sorrow from senior officials. There have been some expressions of regret and remorse by officials. In 2001, during the United Nations Durban conference dealing with racism, the minister for urban policy and integration, Rogier van Boxtel, expressed deep remorse, but stopped short of saying sorry. In 1 July 2008, at the Emancipation Day Activities in Oosterpark, the Dutch prime minister, Jan Peter Balkenende, called slavery 'a shameful episode in our history, a stain on the country's character'.

It should be noted that the idea that slavery was 'a shameful episode in our history, a stain on the country's character' conveys the message that this was just a brief episode; we should forget about it, turn quickly to another page and move on. But this is not the case; the period of modern Dutch state involvement in the Atlantic slavery (circa 300 years) was longer than the period that has elapsed since the legal abolition of slavery (circa 150 years).

It would be more appropriate to call this trend 'anniversaries and the expressions of regret', because activities of this kind rarely include a formal apology – primarily because that might lead to the question of financial obligations and reparations. Instead they provide the first steps that might lead to symbolic reconciliation. While many people have welcomed expressions of regret and apologies for slavery, many others – especially black people and Black organizations – have asked why the apologies have not led to action to combat the legacy of slavery (Christian 2007). The next major anniversary in the Netherlands will occur in 2013 (the 150th anniversary of the abolition of slavery in that nation). A series of activities, from a range of groups, is being planned across the nation, with NiNsee taking the lead nationally. It is highly likely that demands for apologies (and no doubt for reparations) from Black organizations will emerge as part of these plans.

The ways in which these processes unfold, and their impact on societies at large, reflect the highly divergent access of contemporary racial and national groups to knowledge production and political power. At the present time there remains a continuing struggle in the realm of ideology and collective memory among the groups we have just described. It is a struggle that continues to be waged in multiple arenas, from exhibitions, galleries and museums to monuments and memorials; and from government, politics and education to television, the press and the internet. Although the power imbalances among these groups are evident, the outcomes are far from clear.

What all of this means, as we stated at the start of this chapter, is that the main legacy of slavery is emancipation as unfinished business. For far too long the issues of slavery and the 'slave' trade – how they started and how they ended; the meaning of legal abolition and the unfulfilled conditions of full emancipation; and the legacy of slavery throughout the Netherlands, Europe, the Western world – the entire world in fact – have been marginalized. That is now changed for good. Now that Black communities – black citizens of the Netherlands and other nations – are here to stay, they have pushed the issues into the public space, and made it clear that despite any discomfort or upset, they insist on a full, more accurate story being told; and they insist that questions of legacy and questions of reparations must be addressed. Though the outcome of all this is by no means certain, it is certain that the question is here to stay.

7
Conclusion: Parallel Histories and Intertwined Belonging

In this book we have interrogated the relationship between slavery, legal abolition and emancipation. We have identified the links between the transatlantic 'slave' trade, state formation and international trade with Europe and Asia. We have also demonstrated that from the point of view of social formation, issues related to the demographic composition of contemporary Dutch society, memory, belonging and taste are inextricably intertwined with the history and culture of slavery and racism. This in turn has given rise to public and academic discussions about the relevance and appropriateness of a slavery monument, a slavery institute, and, more importantly, about the place of slavery in the Dutch historical and cultural canon.

SOME CONCLUSIONS

Four conclusions can be drawn from this book. The first is that Atlantic slavery was an integral part of state formation in the Netherlands and many other important parts of Europe. Several of the treaties that shaped the formation of some of the major European states in the seventeenth and eighteenth centuries were tied to the control of, or negotiation about, the Atlantic 'slave' trade and slavery system. We can think here, for example, of the treaties of Westphalia, Breda, Rijswijk and Utrecht.

The sustainability of European states depended on the capacity of the leaders of a country to mobilize their citizens, physically, legally, diplomatically and morally, and to defend their countries. Where the mobilization of citizens was not enough, leaders of such countries turned to the annexation or colonization of other peoples' lands and the subjugation of other peoples to *supplement* their own citizens. In the seventeenth, eighteenth and nineteenth centuries in Europe, any respectable country had to have a king; in turn any respectable king had to have a formal or informal colony based on enslaved labour. We speak here of 'formal and informal colonies based on enslaved labour' because even where the notion of slavery was not formally used, subjugated and colonized peoples suffered from coerced and forced labour. As the power of European citizens increased, the appetite for colonies by European kings also increased; after all in the colonies a king did not need to share power with his subjects. On the contrary the king could give the citizens part of the booty. Atlantic slavery thus contributed to massive migration from Europeans to the Atlantic world.

The Atlantic 'slave' trade and slavery were systemic and pervaded several European countries for several hundred years. The long period of colonialism and imperialism that followed the legal abolition of slavery maintained similarly racialized power relations, structures and institutions. These social formations also framed migration to and settlement in the Netherlands by the descendants of the formerly enslaved. And it was the migration of these groups that led to social demands for acknowledgement, remembrance and commemoration of the abolition of slavery, and to discussions about reparations. Thus, just as the legal abolition of Dutch slavery was influenced by developments in Britain, so did the efforts of the Black community in the Netherlands put the Dutch slavery legacy on the political agenda. In other words, the Black community brought the discourse on the legacy of slavery into the public domain and simultaneously gave it an emotional charge.

The second conclusion is that Atlantic slavery has had an enormous influence on the world economy, and the role of Europe within it. The Atlantic economy became complementary to the Asian and European economies. These 'three economies' created the vast network of relations that constitute the global world economy as we understand it in the twenty-first century. The horrors of slavery find their expression in the production processes. These entailed repression, pacification and resistance. Repression implies the violence of coerced labour and whipping; pacification implies the use of Christianity selectively to persuade the enslaved to accept their status as being in accordance with God's wishes; resistance implies escaping enslavement or adopting survival strategies in the context of enslavement.

After the colonization of the Americas, some of the goods the enslaved produced in the Americas, including silver, were transported around the world, especially to Asia, to reinforce trade and strengthen European states. This transportation in turn facilitated the European colonization, first of Asia, and later of Africa. Equally important to note is that one of the legacies of the Atlantic slavery in the world economy is that the goods the enslaved produced – sugar, coffee, tobacco, cotton – have shaped the tastes of consumers around the world and influenced fashion in Europe. This wider array of institutional dynamics has been absolutely central to the unfolding of slavery, legal abolition and its legacies in the twenty-first century.

The third conclusion is that slavery gave rise to parallel histories and intertwined belonging. These parallel histories and intertwined belonging in turn gave rise to different understandings and notions of freedom and emancipation. For the enslaver and the nations that enslaved others, freedom frequently implied the freedom to enslave others; for the enslaved, freedom frequently meant finding a place that they could call home without being hunted and dehumanized and humiliated.

In the context of Dutch history, we have different emancipation trajectories, namely, religion, class, gender and race – though race is downplayed as an intellectual and state project. This makes the analysis of trajectories of emancipation incomplete, state formation Eurocentric, and social thought particularistic. The legal abolition of slavery also made citizenship (as opposed to occupying a common space) an intertwined belonging and parallel memories (as opposed to having different experiences) parallel histories.

This brings us to our fourth and final conclusion, namely, knowledge production on the Atlantic 'slave' trade and slavery, has to this day been partial, distorted and too heavily based on narrow interpretations of archival data. European universalism and Eurocentrism emerged out of Atlantic colonization and slavery. Recall that Africans were free people, who, through abduction, captivity and torture, became unfree people through enslavement. This process has been narrowly classified as the Atlantic 'slave' trade in European historiography. One of the implications of such a classification is that it avoids acknowledgment of the far wider role that transatlantic slavery played in forging state formations and international trade across the oceans linking Europe, Africa, the Americas and Asia. In this book we have raised these questions consistently, so as to open up those connections for interrogation and analysis. One of our goals is to ensure that in future analyses of transatlantic slavery, these issues will be brought to the foreground, rather than being left in the background.

A key aspect of knowledge production, as we have also argued in this book, has to do with what kinds of knowledge are regarded as valid, and what as invalid. For example, career historians have always depended on archive material for their narratives of slavery, and even of its legacies. While we recognize that, to a certain degree, this is laudable, in this book we insist that career historians do not (and should not) have the last word on human histories. It is clear that the scope of Atlantic slavery goes far beyond the archives, in large part because academic narratives also are shaped by power, 'culture', and self-image (Trouillot 1995). Recall once more that one of the main organizing principles of the transatlantic 'slave' trade and slavery was race. Following Fanon, Gordon has noted that racism requires the rejection of another human being's humanity. However since the other human being is a human being, such a rejection is a contradiction of reality (Gordon 1995 and 2000). The information on the 'slave' trade and slavery in the archives was obtained and preserved for a variety of purposes, including maintaining the racial hierarchy, and can therefore be used for the study of social formation – the road to multi-racial societies and how they came about.

Not everything is in the archives. Living people and their memories are not in the archives; that is why the dominant narratives, especially state-sanctioned narratives, are constantly being challenged, contested, contradicted and negated. For instance, in the English-speaking world one can make an analytical distinction between the concepts of 'slave' and 'enslaved'. This has not come about as a result of semantics; it reflects the nature and process of knowledge production. *And it has real consequences.* For example, the term 'slave' was imposed on captives who resisted captivity and enslavement (Rodney 1974).

Not only does the Dutch master narrative lack the analytical distinction, between 'slave' and 'enslaved', it also rejects the concept of race. It is taken for granted that in some distant past, perhaps during slavery and colonialism, there were racist people, but that since the Second World War, as if by some magic, racism has more or less vanished. The words 'race' and 'racism' have no place in the Dutch lexicon or in Dutch society. Any attempt to bring up the issues of race and racism is seen, at best, as looking for problems where none exist, with the express purpose of disturbing the social cohesion; or, at worst, as a fabrication – emotional, subjective and imaginary.

These narrow parameters of knowledge production are now challenged to a point at which they must break down. As the descendants of enslaved people gain more freedom and education, as they continue to enter the institutions of education and knowledge production, and as they exchange ideas and insights across the diaspora, they question the knowledge that has been produced about them by the enslavers and their descendants. In large numbers, they insist that the prevailing interpretations of the causes and consequences of the legal abolition of the 'slave' trade and slavery – especially those produced by career historians – are deficient. For example, in the Netherlands there is a tendency in the academic literature, and in the popular social imaginary (as reflected in collective movements), to represent the legal abolition of the 'slave' trade and slavery as single events; as events that led to consequential and immediately beneficial changes in the lives of the enslaved; and to represent legal abolition as resulting from the morality and magnanimity of the Dutch (with some encouragement from the British). This approach emphasizes specific years – 1814 for the legal abolition of the slave trade; 1863 for the legal abolition of slavery. And it gives rise to the impression that the Dutch government's involvement in the slave trade and slavery ended point blank. Overall, these narratives marginalize the actions and agency of the enslaved in bringing about legal emancipation. They ignore the fact that black people – enslaved, Maroon and legally free – fought slavery from its inception; and that the history of slavery can in fact be told as a history of resistance (Small and Walvin 1994)

These collective representations are both incomplete and far from accurate. In fact the 'slave' trade and slavery were officially abolished in each nation in a series of stages, over the course of many decades; and legal abolition did not lead to full emancipation in the sense of legal, political, economic and social freedom for the formerly enslaved. Instead, slavery continued for a significant period of time after legal abolition of the 'slave' trade – often resulting in changed and frequently worse conditions for the enslaved, including great brutality. And the conditions of servitude immediately after slavery closely resembled slavery in all but legal name, and involved exploitation, oppression and domination, legally, politically, economically and socially. In both Britain and the Netherlands, systems of 'apprenticeship' were first put in place, even before legal freedom was allowed. Racial discrimination and the institutional power of the master enslavers continued to deny black people access to material resources, political power, social equity or social honour. Gender discrimination was a central facet of all these activities, and women faced greater obstacles than men in their efforts to enjoy the fruits of legal abolition.

Rather than resulting from an unequivocal moral imperative, a closer investigation demonstrates that defiance and resistance by the enslaved, social mobilization in Europe and the changing economic interests of the colonial nations, in conjunction with political rivalries between European nations (and the United States), collectively led to legal abolition. After legal abolition, the governments of these nations for lengthy periods continued their illicit trade in enslaved persons, giving sustenance to, and making profit from, other nations that continued to embrace slavery. In other words, a formal legal abolition that is typically regarded as having led to full emancipation for the enslaved, and as having been motivated by morality and immediately consequential, is more accurately understood as a piecemeal and incremental legal measure that did not put an end to British and Dutch complicity in slavery and did not lead to full emancipation. Emancipation was not achieved. And emancipation remains unfinished. The immediate consequences of unfinished emancipation were the maintenance of long-entrenched racialized and gendered systems of inequality and political power. Amongst other things, the unequal access to power that followed slavery ensured that it was the former master enslavers – and the white elites in the metropolises of each empire – who were most able to portray their version of how slavery had ended, and of the meaning and significance of the legacy of slavery. This is why emancipation remains an unfinished business, even today. Especially today.

A FINAL NOTE

With regard to citizenship, knowledge production and unfinished emancipation, we must note one final important issue. That has to do with how the migration of Surinamese to the Netherlands transformed their status from being colonial subjects to being fully fledged Dutch citizens. This in turn has brought the issue of memory and social forgetting of slavery to the foreground of Dutch life and public discussion. It is most vividly represented in the mobilization that led to the unveiling of the National Slavery Monument and the establishment of NiNsee. These two developments resulted directly from the migration of Surinamese to the Netherlands. They also reflect increasing communication across the diaspora by the descendants of the enslaved, from Suriname to the Caribbean, and from the United States and Britain to the Netherlands. Whereas in the past we had overwhelming silence, today we have multiple voices competing to be heard.

Contrary to what some 'frontier historiographers' argue, we are of the opinion that a full and complete study of Dutch Atlantic slavery is in its infancy. By 'frontier historiographers' we mean those who assume that research work on the Atlantic 'slave' trade and slavery is exhausted, so that 'we' should now turn 'our' attention to other slaveries – for example, Arab slavery, African slavery, Indian Ocean slavery. We reject this view and this book challenges it. Instead we call for greater interrogation of the knowledge that has been produced on the 'slave' trade, slavery and their connections with state formation in Europe. We call for greater interrogation of the systems of trade and economics across Europe, the Americas, Africa and Asia that emerged out of the 'slave' trade and slavery. And we insist that Dutch historiography is now opened up to critique and re-examination by a more broadly based set of scholars and analysts than ever before. We believe that since the migration of Surinamese to the Netherlands, and since the active mobilization of the other groups mentioned in this book, these developments are now fully under way. Only with the continuation of these developments will full emancipation ever be achieved.

Bibliography

Abu-Lughod, J. (1989) *Before European Hegemony: The World System AD 1250–1350* (New York: Oxford University Press).
Adelheid, R.M. and Hoefte, L. (1996) *Plantation Labor after the Abolition of Slavery: The Case of Plantation Marienburg (Suriname), 1880–1940* (Ann Arbor: University of Michigan).
Akkerman, T. and Stuurman, S. (1998) *Perspectives on Feminist Political Thought in European History: From the Middle Ages to the Present* (London: Routledge).
Allen, R., Heijes, C. and Marcha, V. (eds) (2003) *Emancipatie en acceptatie : Curaçao en Curaçaoënaars: beeldvorming en identiteit honderdveertig jaar na de slavernij* (Utrecht: SWP).
Amin, S. (1974) *Accumulation on a World Scale: A Critique of the Theory of Underdevelopment* (New York: Monthly Review Press).
—— (1989) *Eurocentricism* (New York: Monthly Review Press).
Anderson, B.R.O. (1983) *Imagined Communities* (New York: Verso).
Ansell, A.E. (1997) *New Right, New Racism. Race and Reaction in the United States and Britain* (New York: New York University Press).
Araujo, M. and Rodriguez Maeso, S. (2010) 'History Textbooks, Racism and the Critique of Eurocentrism: Beyond Rectification or Compensation' (unpublished, University of Coimbra, Portugal).
Arrighi, G. (1994) *The Long Twentieth Century: Money, Power and the Origins of Our Times* (London: Verso).
—— (2006) *Adam Smith in Beijing: Lineages of the Twenty-First Century* (London: Verso).
Asante, M.K. (2007) *An Afrocentric Manifesto: Toward an African Renaissance*. (Cambridge: Polity Press).
AWAD (2009) *The Atlantic World and the Dutch 1500–2000: A Mutual Heritage Project* (KITLV Press: Leiden).
Bales, K. (1999) *Disposable People: New Slavery in the Global Economy* (Berkeley: University of California Press).
Banton, M. (1977) *The Idea of Race* (London: Tavistock).
Beckles, H. (1990) *A History of Barbados: From Amerindian Settlement to Nation-State* (Cambridge: Cambridge University Press).
Berlin, I. (1998) *Many Thousands Gone: The First Two Centuries of Slavery in North America* (Cambridge: The Belknap Press of Harvard University Press).
—— (2003) *Generations of Captivity: A History of African-American Slaves* (Cambridge: Harvard University Press).
Bernal, M. (ed.) (1987) *Black Athena: Afro-Asiatic Roots of Classical Civilization, vol.1: The Fabrication of Ancient Greece 1785–1985* (London: Free Association Books).
Blackburn, R. (2011) *The American Crucible: Slavery, Emancipation and Human Rights* (London: Verso).
Blakely, A. (1993) *Blacks in the Dutch World: The Evolution of Racial Imagery in a Modern Society* (Bloomington: Indiana University Press).

Blight, D. (2001) *Race and Reunion: The Civil War in American History* (Cambridge: The Belknap Press of Harvard University Press).
Blumrosen, A.W. and Blumrosen, R. (2005) *Slave Nation: How Slavery United the Colonies and Sparked the American Revolution* (Napperville: Sourcebooks).
Boahen, A.A. (1966) *Topics in West African History* (London: Longman).
Boomgaard, P. and Oostindie, G.J. (1989) 'Changing Sugar Technology and the Labour Nexus: The Caribbean, 1750–1900', *Nieuwe West-Indische Gids*, 63(1/2).
Brennan, F. (2004) 'Reparations and Human Rights', in Anker, C. van den and Smith, R. (eds) *The Essential Guide to Human Rights* (Hodder Arnold)
—— (2005) 'Are Reparations for Slavery Justified?', Human Rights Global Focus Group, International Human Rights Foundation, India, 3(1) (March).
—— (2008) 'Race, Rights Reparations: Exploring a Reparation Framework for Addressing Trade Inequality', *Hamline Journal of Public Law and Policy*, 30(1) (Fall).
Brundage, W.F. (2005) *The Southern Past: A Clash of Race and Memory* (Cambridge, Mass. and London: Belknap Press of Harvard University Press).
Buddingh, H. (1995) *Geschiedenis van Suriname: een complete, uiterst leesbare geschiedenis van Suriname, van de oorspronkelijke, Indiaanse bewoners tot de plurale samenleving van nu* (Utrecht: Spectrum).
Buiting, H. (1990) 'The Netherlands', in van der Linden, M. and Rojahn, J. (eds) *The Formation of Labour Movements 1870–1914: An International Perspective*, vols 1 and 2 (Leiden: E.J. Brill).
Butler, K.M. (1995) *The Economics of Emancipation: Jamaica and Barbados* (Chapel Hill, N.C. and London: University of North Carolina Press).
Campbell, H. (1985) *Rasta and Resistance: From Marcus Garvey to Walter Rodney* (London: Hansib Publication).
Césaire, A. (1972[1950]) *Discourse on Colonialism* (New York: Monthly Review Press).
Chomsky, N. (1993) 'World Orders, Old and New', in *Facing the Challenge: Responses to the Report of the South Commission* (Geneva: South Centre).
Christian, M. (2007) 'The Age of Slave Apologies: The Case of Liverpool, England', 14 November 2007, keynote address at the International Slavery Museum, Liverpool.
Clark, K.A. (2005) *Defining Moments: African American Commemoration and Political Culture in the South, 1863–1913* (Chapel Hill, N.C.: University of North Carolina Press).
Collins, P.H. (1991) *Black Feminist Thought: Knowledge, Consciousness, and the Politics of Empowerment* (New York and London: Routledge).
Coombes, A.E. (1994) *Reinventing Africa: Museums, Material Culture and Popular Imagination in Late Victorian and Edwardian England* (New Haven and London: Yale University Press).
Dabydeen, D. (1992) 'The Role of Black People in William Hogarth's criticism of Eighteenth-Century English Culture and Society', in Gundara, J.S. and Duffield, I. (eds) *Essays on the History of Blacks in Britain* (Aldershot: Averbury).
Dantzig, A. van (1968) *Het Nederlandse aandeel in de slavenhandel* (Bussum: Fibula-Van Dishoeck).
Darwin, C.R. (1996) *The Voyage of the Beagle* (New York: Plume).
Darwin, J. (2007) *After Tamelane: The Rise and Fall of Global Empires, 1400–2000* (London: Penguin Books).

Davids, K. (2008) *The Rise and Decline of Dutch Technological Leadership: Technology, Economy and Culture in the Netherlands, 1350–1800*, vols 1 and 2 (Leiden: Brill).
—— and Noordegraaf, L. (eds) (1993) *The Dutch Economy in the Golden Age: Nine Studies* (Amsterdam: Nederlandsch Economisch-Historisch Archief).
Davidson, B. (1980) *The African Slave Trade* (London: Back Bay Books).
—— (1992) *The Black Man's Burden: Africa and the Curse of the Nation-State* (James Curry: London).
Davis, R.C. (2003) *Christian Slaves, Muslim Masters: White Slavery in the Mediterranean, the Barbary Coast, and Italy, 1500–1800* (New York: Palgrave Macmillan).
Derveld, F.E.R. and Heilbron, W. (1993) *Economic and Demographic Change in a Post-Slave Society: 1863-1920*, Research Memorandum 518, University of Groningen, Netherlands.
Desmond, A. and Moore J. (2009) *Darwin's Sacred Cause: Race, Slavery and the Quest for Human Origins* (London: Allen Lane).
Dijk, T.A. van (1993) *Elite Discourses and Racism* (Newbury Park: Sage Publications).
Donner, W.R.W. (2003) 'Enige juridische aspecten van de slavernij: rede uitgesproken voor de Surinaamse vereniging', *De Waterkant*, 9 February 2003.
—— (2009) 'Mythen over de slavernij', *Parbode*, 16 (August):19.
Dragtenstein, F. (2002) *De ondraaglijke stoutheid der wegloopers: marronage en koloniaal beleid in Suriname, 1667–1768* (Utrecht: CLACS).
—— (2004) *'Trouw aan de blanken': Quassie van Nieuw Timotibo, twist en strijd in de 18de eeuw in Suriname* (Amsterdam: KIT Publishers).
Draper, N. (2010) *The Price of Emancipation: Slave-Ownership, Compensation and British Society at the End of Slavery* (Cambridge and New York: Cambridge University Press).
Du Bois, W.E.B. (1961[1903]) *The Souls of Black Folk* (New York: Fawcett World Library).
Dunn, R. (1972) *Sugar and Slaves: The Rise of the Planter Class in the English West Indies, 1624–1713* (New York: W.W. Norton).
Dussel, E. (1985) *Philosophy of Liberation* (Eugene, Ore.: Wipf & Stock).
Eichstedt, J. and Small, S. (2002) *Representations of Slavery: Race, Ideology and Southern Plantations Museums* (Washington, D.C.: Smithsonian Institution Press).
Elliott, J.H. (2006) *Empires of the Atlantic World: Britain and Spain in America 1492–1830* (New Haven, Conn.: Yale University Press).
Eltis, D., Behrendt, S.D., Richardson, D. and Klein, H.S. (eds) (1999) *The Trans-Atlantic Slave Trade: A Database on CD ROM* (Cambridge: Cambridge University Press).
Emmer, P.C. (1993) 'Between Slavery and Freedom: The Period of Apprenticeship in Suriname (Dutch Guiana), 1863–1873', *Slavery and Abolition*, 14(1): 87–105.
—— (1998) *The Dutch in the Atlantic Economy, 1580–1880: Trade, Slavery and Emancipation*, Variorum Collected Studies Series CS614 (Farnham, Surrey: Ashgate).
—— (2000) *De Nederlandse Slavehandel 1500–1850* (Amsterdam: De Arbeiderspers).
—— (2006) *The Dutch Slave Trade 1500–1850* (trans. Chris Emery) (New York: Berghahn).
—— and Mörner, M. (eds) (1992) *European Expansion and Migration: Essays on the Intercontinental Migration from Africa, Asia and Europe* (New York: Berg).

Essed, P. (1991) *Understanding Everyday Racism: An Interdisciplinary Theory* (Newbury Park, Calif.: Sage Publications).
—— (1996) *Diversity: Gender, Color and Culture* (Amherst, Mass.: University of Massachusetts Press).
—— and Nimako, K. (2006) 'Designs and (Co)-incidents: Cultures of Scholarship and Public Policy on Immigrants/Minorities in the Netherlands', *International Journal of Comparative Sociology*, 47: 281–312.
Fogel, R.W. (1989) *Without Consent or Contract: The Rise and Fall of American Slavery* (New York: W.W. Norton).
Foner, E. (1983) *Nothing but Freedom: Emancipation and Its Legacy* (Baton Rouge: Louisiana State University Press).
—— (1998) *The Story of American Freedom* (Basic Books).
Frank, A.G. (1978) *World Accumulation, 1492–1789* (New York: Monthly Review Press).
—— (1998) *ReOrient: Global Economy in the Asian Age* (Berkeley: University of California Press).
Fryer, P. (1984) *Staying Power: The History of Black People in Britain* (London: Pluto Press).
Gellner, E. (1983) *Nations and Nationalism* (Oxford: Oxford University Press).
Gifford, A., Brown, W. and Bundy, R. (1989) 'Loosen the Shackles: First Report of the Liverpool 8 Inquiry into Race Relations in Liverpool' (The Gifford Report) (London: Karia Press).
Gilroy, P. (1993) *The Black Atlantic: Modernity and Double Consciousness* (Cambridge, Mass.: Harvard University Press).
Gobardhan-Rambocus, L. (2003) 'Berichten over de Surinaams-Creolse cultuur: hoe werd er over deze cultuur geschreven?', *Interactie*, 6 (Paramaribo, Suriname: Anton de Kom Universiteit): 3–19.
——, Maurits S.H. and Egger J. (eds) (1995) *De erfenis van de slavernij* (Paramaribo, Suriname: Anton de Kom Universiteit).
Goldberg, D.T. (1993) *Racist Culture: Philosophy and the Politics of Meaning* (Cambridge: Blackwell Publishers).
Gomes, P.D. (2003) *Over 'natuurgenooten' en 'onwillige honden' : beeldvorming als instrument voor uitbuiting en onderdrukking in Suriname 1842–1862* (Amsterdam: Aksant).
Gordon, L.R., (1995) *Fanon and the Crisis of European Man: An Essay on Philosophy and the Human Sciences* (New York: Routledge).
—— (2000) *Existentia Africana: Understanding Africana Existential Thought* (New York: Routledge).
—— (2008) *An Introduction to Africana Philosophy* (Cambridge: Cambridge University Press).
—— (2009) 'The Black, the African, and the European: Melancholic Convergence and Distinction in the Formation of Modern Reason', paper presented at the NiNsee *Symposium on Trajectories of Emancipation*, Amsterdam, 29–30 June.
Goslinga, C.C. (1985) *The Dutch in the Caribbean and in the Guianas, 1680–1791* (Assen, Netherlands: Van Gorcum).
—— (1990) *The Dutch in the Caribbean and in Surinam 1791/5–1942* (Assen: Van Gorcum).
Gossett, T. (1965) *Race: The History of an Idea in America* (New York: Schocken Books).
Gould, S.J. (1996) *The Mismeasure of Man*, 2nd edn (New York: Norton).

Greven, J. (2005) *Leren en herinneren: het Nederlandse slavernijverleden, kernleerplan 10–15 jarigen* (Enschede: Stichting Leerplanontwikkeling (SLO)).
Grever, M. and Stuurman, S. (2007) *Beyond the Canon: History for the Twenty-First Century* (New York: Palgrave Macmillan).
Groot, S.W. de (2003) *Surinam Maroon Chiefs in Africa in Search of Their Country of Origin* (Amsterdam: Silvia W. de Groot).
Grosfoguel, R. and Mielants, E. (2006) 'The Long-Durée Entanglement Between Islamophobia and Racism in the Modern/Colonial Capitalist/Patriarchal World-System: An Introduction', *Human Architecture: Journal of the Sociology of Self-Knowledge*, 5(1) (Fall): 1–12.
Haller, J.S. (1995) *Outcasts from Evolution: Scientific Attitudes of Racial Inferiority, 1859–1900* (Carbondale, Ill.: SIU Press).
Hartog, J. (1961) *History of the Netherlands Antilles* (Oranjestad, Aruba: De Wit).
Heijer, H. den (1994) *Geschiedenis van de WIC* (Zutphen: Walburg Pers).
—— (1997) *Goud, ivoor en slaven: scheepvaart en handle van de Tweede Westindische Compagnie op Afrika, 1674–1740* (Zutphen: Walburg Pers).
Helstone, H., Hove, O. ten and Hoogbergen, W. (2004) *Surinaamse Emancipatie 1863: Paramaribo: slaven en eigenaren* (Amsterdam: Rozenburg Publishers).
Henry, C. (2007) *Long Overdue: The Politics of Racial Reparations* (New York: New York University Press).
Hine, D.C., Keaton, T.D. and Small S. (eds) (2009) *Black Europe and the African Diaspora* (Champaign: University of Illinois Press).
Hochschild, A. (2005) *Bevrijd de slaven! het verhaal van de eerste mensenrechtencampagne* (trans. A. Klootwijk and E. de Boer) (Amsterdam: Meulenhoff).
—— (2006) *King Leopold's Ghost: A Story of Greed, Terror and Heroism in Colonial Africa* (London: Pan Books).
Hoetink, H. (1971) *Caribbean Race Relations: A Study of Two Variants* (Oxford, New York and London: Oxford University Press).
—— (1973) *Slavery and Race Relations in the Americas: Comparative Notes on Their Nature and Nexus* (London: Harper & Row).
Hondius, D. (2009) 'Blacks in Early Modern Europe: New Research from the Netherlands', in Hine, D.C., Keaton, T.D. and Small S. (eds) *Black Europe and the African Diaspora* (Champaign, Ill.: University of Illinois Press).
Horton, J. and Horton, L. (2005) *Slavery and the Making of America* (New York: Oxford University Press).
—— and Kardux, J.C. (2005) 'Slavery and Public Memory in the United States and the Netherlands', *New York Journal of American History*, 46(2) (Fall/Winter, 2005): 35–52.
Hove, O. ten and Dragtenstein, F. (1997) *Manumissies in Suriname, 1832–1863* (Utrecht: CLACS & IBS).
Huntington, S.P. (1993) 'The Clash of Civilizations?', *Foreign Affairs*, 72(3) (Summer): 22–49.
James, C.L.R. (1980[1938]) *The Black Jacobins: Toussaint L'Ouverture and the San Domingo Revolution* (London: Alison & Busby).
Jordan, W. (1968) *White over Black: American Attitudes towards the Negro, 1550–1812* (Chapel Hill, N.C.: University of North Carolina Press).
Jurna, N. and Accord, C. (2003) *Met eigen ogen: een hedendaagse kijk op de Surinaamse slavernij* (Amsterdam: KIT Publishers).
Kennedy, P. (1987) *The Rise and Fall of Great Powers: Economic Change and Military Conflict From 1500–2000* (New York: Random House).

Klein, A.N. (1969) 'The Atlantic Slave Trade', in Foner, L. and Genovese, E.D. (eds) *Slavery in the New World: A Reader in Comparative History* (Englewood Cliffs, N.J.: Prentice Hall).
Klooster, W. (1997) *Illicit Riches: The Dutch Trade in the Caribbean, 1648–1795* (Leiden: KITLV Press).
Kom, A. de (1999) *Wij Slaven van Suriname* (Amsterdam: Contact).
Lamur, H.E. (2001) 'The Evolution of Afro-Surinamese National Movements (1955–1995)', *Transforming Anthropology*, 10(1): 17–28.
—— (2004) *Family Name and Kinship of Emancipated Slaves in Suriname: Tracing Ancestors*, vols 1 and 2 (Amsterdam: KIT Publishers/NiNsee).
Legêne, S. and Waaldijk, B. (2007) 'Mission Interrupted: Gender, History and the Colonial Canon', in Grever, M. and Stuurman, S. (2007) *Beyond the Canon: History for the Twenty-First Century* (New York: Palgrave Macmillan).
Lijphart, A. (1968) *Verzuiling, pacificatie en kentering in de Nederlandse politiek* (Haarlem: Becht).
Littler, J. and Naidoo, R. (2005) (eds) *The Politics of Heritage: The Legacies of 'Race'* (London: Routledge).
Lovejoy P (2000) *Transformations of Slavery: A History of Slavery in Africa* (New York: Cambridge University Press).
Magubane, Z. (2006) 'Africana Sociology: A Critical Journey from Pluralism to Postcolonialism', in Zeleza, P.T. (ed.) (2006) *The Study of Africa, vol.1: Disciplinary and Interdisciplinary Encounters* (CODESRIA, Dakar 2006).
Mama, A. (2005) 'Gender Studies for Africa's Transformation', in Mkandawire, T. (ed.) *African Intellectuals: Rethinking Politics, Language, Gender and Development* (London: Zed Books).
Mamadeus, R. (2007) 'Paramaribo Post: Mythen', *Parbode*, 18 (October): 34.
Marshall, E.K. (2003) *Ontstaan en ontwikkeling van het Surinaams nationalism: natievorming als opgave* (Delft: Eboron).
Martinus, E.F. (1996) *The Kiss of a Slave: Papiamentu's West-African Connection* (dissertation) (Amsterdam: Universiteit van Amsterdam).
Martinus-Guda, T. and de Bruin, H. (2005) *Drie eeuwen banya: de geschiedenis van een Surinaamse slavendans* (Paramaribo: Ministerie van onderwijs en volksontwikkeling).
Mazrui, A.A. (2001) 'Ideology and African Political Culture', in Kiros, T. (ed.) *Explorations in African Political Thought: Identity, Community, Ethic* (New York: Routledge).
Mignolo, W. (2007) *The Darker Side of the Renaissance: Literacy, Territoriality, and Colonization* (Ann Arbor, Mich.: University of Michigan Press).
—— (2009) Epistemic Disobedience, Independent Thought and De-Colonial Freedom, *Theory, Culture and Society*, 26(7–8): 1–23.
Miles, R. (1982) *Racism and Migrant Labour* (London: Routledge & Kegan Paul).
—— and Phizacklea, A. (1984) *White Man's Country: Racism in British Politics* (London: Pluto Press).
Moitt, B. (2001) *Women and Slavery in the French Antilles, 1635–1848* (Bloomington: Indiana University Press).
Monteiro, L. (2009) 'Beyond Awareness: British Museums and "Abolition 200"', paper presented at the *Annual Meeting of the Organization of American Historians*, Seattle, Wash., 26–29 March.
Mullard, C. (1988) 'Racism, Ethnicism and Etharchy or Not? The Principles of Progressive Control and Transformative Change', in Skutnabb-Kangas, T. and

Cummins, J. (eds) *Minority Education: From Shame to Struggle* (Philadelphia: Clevedon Multilingual Matters).
——, Nimako, K. and Willemsen, G. (1990) *De plurale kubus: een vertoog over emancipatiemodellen en minderhedenbeleid* (s'Gravenhage: Warray).
Muller, J. (2008) 'Us and Them: The Enduring Power of Ethnic Nationalism', *Foreign Affairs* (New York), 87(2) (March/April): 18–35.
Munford, C.J. (1996) *Race and Reparations: A Black Perspective for the 21st Century* (Trenton, N.J. and Asmara, Eritrea: Africa World Press).
Nationaal instituut Nederlands slavernijverleden en erfenis (NiNsee) (2003) *Slavernij moment nu: gedeeld heden, verdeeld verleden* (Amsterdam: NiNsee).
Neus-van der Putten, H. (2003) *Susanna du Plessis: portret van een slavenmeesteres* (Amsterdam: KIT Publishers).
Nimako, K. (1991) *Economic Change and Political Conflict in Ghana, 1600–1990* (thesis) (Amsterdam: Amsterdam Thesis Publishers).
—— (1998) *Beyond Multiculturalisation: Amsterdam Southeast as Strategic Location* (Rotterdam: Gramo de Combinatie).
—— (2008) 'Post/Anti-Slavery Issues: Current Global Trends', paper presented at the conference *Africa: An Outlook from the Centre and Observatories*, organized by the Observatory of the African Social Reality fostered and run by the Autonomous University of Madrid and Carlos de Amberes Foundation in Madrid, 15–17 December (Madrid: Autonomous University of Madrid).
—— and Small, S. (2009) 'Theorizing Black Europe and the African Diaspora: Implications for Citizenship, Nativism and Xenophobia', in Hine, D.C., Keaton, T.D. and Small S. (eds) *Black Europe and the African Diaspora* (Champaign, Ill.: University of Illinois Press).
—— —— (2010) 'Collective Memory of Slavery in Great Britain and the Netherlands', paper presented at the *American Sociological Association Annual Conference*, 13–16 August (Atlanta, Ga.: ASA).
——, Cain, A. and Small, S. (2010) 'Enclave Formation and the Emergence of the "Black Problem" in Europe: A Preliminary Survey', paper presented at the Association of American Geographers, Washington, D.C., 14–18 April.
Omi, M. and Winant, H. (1994) *Racial Formation in the United States: From the 1960s to the 1980s* (2nd edn) (New York: Routledge).
Oostindie, G. (1989) *Roosenburg en Mon Bijou: twee Surinaamse plantages, 1720–1870* (Dordrecht: Foris).
—— (ed.) (1996) *Fifty Years Later: Antislavery, Capitalism and Modernity in the Dutch Orbit* (Leiden: Pittsburg University Press and KITLV Press).
—— (1998) *Het paradijs overzee: de 'Nederlandse' Caraïben en Nederland* (Amsterdam: Bakker).
—— (2001) *Facing up to the Past: Perspectives on the Commemoration of Slavery from Africa, the Americas and Europe* (Kingston: Ian Randle).
Page, W.F. (1997) *The Dutch Triangle: The Netherlands and the Atlantic Slave Trade, 1621–1664* (New York: Garland Publishing).
Palmer, R.R. and Colton, J. (1978) *A History of the Modern World* (New York: Alfred A. Knopf).
Paquette, R.L. and Engerman, S.L. (1996) *The Lesser Antilles in the Age of European Expansion* (Gainesville, Fla.: University Press of Florida).
Patterson, O. (1973) *The Sociology of Slavery* (London: Granada Publishing).
—— (1991) *Freedom in the Making of Western Culture* (Basic Books)

Pieterse, J.N., (1990) *Emancipation and Empire: Power and Liberation on a World Scale* (London: Pluto Press).
Poldervaart, S. (1993) *Tegen conventioneel fatsoen en zekerheid* (Amsterdam: Van Gennep).
Pomeranz, K. (2000) *The Great Divergence: China, Europe, and the Making of the Modern* (Princeton: Princeton University Press).
Popkin, J.D. (ed.) (2007) *Facing Racial Revolution: Eyewitness Accounts of the Haitian Insurrection* (Chicago: University of Chicago Press).
Postma, J.M. (1990) *The Dutch in the Atlantic Slave Trade, 1600–1815* (Cambridge: Cambridge University Press).
—— (2003) *The Atlantic Slave Trade* (Gainsville, Fla.: University Press of Florida).
—— and Enthoven, V. (2003) *Riches from Atlantic Commerce: Dutch Transatlantic Trade and Shipping, 1585–1817* (Leiden: Brill).
Quijano, A. (2000) *The Coloniality of Power, and Eurocentricism, and Latin America* (Durham, N.C.: Duke University Press).
Rego, C. do and Janga, L. (2009) *Slavery and Resistance in Curacao: The Rebellion of 1795* (Curacao: Fundashon Parke Nashonal).
Richardson, D. (ed.) (1985) *Abolition and Its Aftermath: The Historical Context, 1790–1916* (London and Totowa, N.J.: Frank Cass).
Riehecky, J. (2003) *De afschaffing van de slavernij 1863: de emancipatieproclamatie* (trans. Gert-Jan Kramer) (Harmelen: Ars Scribendi).
Robinson, R. (1972) 'Non-European Foundations of European Imperialism: Sketch for a Theory of Collaboration', in Owen, R., and Sutcliffe, B. (eds) *Studies in the Theory of Imperialism* (London: Longman).
Rodney, W. (1974) *How Europe Underdeveloped Africa* (Washington, D.C.: Howard University Press).
Sachs, W. (2009) Preface to *The Development Dictionary* (2nd edn) (London: Zed Books).
Said, E. (1978) *Orientalism* (New York: Vintage Books).
Sampson, A. (1999) *Mandela: The Authorised Biography* (London: HarperCollins).
Samsom-Rous, L. and Samsom, H. (2003) *Tree of Forgetfulness / Boom der vergetelheid / l'arbre de l'oubli / a bon fu frigiti* (Amsterdam: KIT).
Sherwood, M. (2007) *After Abolition: Britain and the Slave Trade Since 1807* (London: I.B. Tauris).
Shyllon, F. (1977) *Black People in Britain, 1553–1833,* (London: Oxford University Press).
Sivanandan, A. (1982) *A Different Hunger: Writings on Black Resistance* (London: Pluto Press).
—— (1990) *Communities of Resistance: Writings on Black Struggles for Socialism* (London: Verso).
Siwpersad, J.P. (1979) *De Nederlandse regering en de afschffing van de Surinaamse slavernij, 1833–1863* (Groningen: Bouma's Boekhuis).
Small, S. (1994a) *Racialised Barriers: The Black Experience in the United States and England* (New York and London: Routledge).
—— (1994b) 'Racist Ideologies', in Tibbles, T. (ed.) *Transatlantic Slavery: Against Human Dignity* (Liverpool: Liverpool University Press).
—— (1994c) 'The General Legacy of the Atlantic Slave Trade', in Tibbles, T. (ed.) *Transatlantic Slavery: Against Human Dignity* (Liverpool: Liverpool University Press).

—— (1997) 'Contextualizing the Black Presence in British Museums: Representations, Resources and Response', in Greenhill, E.H. (ed.) *Museums and Multiculturalism in Britain* (Leicester: Leicester University Press).
—— and Walvin, J. (1994) 'African Resistance to Enslavement', in Tibbles, T. (ed.) *Transatlantic Slavery: Against Human Dignity* (Liverpool: Liverpool University Press).
Smith, A. (1977[1776]) *The Wealth of Nations* (Harmondsworth: Penguin Books).
Smith, A.D. (1986) *The Ethnic Origins of Nations* (Oxford: Blackwell).
Stipriaan, A. van, (1989) 'The Suriname Rat Race: Labour and Technology on Sugar Plantations, 1750–1900', *Nieuwe West-Indische Gids*, 63(1/2).
—— (1993) *Surinaams contrast: roofbouw en overleven in een Caraïbische plantagekolonie 1750–1863* (2nd edn) (Leiden: KITLV Uitgeverij).
—— (1996) 'Suriname and the abolition of slavery', in Oostindie, G (ed.) *Fifty Years Later: Antislavery, Capitalism and Modernity in the Dutch Orbit* (Pittsburg and Leiden: Pittsburg University Press and KITLV Press).
—— (2005) 'Slavery in the Dutch Caribbean: The Books No One Has Read', in De Barros, J., Diptee, A. and Trotman, D.V. (eds) *Beyond Fragmentation: Perspectives on Caribbean History* (Princeton: Markus Wiener Publishers).
—— (2007) 'Disrupting the Canon: the Case of Slavery', in Grever, M. and Stuurman, S. (2007) *Beyond the Canon: History for the Twenty-First Century* (New York: Palgrave Macmillan).
Stuurman, S. (1983) *Verzuiling, Kapitalisme en Patriarchaat* (Nijmegen: SUN).
Spufford, P. (2006) 'From Antwerp and Amsterdam to London: The Decline of Financial Centres in Europe', *De Economist*, 154(2) (June): 143–75.
Temperley, H. (ed.) (2000) *After Slavery: Emancipation and Its Discontents* (London and Portland, Ore.: Frank Cass).
Tibbles, A. (ed.) (1994) *Transatlantic Slavery: Against Human Dignity* (Liverpool: Liverpool University Press).
Tilly, C. (1986) 'War Making and State Making as Organized Crime', in Evans, P., Rueschemeyer, D. and Skocpol, T. (eds) *Bringing the State Back In* (Cambridge: Cambridge University Press).
—— (1990) *Coercion, Capital and European States, AD 990–1990* (Cambridge: Blackwell).
Thornton, J. (1999) *Africa and Africans in the Making of the Atlantic World, 1400–1800* (Cambridge: Cambridge University Press).
Trouillot, M.-R. (1995) *Silencing the Past: Power and the Production of History* (Boston: Beacon Press).
Tulloch, C. (2005) 'Picture This: The "Black" curator', in Littler, J. and Naidoo, R. (2005) (eds) *The Politics of Heritage: The Legacies of 'Race'* (London: Routledge).
Verwey-Jonker, H. (ed.) (1983) *Emancipatiebewegingen in Nederland* (Deventer: Van Loghum Slaterus).
Voorhoeve, J. (1985) *Peace, Profits and Principles: A Study of Dutch Foreign Policy* (The Hague: M. Nijhoff).
Vreis, J. de and Woude, A. van der (1997) *The First Modern Economy: Success, Failure and Perseverance of the Dutch Economy, 1500–1815* (Cambridge: Cambridge University Press).
Wallace, E.K. (2006) *The British Slave Trade and Public Memory* (New York: Columbia University Press).

Wallerstein, I. (1974) *The Modern World-System, vol.1: Capitalist Agriculture and the Origins of the European World-Economy in the Sixteenth Century* (New York and London: Academic Press).

—— (1986) 'The Three Stages of African Involvement in the World-Economy', in *Africa and the Modern World* (Trenton, N.J.: Africa World Press).

—— (2004) *World System Analysis: An Introduction* (Durham, N.C.: Duke University Press).

—— (2006) *European Universalism: The Rhetoric of Power* (New York: The New Press).

—— (2009) 'Reflections on Fanon', *New Left Review*, 57 (May/June): 117–25.

Walvin, J. (1973) *Black and White: The Negro in English Society, 1555–1945* (London: Allen Lane).

Wekker, G. (2009) 'Another Dream of Imagining Europe', in Hine, D.C., Keaton, T.D. and Small, S. (eds) *Black Europe and the African Diaspora* (University of Illinois Press, Chicago).

Willemsen, G. (1980) *Koloniale politiek en transformatie processen in een plantage-economie: Suriname 1873–1930* (dissertation) (Rotterdam: Erasmus Universiteit).

—— (2006a) *Dagen van gejuich en gejubel: viering en herdenking van de afschaffing van de slavernij in Nederland, Suriname en de Nederlandse Antillen* (Den Haag: Amrit/NiNsee).

—— (2006b) 'Commemoration and Commemorators', speech given at the Gilder Lehrman Institute for the Study of Slavery, Abolition and Emancipation, 2–4 November (New Haven, Conn.: Yale University).

—— and Nimako K. (1993) 'Multiculturalisme, verzuilde samenleving en verzorgingsstaat: naar een pluralistische democratie', in Pas, G. (ed.) *Achter de coulissen: gedachten over de multi-ethnische samenleving* (Amsterdam: Wetenschappelijk Bureau Groen Links).

—— —— (2007) 'Abolition without Emancipation: Debating Freedom on the Eve of the Abolition of Dutch Slavery', paper presented at the conference *Slavery: Unfinished Business*, at the University of Hull/WISE in Hull, UK, 16–19 May.

—— —— (2008) 'Chattel Slavery, Humanity, and the Free Soil Ideology in the Dutch Orbit', paper presented at the symposium *Reflections on the Decolonial Option and the Humanities: An International Dialogue*, at the Center for Global Studies and the Humanities, Duke University, Durham, N.C.: 21–3 February.

Williams, E. (1994[1944]) *Capitalism and Slavery* (Chapel Hill, N.C. and London: University of North Carolina Press).

Winbush, R.A. (ed.) (2003) *Should America Pay? Slavery and the Raging Debate on Reparations* (New York: Amistad).

Wolf, E.R. (1982) *Europe and the People Without History* (Berkeley: University of California Press).

Wooding, C.J. (1972) *Winti: een Afroamericaanse godsdienst in Suriname: een cultureel-historische analyse van de religieuze verschijnselen in de Para* (Meppel: Krips Repro).

Young, L. (2002) 'Rethinking Heritage: Cultural Policy and Inclusion', in R. Sandell (ed.) *Museums, Society, Inequality* (New York and London: Routledge).

Zunder, A. (2010) *Herstelbetalingen: de 'Wiedergutmachung' voor de schade die Suriname en haar bevolking hebben geleden onder het Nederlands kolonialisme* (Den Haag: Amrit).

Index

abolition/legal abolition
  Article 2, 111
  as consequence of pressure from Britain, 155, 165, 185, 188
  as key concept, xv, 5, 11–12
  British abolition of slavery, 68, 69, 71, 88
  British abolition of slave trade, 23, 68
  celebrations of, 11, *see also* anniversaries and apologies; remembrance and commemoration; Slavery Emancipation Day; NiNsee
  comparisons to Great Britain, 10, 36, 46, 47, 104, 111–14, 156, 171, 173
  compensation for enslavers and, 111, 119, 138–41, 142, 144, 156
  complete abolition, 120–1
  debate and race relations, 122
  decline of slavery economy during, 141
  delayed abolition, 9–10, 141
  distinct from emancipation, 10, 100, 102, 123, 134, 188
  Dutch academic literature on, 3, 188
  Dutch Atlantic slavery and, 1
  Dutch Parliament and, 104–8, 112, *see also* Bosse, Pieter Philip van; State Committee; Baud, J.C.
  Dutch postponement of, 86
  Dutch public opinion, 94
  Dutch system of state control, 112–17, 119, *see also* progressive control
  emancipation discourse and, 124, 126–7
  financed through Dutch colony Indonesia, 143
  French declaration of, 22, 82
  gender discrimination and, 188, *see also* gender
  King Willem III, 85, 118, 156, 158
  lack of Dutch national abolition heroes, 47
  legal abolition debate and Dutch citizenship, 112
  legal abolition defined as, 100
  limitations of, xiv
  manumission and, 135–6
  old slave trade abolition movement, 8
  partial abolition, 83, 188
  Partition of Africa and, 51
  plantation economy and, 69–71
  post-abolition freedmen experiences, 146–8, *see also* gender
  role of Christian missionaries, 79
  segregation as result of, 124, *see also* segregation
  translation of Dutch abolition laws into Sranan, 119
  without emancipation, xvi, 87
  see also emancipation; transformative change; Netherlands; African diaspora; reparations
Africa
  African nationalism, 151
  age of banditry, 3, 14–15, 17–20, 41, 47, 49, 64
  as source of captives, 13
  as source of gold, 15
  dignitarian impulse, 151
  in slave trade, 3
  Las Casas and, 16
  location for enslavement, 134
  see also Africana, Africans
Africana
  definition of, 151
  dignitarianism, 151
  dignitarian tradition, 151–4
  see also individual intellectuals

Africans
    abduction, 3, 6, 14, 15, 19, 45–9, 186
    as captives, 3, 5, 6, 17, 19, 21–8,
        40, 45, 48, 50, 56–8, 66, 75, 77,
        80, 81, 85, 87, 89, 120, 187, see
        also enslaved
    as instruments of conquest, 17
    as slaves, xvi, 6, 16, 17, 18, 23, 24,
        28, 31, 33, 40, 45–50, 57, 61–2,
        67, see also chattel slavery;
        enslaved; Las Casas
    Middleburg and, 18, 33
    migration to Netherlands
    shared social spaces with Europeans,
        xvii
    see also African diaspora; enslaved;
        enslavement; Rodney, Walter;
        slavery; transatlantic slave trade
African diaspora
    abolition and, 174
    Black nationalism and, 175
    chattel slavery and notion of, 29
    discourse and, 159
    see also Africa; Africana; Africans
Afro-Dutch, 11, 157, 173, 178
Afro-Eurasian world market, 15, 54
Afro-European Feminist Movement,
    161
Afro-Surinamese Cultural Center
    (ASCC), 156, see also
    remembrance and
    commemoration movement;
    emancipation; NiNsee
allochtonen
    autochtonen and xvii, 167–9
    defined as, 167
    policy (Netherlands), 167
    see also autochtonen; pillarization;
    Dutch integration policy;
    ethnic-minorities; Dutch
    ethnic-minorities policy
Amsterdam
    Afro-Dutch community in, 11, 173
    Amsterdam Historical Museum,
        176–7
    Black organizations in, 161, 173
    chocolate making in, 66
    commemoration of legal abolition,
        160–3, 182, see also anniversaries
        and apologies trend; NiNsee

demand for and refining of sugar,
    69, 72–4, see also sugar
Dutch banking in, 125
financial center of Europe, 53
first trade union, 128
liberated Surinamese in, 104
National Slavery Monument, see
    National Slavery Monument in
    Amsterdam; NiNsee
Tropical Museum (KIT), 176
reparations movement in, 179
segregated neighborhoods in, xvii
Surinameplein, 161, 163, see also
    Netherlands
University of Amsterdam, 37
United East India Company, 37–8,
    see also Dutch East India
    Company (VOC); Dutch West
    India Company (WIC)
anniversaries and apologies trend, 7,
    158, 159, 161, 176, 178, 181–2
Antilles, see Dutch Antilles
anti-racism
    Paul Scheffer and, 168
    World Anti-Racism Conference, 163
anti-slavery
    definition of, 7
    Dutch parliament and, 104, 109
    public debate, 87
    new movement, see new anti-slavery
        movement
    revolution in Haiti, 51
    resistance and revolts, 78–9
    slave codes in response to, 79
Antwerp, 18, 53, 62
apartheid, 151, 154
Aruba, 17, 66, 89, 143, 162, 179, see
    also Dutch Antilles
Asia, 9, 11, 13, 15, 30–2, 37–9, 52–6,
    58, 59, 70, 75, 95, 151, 154, 184,
    185, 186, 190
assimilation, 10, 123, 134, 166, 168,
    169, see also Dutch integration
    policy
autochtonen
    allochtonen and, xvii, 167–9
    defined as, 167
    see also allochtonen; ethnic-
        minorities; Dutch
        ethnic-minorities policy; Dutch
        integration policy

INDEX 203

Batavia, *see* Indonesia
Baud Committee, 82, 90, *see also* State Committee; Baud, J.C
Baud, J.C., 66, 90–1, 121, *see also* Baud Committee; State Committee
Beckles, Sir Hilary, 31, 60, 63, 78–9
Biekman, Barryl, 161, *see also* Sophiedela
Berlin, Ira, 145, 146
Blumenbach, Johann Friedrich, 42
Bonaire, 17, 65, 89, 143, *see also* Dutch Antilles
Bordeaux Declaration
Brazil, 16–17, 28, 31, 62–5, 72–5, 112, 149, 150
Britain, *see* England; Great Britain
Bosse, Pieter Philip van, 96, 105–8, 110, 117, 118, 138, 139, 147
Boxtel, Rogier van, 162, 163

Cain, Artwell, xix–xxi, *see also* NiNsee
Caribbean, *see* Dutch Antilles; French West Indies; *particular Dutch colonies*
Catholicism/Catholics, 10, 14, 79, 124, 126–7, 128, 133, 148, 164, 167, *see also* emancipation
Césaire, Aimé, 151, 152–3
chattel slavery
  abolition of, 123
  African diaspora and, 29
  age of bandity and, 20
  as key concept, 12
  as legal and economic system, 87
  as legal institution, 7, 29, 152
  Atlantic economy built around, 11, 36
  colonies and revolt, 149
  debates over, 15–16, *see also* Las Casas; Sepúlveda
  definition of, 29, 46, 97
  discourse of, 51
  Dutch abolition of, 136
  economic interests, 147
  emigration and, 20
  family structures of, 142
  free soil ideology, 26, 29
  international relations and, 20
  legacy of, 51
  making of European world order, 13, 53
  modalities of abolition, 97
  nationalism and, 20
  national sovereignty and citizenship in Europe, 9, 20, 29, 50
  overthrow of system, 87
  race as main organizing principle, 32, 51, 124, 152
  regulated under European states, 19
  regulation of, 20
  religion and, 41, *see also* Las Casas; Sepúlveda
  role of states in, 19, 40, *see also* slavery/Atlantic slavery
  science and, 41, 43
  sugar and salt, 52, *see also particular commodities*
  territorial control and, 20
  trajectories of emancipation and, 5
  wars of peoples and, 32
  see also Africa; Africans; Dutch Antilles; Europe; Peace of Westphalia; slavery; sovereignty; transatlantic slave trade
Chomsky, Noam, 13, 27
Christianity/Christians, 42, 79, 111, 116, 185
class
  absence of permanent African slave-trading class, 47
  Christianity and ruling classes, 79
  contrasts between pillars in Dutch society, 127–8, 133, *see also* pillarization
  differentiation within black population after manumission, 82, *see also* gender; abolition
  emancipation of working-class, 10, 124, 128, 148, *see also* emancipation
  emancipation struggles and class struggles, 124
  ethnic, race, gender relations and, 29, 124
  international division of labor and class relations, 24
  race and, 152–3, *see also* Césaire, Aimé

class *continued*
  ruling class and abolition, 119, *see also* enslavers/master enslavers
  trajectories of emancipation, 123, 186
  unions and, 132
  working-class movements, 128, 131, 133, *see also* emancipation; gender; women
  working-class women and women's movement, 131–3, *see also* emancipation; gender; women
cocoa, 66, 69, 71–2
coffee, 59, 63, 67–72, 91, 119, 186
collaboration theory, 49–50
collective memory, 11, 149, 169, 171, 182
colonialism
  changing systems of sovereignty and, 50
  dignitarianism as response to, 151–3, 155, *see also* Africana, dignitarianism
  Dutch 'Ethical Policy', 39
  former enslaved as racialized colonial subjects, 150, 185
  legal abolition of slavery and, 185
Columbus, Christopher
  arrival in Americas, 27
  looking for alternative routes to Asia, 53, 54
  post-Columbus expeditions, 37
  voyages, 15
cotton, 55, 57, 59, 60, 65, 68–72, 77, 91, 186
Cuba, 62, 63, 121
Curaçao
  emigration to Suriname, 82
  Tula, 36
  see also Dutch Antilles

Darwin, Charles, 42–3
Davids, Karel, 31
De Stichting Eer en Herstel, Betaling Slachtoffers van de Slavernij in Suriname (Foundation for the Honour, Restoration and Compensation of Victims of Slavery in Suriname), 162

Du Bois, W. E. B., 151–2, *see also* Africana
Dutch Antilles, xvi, 1, 2, 10, 11, 29, 65, 75, 80, 82, 88, 89, 95, 96, 109, 118, 121, 122, 124, 140, 160, 179, *see also* Sint Maarten; Sint Eustatius; Saba; Curaçao; Bonaire; Aruba
Dutch Antillean
  agency of, 165
  as Dutch citizens, 173
  as 'free blacks', 80
  communities in Netherlands, 11, 149
  demands for a slavery monument, 164
  organizations, 162
  youth in the Netherlands, 154
Dutch East India Company (VOC), 31, 37–40, 55, 56, 58, 59, 70, 75
Dutch ethnic-minorities policy, 162–9
Dutch historiography, 8, 10, 124, 190
Dutch integration policy, 164–5, *see also* allochtonen; assimilation; autotochnen; pillarization; multiculturalism; segregation
Dutch West India Company (WIC), 25, 37, 39, 40, 43, 58, 59, 60, 72, 74–5, 76, 85
Dutch Working Men's Association (Nederlandsch Werklieden Verbond, NWV), 128

Eighty Years' War, 14, 65
Elliot, J.H., 30
emancipation
  abolition and, 10
  abolition without, 87
  absence of debate in Netherlands, 87
  assimilation and, 123, 134
  as sociological phenomenon, 123
  as unfinished business, 7–8, 10, 12, 149–53, 163, 183, 189
  cash flow out of Suriname after, 141
  circumstances of, 2
  complete emancipation, 83, 96, 171–2, 183, 190, *see also* Sint Maarten; Suriname

continuous postponement, 86, 122, *see also* Suriname
compensation for enslavers and, 83, 144, *see also* enslavers/master enslavers
decolonization and, 147, 152
definition of, 103, 138
dignitarianism and, 151, *see also* Africana
distinction between abolition and, 10, 100, 102, 103, 123, 124, 134, 188–9
Dutch historiography and question of, xiv
Dutch Parliament and, 104–8, 112, *see also* Soeterwoude, Elout van; Bosse, Pieter Philip van; Hogelanden, Boreel van; Luynden, Willem van; Nolthenius, Tutein; Nyevelt, Julius van Zuylen
Dutch system of state control and, 112–17, 119, *see also* progressive control
emancipation of the working class, 10, 124, 148
Emancipation Register, 144
enslaved paying for, 95
equality demand for, 164
ethnic minorities policy and, 167
ideas of, 66
integration and, 124, 134, 164
literature on, 3
mainstream Dutch historiography and, 10, 79, 124
moral emancipation, 159
social harmony and the state, 164–6
State Committee and, 91–4, 96, *see also* Baud Committee; Baud, J.C.
parallel histories and intertwined belonging and, 11, 184–6, 188
pillarization and, 124, *see also* pillarization
political emancipation of the Catholics, 10, 79, 124, 148, 164, 167
racialized, 10, 124
race and, 124, 134
religion and, 125–7

Scheffer, Paul and, 169, *see also* anti-racism; progressive control; Scheffer, Paul
segregation and, xvii, 123–4, 134
separation and, 124, 134
social forgetting and, 173
state management of, 95
the slave's nature and, 98, 101
trajectories of, 5, 122, 124
transformative change and, 97, 103, 124
women and, 10, 124, 131–3, 148, 164, 167, *see also* gender; Verwey-Jonker
working class movements and, 128–31, 164, 167
see also Amsterdam; Sint Maarten; Suriname; Surinamese; Sint Eustatius; Saba; Slavery Emancipation Day; NiNsee; National Slavery Monument; England; progressive control
Emmer, Pieter, 18, 74, 75, 102
England
  apology for slavery, 181
  American colonies revolt, 149
  as Protestant state, 14
  as slave trading nation, 32
  Church of England, 181
  commercial expansion, 23
  commercial warfare with Holland, 21
  emancipation debates, 111, 113
  James Somerset case, 34
  literacy in, 87
  museums and galleries in, 178
  Netherlands and, 94, 104
  Peace of Ryswick and, 21
  profits from slavery, 76
  status of slaves in, 33, 35
  sugar imports, 22
  tobacco cultivation, 59
  see also Great Britain
enslaved
  Africans as, 4, 17, 45, 49, 57, 61, 62, 64, 78, 134
  age of banditry and, 15
  archives not recorded by, 6
  as concept in Dutch discourse, 157–8

enslaved *continued*
  as savages, 92, *see also* progressive control
  as subhuman, 78, 95, 112, *see also* progressive control
  categorization as slaves, 49, 80, 187
  Christians/Christianization and, 18, 34, 185
  Coloured and manumission, 81
  compensation for, 111–12, 117, 137–8, 140, *see also* Soeterwoude, Elout van
  concept of slave trade and, 47–9
  decline of enslaved populations, 90–1
  defintion of, 26, 44, 45–6, 52, 78, *see also* chattel slavery
  descendants and claims of, xvi, 2, 6, 12, 157–60, 162, 163, 164, 169, 171, 174, 176, 179, 187
  descendants and migration to Netherlands, 185, *see also* African diaspora
  distrust between enslavers and, 114
  division of labour between enslavers and, 5, 52, 78, *see also* enslavers/master enslavers
  Dutch book-keeping model, 76–7
  Dutch slave trade vs. enslavement, 75
  emancipation of, 2, 72, *see also* abolition; emancipation; Suriname
  escape of, 83, 119, 122, 136
  emigration of Europeans and, 26
  enslaved population figures, 88–90
  European consumption of goods, 14
  family structures, 142
  former enslaved as racialized colonial subjects, 134, 150, 185
  freedom and, 5
  interpreted notion of freedom, 1, 144–6, 148, 150, 186
  labour, 3, 8, 31, 52, 54, 56, 59, 67, 70, 71, 90, 184, *see also* sugar production; *particular commodities*
  Las Casas- Sepúlveda debate, 15–16
  legal freedom and, 10, 34–5, *see also* abolition; emancipation
  management of, 77–8, 79, 83
  manumission, 81–2, 116, 135–6
  Maroons/Maroonage, 83, 119, 136
  numbers of enslaved who became free, 143
  revolt of, 35, *see also* Haitian Revolution; Tula
  role of missionaries and, 79
  shared spaces with enslaver, 5, *see also* parallel histories and intertwined belongings
  slave codes, 79, 81
  societies in Suriname and Antilles, 65
  State Committee debates, 92–3
  Statement of Registration, 144, *see also* Lamur, Humphrey
  Unie van Slaven (Union of Slaves), 36, *see also* Tula; Curaçao
  wars of people and, 32
  women and rape, 81
  see also chattel slavery; slavery; collaboration theory, enslavement; enslavers/master enslavers; emancipation; transatlantic slave trade; *particular nations; particular Dutch colonies*

enslavement
  abduction and, 6, 19, 186
  Africans responsible for, 47
  Africa as location for, 13, 134
  Atlantic slavery refers to, 46
  captivity, 3, 14, 45–7, 49, 82, 186, 187
  concept of 'slave trade' and, 47
  dehumanizing as grounds for, 44
  eligibility and criteria for, 45, 101
  European state construction and, 40
  exportation of silver from colonies, 56
  Frantz Fanon and, 153
  histories of, 5
  in the Americas, 48
  other groups and, 151
  remorse, 163
  resistance to, 134–5, 185
  Rodney, Walter and concept of, 49, 187

INDEX 207

slaves vs. enslaved, 49
sugar production and, 60, 63, *see also* sugar
transport of African captives and, 19, 26
VOC and, 39–40, *see also* Dutch East India Company
WIC and, 59, *see also* Dutch West India Company
see also Africa; Africans; chattel slavery; slavery; transatlantic slave trade, *particular Dutch colonies*
enslavers/master enslavers
advocate progressive control, 98–9, 103
as citizens, 112
as free people, 78
assigning value to enslaved, 77, 95
bringing slaves to Netherlands, 33–4, *see also* James Somerset
churches of, 79
compensation for, xvi, 6, 9, 112, 119, 137–44, 156, *see also* Bosse, Pieter Philip van
concept of slave as used by, 158
criteria for enslavement, *see also* Africans; enslavement; slavery; enslaved
distrust between enslaved and, 114
division of labour between enslaved and, 52, 78
Dutch enslavers and WIC, 25, 43
English apprentices and, 110
efforts to obliterate ethnicity of African captives, 85, *see also* identity
fear of rebellion, 83–5, 119, 120
French state subsidizing, 22
interpreted notion of freedom, 1, 102, 144
intervention in social life of enslaved, 71, 81
investing in enslaved population, 111
legal abolition debate, 112, 114, *see also* abolition; emancipation
legal provisions passed by, 83–4
manumission and, 81–2, 136
misidentified as planters, 71

partial abolition and, 83
post-abolition conditions of servitude, 188
power over legacy of slavery, 189
rape of enslaved women by, 81, *see also* women
rejection of emancipation motions, 94
repression and pacification, 52
revolts against mother countries, 150
sexual exploitation of women by, 145, *see also* women
shared spaces with enslaved, 5
slavery as conceived by, 45
sources/records of, 6, 12, 43
state and, 97
state replaces authority of, 93
Statement of Registration, 144, *see also* Lamur, Humphrey
Suriname ratio of enslaved to, 80, *see also* Suriname; Surinamese
Unie van Slaven (Union of Slaves) and, 36, *see also* Tula
Essed, Philomena, 47, 157, 166, 168, 169, 171
ethnic minority groups in the Netherlands
Mollucans, 168
Moroccans, 165, 167
Turks, 165, 167
see also Antillean; Dutch ethnic-minorities policy; Surinamese
EU, *see* European Union
Europe
age of sovereignty, 20
citizenship, 9, 12, 19, 29, 32 41–2
colonization, 27, 41
emigration from, 20, 26–9, 41
European world order, 9
expansion, 4, 27, 29, 31, 32, 41, 54, 61
free soil ideology, 26, 29, 32, 33
international relations, 3, 20, 26
nationalism, 20, 24–5, 42, 50, 127
nation states formation and consolidation, 20
slave trade and, 3
slavery system as a whole, 3

Europe *continued*
  territorial control, 20–3
  wars of peoples, 32
  see also Eighty Years' War; Peace of Ryswick; Peace of Westphalia; Peace of Utrecht; Thirty Years' War; *particular nation states*; European Union (EU), 50
Executive Committee to Abolish Slavery (Maatschappij tot Afschaffing van de Slavernij), 104

Family Names and Kinship of Emancipated Slaves in Suriname, 144, *see also* Lamur, Humphrey
Fanon, Frantz, 151, 152–3, 187, *see also* Africana
First World War, 50
Fogel, R.W., 17, 29, 45, 60–4, 69, 97
Foner, Eric, 78
Fortuyn, Pim, 168
France
  abolition of slavery in colonies, 82, 94
  as Catholic state, 14
  Atlantic presence, 75
  diasporic connections and exchange, 175, 179
  Dutch export of cocoa beans to, 66
  export of raw salt, 65
  export of raw sugar, 73
  French Caribbean, 63, 152
  Great Britain and competition, 36
  involvement in slave trade, 22, 32
  Napoleonic Occupation, 35
  Sint Maarten, 122, 140
  status of black people on French soil, 35
  sugar production, 62, 63
  support of American Revolution, 36
  transport of African captives, 22–3
  war with Spain, 125
  see also Europe; French Revolution; French West Indies; Haitian Revolution; Haiti
Frank, André Gunder, 30, 38, 53, 54
French Revolution, 20, 22, 26, 30, 32, 37, 41, 112, 126
French West Indies, 22, 23, *see also* Haiti; France

Gama, Vasco de, 15
gender
  Afro-European Feminist Movement, 161
  as divisive issue, 170
  differentiation, 82
  demographics, 133
  discrimination, 188
  emancipation and, 131–3
  gendered nature of white elites' lifestyles, 177
  gendered systems of inequality, 189
  ideology, 148
  male-dominated working-class unions, 132
  post-abolition experiences for men and women, 146–8
  relations, 29
  roles in political parties and organizations, 132
  three pillars and, 133
  trajectories of emancipation and, 123–4, 186
General Dutch Union of Typographers (Algemeene Nederlandsche Typografenbond, ANTB), 128
Germany
  as Protestant state, 14
  Dutch arms manufacture, 32
  Dutch export of cocoa beans to, 66
  Nazi Germany occupation in Europe, 165
  see also Europe; Nazi Holocaust; Second World War
Ghana, 57
Ghanaians, 57, 152, *see also* Nkrumah, Kwame
globalization, 170
Golden Triangle, 52–3
gold, 15, 54, 55, 56, 62
Gordon, Lewis, 43–4, 78, 187
Great Britain
  abolition of slave trade, 36, 58, 68, 81, 87, 97 108, 171
  anniversaries and apologies in, 7, 181
  as mirror to Dutch policy, 114
  Atlantic presence, 75
  British Empire and Commonwealth Museum, 178
  British Museum, 178

British Race Relations Act, 166
depiction of Black people in paintings, 176
diasporic connections and exchange, 189
dominant nationalist self-reference frame, 173
dramatic social transformation, 177
European expansion, 29
International Slavery Museum, 177
Haitian Revolution and, 26, 36
Horniman Museum, 178
industrial revolution, 75
international division of labour and, 56–8
legal abolition of Dutch slavery and, 155, 156, 165, 185, 188
London Docklands Museum, 178
loss of American slave colony, 58
Merseyside Maritime Museum, 177
migration and settlement of black people in, xv
museum heritage and artefacts trends, 7
national abolition heroes, 47
new anti-slavery movement, 8
old slave trade abolition movement, 8, 10
reparations movement, 7, 178–81
role of Black communities, 174
Smith, Adam and, 44
suppression of transatlantic slave trade and Atlantic slavery, 46
sugar production, 58, 62, 63
support for Portugal, 26
transport of African captives, 19, 22–3
Wilberforce House Museum, 177
Wilberforce, William, 156
see also England; Europe; Treaty of Methuen
Groenberg, Roy, 162, *see also* De Stichting Eer en Herstel, Betaling Slachtoffers van de Slavernij in Suriname
Grosfoguel, Ramon, 16
Gupta, Samir das, 38

Haiti, 25, 26, 35, 36, 51, 62, 63, 87, 149, 150, 152

Haitian Revolution, 35–6
Haakmat, André, 178–9
Haegen, Pieter van der, 18
Hegel, Georg Wilhelm Friedrich, 44–5
Herstelbetalingen (Reparations), 179, *see also* Zunder, Armand
Hogelandenm, Boreel van, 109
Hondius, Dienke, 18, 33

identity
cultural identity in Netherlands, 166
emancipated slave names with no link to slave owners, 144
emergence of black, 44
enslavers' efforts to destroy African ethnic identities, 85
legacy of slavery and racial identities, xvii
religious, 126
see also allochtonen; autochtonen
immigration, *see* assimilation; migration; Netherlands
India, 13, 15, 25, 36, 54, 55
Indonesia, 9, 38, 39–40, 95, 143, 165–6
integration, 10, 124, 134, 162, 164–6, 167, 169, 182, *see also* assimilation; Dutch integration policy; multiculturalism; segregation
international division of labour, 13, 14, 15, 17, 29, 56
international relations, xv, 20, 26, *see also* sovereignty
international trade, 30, 37, 38, 54, 55, 58, 184, 186
Islam/Muslims, 164, 167, 168
Italy
Catholicism as dominant religion, 14
Dutch arms manufacture and, 32
Italian entrepreneurs and sugar refining, 62
Columbus and, 24, *see also* Columbus, Christopher

James, C.L.R., 151, 152
Japan/Japanese, 165, 180

Kaikusi, *see* Groenberg, Roy; De Stichting Eer en Herstel, Betaling Slachtoffers van de Slavernij in Suriname
KetiKoti, xix
King, Martin Luther, 154
Kom, Anton de, 151, 153, 154, 162, *see also* We the Slaves of Suriname

Jews/Jewish communities in Netherlands
 anti-semitism, 31
 as Dutch merchants in Barbados, 31
 as enslavers in Suriname, 162
 reconciliation with Surinamese community in Netherlands, 162, *see also* Groenberg, Roy
 reparations after Second World War, 179–80
 see also Nazi Holocaust

Lamur, Humphrey, 144
Landelijk Platform Slavernijverleden (Nationwide Platform for the History of Slavery) (LPS), 162–3, *see also* National Slavery Monument
language
 aliens policy and adult language education, 167
 cultural nationalism and, 154, *see also* Curaçao; Suriname
 Dutch authorities and, 94
 enslaved and, 85, 111
 European colonization and, 27
 Papiementoe and Curaçao, 154
 Sranan Tongo and Suriname, 119, 154
 translation of Dutch abolition laws, 119, 142
 slave trade and, 50
 Suriname and, 82
 see also Tula
Las Casas, Bartolemé de, 15–16, 41, 112
 cultural racist discourse and, 16
 Sepúlveda, Gines and, 15–16, 41
Legêne, Susan, 39–40, 165

Linnaeus, Carolus, 42, *see also* racism
Lovejoy, Paul E., 46
Luckhardt, Cees, 74
Luynden, Willem van, 110
lynching, 151

Mama, Amina, 43
Mandela, Nelson, 154
Mazrui, Ali, 151
Middleburg, 17, 18, 33, 35, 38, 67, 176, 177
Mielants, Eric, 16
migration
 Europeans to colonies, 76, 185, *see also* Europe
 globalization, post-coloniality and, 170
 mass migration from Suriname, 11
 social formations in Netherlands and, 185
 Surinamese migration to Netherlands, 161, 189–90
 to Europe from colonies, 174, 180
minorities, *see* ethnic minority groups in the Netherlands
Mullard, Chris, 97, 98, 103, 123, 159, 169
multiculturalism, 164, 166, 168, 170
museum heritage and artefacts trend, 7, 172, 176–7, 180, 181

nation states, *see individual nation states*
National Slavery Monument in Amsterdam, xv, 1, 163—164, *see also* NiNsee
Nazi Holocaust, 151, *see also* Germany; Second World War
Netherlands
 Afro-Surinamese Cultural Centre (ASCC), 156
 as Protestant state, 14
 Atlantic presence, 75
 black Dutch groups in, 1
 Dutch citizenship, 5, 35, 37, 112, 133, 164, 168, 169, 171, 186, 189
 Dutch East Indies, xvi, 9

Dutch National Institute for the Study of the Slavery Past and its Legacy (NiNsee), *see* NiNsee
Dutch Republic, 14, 32, 39, 66, 75, 125
Dutch West Indies, 9
Golden Age, 176
Holland, 21, 22, 39, 54, 65, 76
King William II, 90
King Willem III, 85, 118, 156
Ministry of Education, Culture and Science, 170
Napoleonic occupation of, 35, 148
National Slavery Monument, *see* National Slavery Monument in Amsterdam; NiNsee
organizations in, 3
Queen Beatrix, 163
racism in, *see* racism
slavery and collective consciousness, 10
slavery on Dutch soil, 33, *see also* Middleburg
Slavery Emancipation Day in Netherlands, 2, 159, 182, *see also* Amsterdam; emancipation; NiNsee
States of Zeeland, 18, 38, 67, 76, *see also* Middleburg
Surinameplein, 161, 163, *see also* Amsterdam
United East India Company, The, 38
University of Amsterdam, 37
see also Amsterdam; Antwerp; Eighty Years' War; Europe; Middleburg; The Hague; Rotterdam; *individual organizations*
NederlandschVerbond van Vakvereenigingen (NVV), 130, 132–3, *see also* women
new anti-slavery movement, 7, 8
Nimako, Kwame, xiv, xv, xvii, xviii, xx, 7, 25, 2, 7 47, 123, 12, 7 152, 157, 16, 0 164, 166, 167, 168, 169, 173
NiNsee, xiii, xv, xix–xxi, 1, 11, 160, 163, 169–75, 177, 179, 182, 189
Nkrumah, Kwame, 151, 152
Nolthenius, Tutein, 107–8

Nyevelt, Julius van Zuylen van, 103–4

Padmore, George, 151, *see also* Africana
parallel histories and intertwined belonging
  Atlantic slavery and, 11, 186
  central organizing feature, xvii, 8
  definition of, 4–5
  enslaved and enslavers, 5
  Dutch social formation and, 173
  Dutch society, memory, taste and, 184
  freedom and emancipation and, 5
  Glenn Willemsen and, 12
  parallel memories, 5, 186
  nationalism and, 24
  trajectories of emancipation and, 124
Peace of Ryswick, 20, 21, 37
Peace of Utrecht, 20, 21–2, 23, 37, 64, *see also* Treaty of Utrecht
Peace of Westphalia, 14, 18–20, 23, 24, 26, 30, 32, 37, 50, 125, *see also* Europe; *particular nations*
pillarization, 10, 124, 128, 166–8, *see also* alloctonen; assimilation; autochtonen; Dutch integration policy; multiculturalism; segregation
Portugal
  as Catholic state, 14
  Atlantic presence, 75
  Brazil revolts, 149, 150
  British support, 26
  Columbus and, 15, *see also* Columbus, Christopher
  export of raw salt, 65
  Pope Alexander VI and, 51
  separation from Spain, 26, 64
  Spanish domination over, 30
  transport of African captives, 19, 22, 28
  sugar production, 31, 61, 62, 64
  Tula in, 36 See *Tula* and *Curaçao*
  VOC (Dutch East India Company) and, 37
  see also Brazil; Europe; Treaty of Methuen; Tula
Postma, Johannes, 40, 47–8, 60–1, 69

progressive control, 97–8, 102–3, 105, 111, 116, 118, 123, 159, 169, *see also* abolition; emancipation
Protestantism/Protestants, 14, 125, 126–8, 167
Prussia, 22, *see also* Peace of Utrecht

race
  abolition of slavery, 134
  absence in Dutch lexicon, 187, *see also* racism
  as organizing principle of slavery, 16, 17, 25, 26, 32, 134, 171, 187
  British Race Relations Act, 166
  chattel slavery and, 46, 51
  citizenship and, 164
  class and, 152–3, *see also* Césaire, Aimé
  colonialism and, 153
  Dutch debates and relations, 122
  Dutch mainstream academia and, 171, 175, *see also* racism
  Dutch master narrative and, 187
  Dutch nation state and, 4
  emancipation and, 124, 186
  ethnic, class, gender relations and, 29, 124
  ethnic-minorities policy in Netherlands and, 166
  ethnic studies and, 157
  gender, ethnicity and, 170
  intellectual and political tradition and, 155
  international division of labour and, 29
  Linnaeus, Carolus and theory of separate races, 42–3
  memory of racial humiliation and, 51
  NiNsee and, 171
  racial identification, 80, 134
  reinforcing nationalism, 25
  religion and, 15–16, 42, *see also* Las Casas; Sepúlveda
  scientific community and, 43
  variations within slavery, 152
  see also racism
racism
  absence in Dutch lexicon, 187, *see also* race

  acknowledgement as part of history, 149
  after Second World War, 187
  awareness of current, 154
  as fundamental component of slavery, 4
  as obstacle to equality, 148
  cultural racism, 42, *see also* Darwin, Charles
  denial of humanity, 187
  dignitarianism and, 151
  Dutch mainstream academia and, 171
  Dutch social memory and belonging, 184
  endemic to former slave-trading nations, 174
  high intensity discourse, 164
  information dissemination about, 156
  modern racism, 9
  new racism, 171–2
  NiNsee and, 171
  related to freedom and emancipation, 12
  religious, 171, *see also* Las Casas; Sepúlveda
  reparations and, 116
  role of Black communities, 174–5
  scientific, 171, *see also* race; Darwin, Charles; Linnaeus, Carolus
  slavery and, 4, 47, 171
  trajectories of emancipation and, 5
  two forms of, 16, *see also* Las Casas; Sepúlveda
  see also Boxtel, Rogier van; chattel slavery; race; Scheffer, Paul; slavery; transatlantic slave trade; World Anti-Racism conference
racist discourse
  cultural racist discourse, 16, *see also* Las Casas
  biological racist discourse, 16, see *also* Sepúlveda
religion
  abolition and, 96
  Christendom, 43
  emancipation struggles and, 124–6
  emancipation trajectories, 186

INDEX 213

European states and, 14, *see also particular countries*
ideology and, 127
Moravian bretheren in Suriname, 111
race and, 15–16, *see* Las Casas; Sepúlveda
role of Christian missionaries, 79, 145
tambu and, 85
three pillars of Dutch society, 127, *see also* pillarization
tool for pacification, 79
science and, 42
see also Catholicism; Christianity; Protestantism; Islam
Reesee, J.J., 74
remembrance and commemoration movement, 7, 157, 158–60, 170, 172–3, 174, 181, 185
reparations movement, xvi, 6, 7, 116, 153, 174, 178–83, 185
Rodney, Walter, xvi, 3, 5, 14, 19, 27, 49, 56, 120, 187
Rotterdam, xvii, 11, 73, 129, 158, 161, 162, 173
Russia, 125

Saba, 17, 66, 89, 111, 143
Sachs, Wolfgang, 154–5
salt, xv, 52, 54, 65–6
Second World War, 50, 160, 161, 166, 167, 179, 187
segregation, 10, 79 123–4, 134, 151, 168–9, *see also* assimilation; integration; Dutch integration policy; multiculturalism; pillarization
Sepúlveda, Gines de
biological racist discourse and, 16
Las Casas and, 15–16, 41
Scheffer, Paul, 168–9
Sherwood, Marika, 68, 89
silver, 9, 30–1, 53, 55–6, 58, 59, 60, 63, 185
Sint Eustatius, 17, 65, 66, 89, 111, 160, *see also* Dutch Antilles
Sint Maarten, 17, 65, 82, 89, 109, 122, 140, *see also* Dutch Antilles

slavery
abduction and captivity, 3, 6, 14, 15, 19, 45, 46, 47, 49, 186, *see also* Africa; Africans; transatlantic slave trade
as cooperative effort, 47–9
Atlantic slavery, 3, 11, 13, 15, 17, 19, 22, 26, 41, 45, 46
archival sources of, 5–6
collective memory, xvii
distinction between Atlantic slavery and transatlantic slave trade, 46
Dutch collective consciousness and, 10
Dutch historiography xiii–xv, xvi
Dutch society and, xiii
legacy of, xvii, 1, 3, 7, 10–12, 149, 151, 172, 174, 182, 183, 185, 189, *see also* colonialism; racism remembrance and commemoration movement
legitimacy and the state, 40–1
Middle Passage, 40, 64
National Slavery Monument, *see* National Slavery Monument in Amsterdam; NiNsee
nation state formation, *see* state formation and *particular nation states*
new social formations and, 3
plantation owners and, 9, 10, 27, 106, 112, 113, 116, 117, 118, 141, 147, *see also* enslavers/master enslavers
post-slavery, 7
production of goods by, 9, 14, 52
remembrance and commemoration, 7
reparations and, xvi, 7
role of Dutch in xiii, xv, 3
science and, 5, 12, 19, 24, 37, 41–2, 45
slaves vs. enslaved, xvi, *see also* Rodney, Walter, *see also* chattel slavery; enslaved; enslavers/master enslavers
slave hunters, 43
slave traders, 25, 31, 40
see also chattel slavery; enslaved; enslavers/master enslavers; enslavement; transatlantic slave trade

Slavery Emancipation Day
  Afro-Surinamese rallies, 159
  as vehicle for anti-colonialist ideas, 159
  in Curaçao, 160
  in Sint Eustatius, 160
  in Dutch Antilles, 2, 182
  in Netherlands, 2, 182
  in Suriname, 2, 182
  see also KetiKoti; National Slavery Monument; Netherlands; NiNsee
slave trade/Atlantic slave trade, see transatlantic slave trade
Small, Stephen, xii–xvii, 7, 29, 78, 156, 160, 171, 175, 176, 177, 178, 180, 181, 188
Smith, Adam, 44
Social Democratic League, 128–9
Soeterwoude, Elout van, 104
Somerset, James, 33–4
Sophiedela, 161, 162
sovereignty
  age of, 20
  emigration and, 20, 26–7
  international relations and, xv, 20, 26
  nationalism and, 20, 24–5
  territorial control and, 20–1
  United Nations, 50
  see also chattel slavery; Europe; Peace of Westphalia
Spain
  as Catholic state, 14
  Atlantic presence, 75
  declining international power, 30
  demand for sugar, 61–3
  Dutch export of cocoa beans to, 66
  export of raw salt, 65
  Latin American countries revolt against, 149
  Portugal separates from, 26
  Pope Alexander VI and, 51
  Spanish America, 66
  Spanish loan, 125
  transport of African captives, 23
  war with France, 125
  see also Eighty Years' War; Elliot, J.H.; Europe; Las Casas; Sepúlveda
State Committee, 91–3, 96, see also Baud Committee; Baud, J.C.

state formation
  slavery system and, xv, 4, 11
  Atlantic slavery and, 11, 184, 190
  Atlantic slave colony revolt and, 150
  Ashanti and Dahomey, 48
  Dutch state formation, 124
  Eurocentric, 186
  sugar trade and, 63
  transatlantic slave trade and, 184, 186, 190
  see also particular nation states
St. Maarten, see Sint Maarten
Stripriaan Luïscius, Alex van, 67, 72, 158
sugar
  abolition debates, 91, 94, 121
  Amsterdam Historical Museum and exhibit on, 176–7
  Asian cultivation and trade, 58–9
  Barbados and, 31, 63
  Brazilian production of, 17, 31, 62, 63, 72
  British Caribbean/British West Indies and, 63
  coffee production and, 68–9
  cultivation linked to transatlantic slave trade, 16, 63, 64
  dictates need for enslaved labor, 61, 70
  Dutch capture of Brazil and, 17, 64, 72
  Dutch enslavement and, 90
  Dutch involvement in production, 63
  enslaved African labor and, 31, 64
  enslaved women and, 147
  European taste/demand for, 61, 64, 69, 77
  French West Indies and, 73, see also Haiti
  frontier historiography and, 60–1
  Haiti and production, 63, see also Haiti
  import to England, 22, see also England
  Jamaica and, 63
  legacy of slavery and, 186
  Netherlands and sugar industries, 72–4
  Portugese Brazil and, 31

INDEX 215

Portugese enslavement of Africans for production, 61, 62
refineries in Amsterdam, 72–4
refineries in Antwerp, 62
refineries in Dordrecht, 73
refineries in Rotterdam, 73
shifts in market share, 62–3
Sint Eustatius and, 65
Sint Maarten and, 65
slavery and Caribbean cultivation, 60
state control and production, 110–11 See also Suriname
Spain and trade in, 63
steam power and processing, 70, 72
Suriname and, see Suriname
Suriname
abolition and financing of, 95
abolition of slave trade by British and, 81
Amsterdam Historical Museum and, 176–7
as non-profitable colony, 76–7
bill to abolish slavery in Dutch West Indian colonies, 96, 118
cocoa supplier and exporter, 66, 72
coffee exporter, 71, 72
cotton exports to Netherlands, 72
commemoration, 158 160
compulsory education in, 117
cultural nationalist movement, 154
day of legal abolition, 1, 2, 122
diasporic connections and exchange, 179, 189
Dutch debates over emancipation in, 99, 104, 107, 114, 115
Dutch debates over enslaver compensation, 139–40
emancipation linked to abolition, 10, 124
emancipation as unfinished business, 10–11
emancipation in Dutch Antilles and, 109–11
emancipation to preserve colony, 90, 94–5, 121
enslaved in Curaçao and, 122
enslaved population figures, 88–90, 91
free labour in Ghana and, 57
knowledge production in, 11
migration from, 11, see also migration
military action in, 119–20
nationalism, 159
post-emancipation apprenticeship, 135
post-emancipation and demand for education, 147
racial identification, 80
ratio of enslaved to enslavers, 80
revolts in, 82, 84–5, 86, 134
slavery based plantation economy, 67–9
slavery in Dutch Antilles and, 82, 121
state control over freedmen, 116
sugar imports from to Netherlands, 71
sugar production, 64–5, 70, 72, 74
textile imports, 70
treatment of enslaved, 80
use of steam mills, 72
Van Bosse and, 106, see also van Bosse, Pieter Philip
WIC and, 72
Zunder, Armand and, 179
Surinamese
Afro-Surinamese, 159, 162
armed forces, 84
collective memories, 165
communities living in Netherlands, 11, 149, 161
compensation for Surinamese enslavers, 119, 139, 142
Dutch citizenship, 161, 173, 189
Dutch ethnic-minority policy, 164
enslavers bring to Netherlands, 33
freedmen and conflict over wages, 147
freedmen travelling, 146
historiography, 106
migration to Netherlands, 189, 190
odos, 145
pillarization, 167
rebellion leaders, 153
Sranan Tongo, 154
tambu, 85–6
see also Amsterdam; Kom, Anton de; *We The Slaves of Suriname*

The Hague, xvii, 11, 21, 161, 166
Thirty Years' War, 20, 125
Tocqueville, Alexis de, 113
transatlantic slave trade
  Africa as source, 15
  abolition of, 88–9, see also abolition
  distinct from Atlantic slavery, 46–7
  Dutch involvement in xiii, xv, 3
  European expansion and colonization and, 27
  European historiography and, 186
  Golden Triangle, 52–3
  Las Casas- Sepúlveda debate and, 15
  legacy of, 6
  relation to state formation and slavery system, 4, 184
  Walter Rodney and, 49–50, see also Rodney, Walter
  Willemsen's lectures on, 1–2, see also Willemsen, Glenn
  see also Africa; Africans; enslaved; enslavement; enslavers/master enslavers; slavery
transformative change, 97, 103, 111, 123, 124, 159, 169, see also emancipation; abolition; progressive control
transnational institutions, see European Union; United Nations
Treaty of Breda, 20
Treaty of Methuen, 30
Treaty of Utrecht, 22, 64, see also Peace of Utrecht
Tula, 36, see also Curaçao; Portugal
Twist, Duymaer van, 101–2

Uhlenbeck, Gerhard Hendrik, 96, 113, 114, 117
United Kingdom, see Great Britain
United Nations, 50, 51, 175, 182, see also World Anti-Racism Conference
United States
  abolition of slavery through civil war, 87
  anniversaries and apologies in, 7, 181
  Black Nationalism, 180
  Black Power, xv
  Civil Rights Movement, xiv, 154, 180, see also King, Martin Luther
  colonial revolt, 149
  diasporic connections and exchange, xv, 175, 179, 189
  dramatic social transformation, 177
  European citizens as colonists, 112
  freedmen experience liberation in, 146
  Haiti and, 26
  legal abolition in, 189
  museum heritage and artefacts trends, 7
  political rivalries and abolition, 189
  political upheaval in, 25
  reparations for Japanese, 180
  reparations movement, 178, 180
  role of Black communities, 174
  role of decolonization, 165
  slave drivers in U.S. South, 78
  Women's Movement in, xv

Varma, Tara Oedayraj Singh, 161, see also Sophiedela
Vereniging Ons Suriname (Union of Suranmese in the Netherlands), 179
Vereniging voor Vrouwenbelangen (Association for Women's Interests), 133
Verwey-Jonker, Hilda, 124, 131–2
Vrouwenarbeid en Gelijk Staatsburgerschap (Women's Labour and Equal State Citizenship), 133

Waaldijk, Berteke, 39–40, 165
Wallerstein, Immanuel, 5, 13, 19, 21, 22, 23, 29, 32, 76, 126, 153
Wekker, Gloria, 173
We the Slaves of Suriname, 153–4, see also Kom, Anton de
Wilberforce, William, 47, see also Great Britain
Willemsen, Glenn, xiv, xv, xvii, xviii, xx, 1–2, 3, 6, 12, 76, 106, 111, 114, 175

Williams, Eric, 3, 4, 14, 21, 29, 60, 62, 75
women
   Afro-European Feminist Movement, 161
   enslaved women and rape, 81
   NVV, see NederlandschVerbond van Vakvereenigingen
   post-abolition experiences for women, 146–8
   sexual exploitation of women by enslavers, 145
   Social Democratic Women's Propaganda Club, 133
   socialism and, 133
   sugar and enslaved women and, 147–8
   women's emancipation movements tied to working-class movements, 130
   women organizing, 132–3, *see also* *individual organizations*
   working class women, 131–2
   universal suffrage and, 133
   see also emancipation; class; gender
World Anti-Racism Conference, 163, 175, 176, *see also* racism; Boxtel, Rogier van; Scheffer, Paul
World War I, *see* First World War
World War II, *see* Second World War

Zijderveld, Anton, 166–7, *see also* pillarization
Zunder, Armand, 67, 74, 76, 179

www.ingramcontent.com/pod-product-compliance
Lightning Source LLC
Chambersburg PA
CBHW030529010526
44110CB00048B/785